HENRY JAMES AND THE OCCULT

The Great Extension

Martha Banta

HENRY JAMES
AND
THE OCCULT

The Great Extension

Indiana University Press

BLOOMINGTON / LONDON

Published in Canada by Fitzhenry & Whiteside
Limited, Don Mills, Ontario

Library of Congress catalog card number:
72-75386
ISBN: 0-253-32732-6

Manufactured in the United States of America

To my parents,
who were never bored,

and Henry James,
who was seldom boring

Acknowledgments

I wish to thank those who have helped me in thinking through the material of this book from its earliest conception as a dissertation written under the penetrating eye of Edwin H. Cady to its present, greatly altered form. Receiving special thanks are those who read and commented upon the manuscript in its several guises and gave me that encouragement which is as necessary to the completion of such a book as typing paper and dictionary: Pamela R. Byrne, E. Fred Carlisle, James M. Cox, Alfred H. Marks, Joseph N. Satterwhite, Lawrence Willson, and of course, Edwin Cady.

Certain portions of the book are considerably amplified from articles that appeared in the *New England Quarterly* and the *Yale Review.*

Contents

One must have seen a great deal before one concludes; the world is very large, and life is a mixture of many things; she by no means eschews the strange, and often risks combinations and effects that make one rub one's eyes.

. . . the question has ever been for me but of wondering and, with all achievable adroitness, of causing to wonder, so the whole fairy-tale side of life has used, for its tug, at my sensibility, a cord all its own.

. . . if he were not constantly, in his commonest processes, carrying the field of consciousness further and further, making it lose itself in the ineffable, he shouldn't, in the least feel himself an artist.

He values it, all sublimely and perhaps a little fatuously, for itself—as the great extension, great beyond all others, of experience and of consciousness.

HENRY JAMES

HENRY JAMES
AND THE OCCULT

The Great Extension

Part One

THE FIELDS OF CHOICE

Introduction

Four words are used recurrently in this book: supernatural, occult, psychical, and transcendent. They do not refer to outside influences such as demons, nature spirits, gods, the stars or the planets. They apply solely to hidden powers of the human mind that go sufficiently beyond the "ordinary" to grant it that metaphoric stature of the "exceptional" that Henry James often sought for his privileged characters. Theirs is the exceptionality that proves the rule of their humanity rather than denies it.

The non-credo of Henry James is readily made out. He did not believe in those tenets of the Christian orthodoxy that speak of other beings, other worlds, or other lives than those discernible by the human eye and the human heart in this world and this time. He did not believe in the quasi-religious propositions of the cultists and occultists that glorified the revelations of the séance room and the realms of ectoplasmic existence. Nor did he believe in the hypotheses of science that elevated the new dogmas of the laboratory. He did not believe these things since he did not desire them.

Henry James was a secular man who felt no shame, anxiety, or doubt about his secularism. He was of the generation (unlike Herman Melville's) and of the temperament (unlike Henry Adams's) that enabled him to be at ease in a world viewed humanistically and agnostically. Christianity, Transcendentalism, and Spiritualism were rejected without travail by a man whose full faith in the powers of the human consciousness sufficed as the only religion he knew or needed.

The religion of consciousness exacts much from its followers; it also promises much. If one believes, as did Henry James, that religion is lived out by means of the creative act, it becomes an art defined in terms of drama, style, experimentation, and extension. Because the séance rooms and the scientific laboratories of James's generation lacked just such qualities, he rejected their self-assertions as True Faiths. And yet, even as James repudiated—with wit and bite—the inanities, the absence of style, and the self-imposed limitations of scientific empiricalism and spiritualist vaporizing, he took note of what they said about the human consciousness. He took warning of their follies; occasionally, he took fire over the possibilities for his art that they offered to his probing artistic eye.

This book is concerned as deeply with the rejections Henry James made as with his acceptances from the broad areas of "mental science" and occultism. Negations, rightly viewed, are as illuminating to the student as positives. What a writer chooses *not* to select from a possible range of choices for his art is highly significant. This is especially true when that writer cogently expresses why he decides against making use of what others have uncritically accepted to dress up their lives or their art.

As a commentator *about* his fiction, James often made precise statements about the reasons for his rejection of occult material or for his renunciation of the conventional handling of such material. *Within* his fiction we do not see James in the act of renouncing the questionable aspects of the occult; we can only make out those blanks where such occultism might have figured.

A study of James's fiction of the supernatural ought not, of course, to be based upon instances of total negation. It would be fruitless to go through the pages of his stories or novels attempting to detect what-might-have-been. We can be instructed in the ways of Jamesian choices only if they show themselves in some positive form. Denials, when dramatized, are positives of this kind. When in *The Bostonians* James twits séance mediums for their tawdry ineffectuality and members of the Society for Psychical Research for excessive earnestness, he goes beyond the opinions voiced in his prefaces, essays, or letters. He is transforming private opinions into specific personae. He is creating figures who act out necessary conditions for the dramatic pull and push of his narratives.

Still, it is not enough for a book to present a review, first, of what James left out and, second, of what he inserted in order to deny it validity. It must set itself to the task of discovering what positive joys James drew from his age's interest in the powers of the human consciousness. It must show not only what he used in affirmation of others' beliefs in psychic sensitivity and the expanded vision; it must also reveal what he took possession of in his own way. Once James shed what he did not need, and retained what he liked, he could then move quickly to transform it into distinctly Jamesian elements of art. Ultimately, that point is reached in his fiction where one may paraphrase the old line of disavowal to read, "Any resemblance between the refined material used in these stories and its original raw state is purely coincidental."

The process goes something like this: When Henry James used notions extracted from contemporary attitudes toward the supernatural (whether viewed by followers of the spiritualist movement or members of the S.P.R.), he usually dramatized his denial of the worth of those attitudes, as in "The Ghostly Rental" or *The Bostonians*. When James took the middle ground of suspended disbelief (as in "Sir Edmund Orme" or *The Sense of the Past*), he wrote ghost stories heightened by certain significant Jamesian touches and concerns. When he acted to affirm something of special value in psychic powers profoundly central to his entire vision of life, his artistic manipulation so transforms the basic notions that he no longer seems to be writing about the occult as we, prosaically, tend to define its nature.

In order to make this movement clearer the matter of this book is divided into three parts. Chapters 1 through 3 deal with the intellectual and emotional milieu of James's choices to use or not to use supernatural material—a milieu in which his brother William figures largely and illuminatingly. Chapters 4 through 7 examine his application of traditional supernatural motifs to his own way of writing fiction. The final chapter pushes into territory distinctly Jamesian in its experimental use of narrative motifs and strategies and its thematic conclusions about consciousnesses living at "the pitch of passion."

The argument of this book is, therefore, admittedly a slippery one. It possesses many of the attributes of the now-you-see-it-now-you-don't realm of the prestidigitator whose arts James himself delighted to refer to. Yet it is, I believe, possible—and valid, and helpful—to make the effort to see what Henry James chose not to choose and what he elected to seize and transform from that oftentimes vague, silly, yet highly provocative welter of occultism that forms much of the intellectual and emotional background for the late nineteenth century.

Between 1881 and 1898 James was exposed to the excitements and controversies stirred up by the Society for Psychical Research. He found new ways of viewing, and expressing, what he had intuited almost from the first about the special nature of psychic sensitivity. Only now he did not need to limit himself to his literary inheritance; he could turn more directly to metaphors and observances taken from the worlds opened up by the séance and the psychologist's study.

It was not that James had a veil rent from his mind during the 1880's and 1890's and could at last comprehend the realities of unreality, the natural truths of the supernatural. Things are rarely that simple and, of all men, one ought not to expect the simple response from Henry James. His was no sweeping conversion on the road to Damascus in either an intellectual, theological, or artistic sense. Long before the 1890's James was enough a pragmatist in matters of art to exploit whatever good literary forms came to his hand. He had early recognized the possibilities latent in the ghostly tale and had had a decade of practice experimenting with the type between 1865 and 1876. By the last decade of the century he was prepared to take up the genre once again—now refining it into a personal mode of expression and an effective method of discovery.

Nor were the changes in James's aesthetic attitudes toward the supernatural superficial. Merely to pick up current jargon is no proof that the implications behind the words and phrases have been assimilated by the artistic consciousness. (Look at the novelists who turn out "Freudian fiction" which is neither Freudian nor good art.) If James had done no more with the language of psychic awareness than he did in stray examples from such early novels as *Watch and Ward* of 1871, there would be no warrant for doing anything more than noting additions to the list of Jamesian "caught images." Nor did the themes prevalent in James's previous handling of the supernatural suddenly disappear after 1890. The moral values James always honored thread both his early and late ghost stories. They are essentially the same, however subtilized and expanded. For instance, the motifs found in "The Ghostly Rental" of 1876 of the obsessed observer, of the burning desire for risk and adventure, and of the need for reverencing the dead continue to appear in James' fiction—natural or supernatural in type.

James's *use* of the supernatural as vocabulary, metaphor, theme, and atmosphere altered greatly, however, in the *degree* of its quality and importance of symbolic essence. James's *conception* of the supernatural changed in *kind* as well; it changed to an instinctive sense that there was more often "something there" to fascinate than to be lightly dismissed.

James consistently placed emphasis upon man's relationship with man. Because of this, not in spite of it, he produced an extensive body of writing that examines such matters as veridical hallucinations, pursuit of ghostly presences, mental telepathy, clairvoyancy, and hauntedness. The reasoned search for the meaning of reality in a universe seen as increasingly hostile, irrational, and unreal remained a constant throughout James's life. Both before and after that significant decade of the 1880's he looked at life with the same disturbing gaze that marks his photographic portraits. In the later years his protuberant eyes bulged further, able to see more clearly that reality might be interior, imperceptible by "Newton's vision" and unprovable by laboratory methods.

James had to come to these conclusions naturally, not by philosophical or theological compulsions, but as the result of his artistic needs. Here we sweep back around the circle. James did not alter his attitudes toward the supernatural merely because of his art; still, whatever the effects of these changes, and whatever their intellectual and emotional causes, they were aesthetic in their consequences. And this is primarily a book about consequences.

In Kenneth Burke's "Prologue in Heaven" (contained within his *The Rhetoric of Religion*) the Lord and Satan discuss whether human beings can "really" talk about the supernatural. Satan agrees that " 'Obviously, by sheer definition, insofar as they are *natural* animals, they *can't* know anything about the supernatural. For if anything of the supernatural crossed over into the natural, then by sheer definition it would be part of the natural.' " The impossibility of such speculation does not stop Burke from such talk; nor James in his way; nor this book in its. The subject must provide its own justification as well as its own absurdities.

CHAPTER I

Strange Bedfellows

Modern Spiritualism as Religion or Science

Whether for good or ill, Modern Spiritualism was one of America's gifts to the western world.[1] Originating in 1848 at the home of John Fox of Hydesville, New York, this particular form of the age-old impulse to penetrate the occult was brought with great success to England in 1852 by the medium Mrs. Hayden. Twenty years later the British National Association for Spiritualists came into being. In 1882 the learned Society for Psychical Research was founded to investigate supernatural activities that spiritualists insisted were indisputably true. Such sparse details hardly indicate the impact Modern Spiritualism had upon the public within a single generation or the problems which arose over where its proper sphere of influence lay: in the worshipful temple of the séance room or in the rigorous questionings of the scientist's laboratory.

Preceding Modern Spiritualism, and far earlier in its origins than science, was "old spiritualism," which viewed spirit as the divine "breath"—the creative life principle—that animates the body. Old spiritualism was totally religious by nature; its belief that reality consists of spiritual forces gave science little to lay its hand upon. In contrast, Modern Spiritualism, a phenomenon of the age of science, narrowly concentrated upon communication between consciousnesses. The living and the dead came into contact by means of the consciousness of yet a third party, the medium who acted as bridge between the worlds of the natural (this earth, we humans) and the supernatural (that other place where the once fleshly exist as discarnate beings). Modern Spiritualism's implied negation of the divine principle permitted the surmise that consciousness might somehow be material; it was, therefore, more immediately accessible to scientific investigation of the actions of mind upon mind. The ambiguities released as a result of the potentially mixed nature of Modern Spiritualism were crucial to its history.

From the outset Modern Spiritualism linked itself with the pseudo-science of mesmerism. This insistence led to difficulties in determining whether it was more concerned with matter than with spirit. In its own social-climbing attempt to gain acceptance as a bona-fide science, mesmerism claimed ancestry in common with the Paracelsian doctrine of animal magnetism once advocated by alchemists. Until the 1830's magnetism was explained as the result of a physical fluid or force emanating from the person of the mesmerist. Then several treatises were written which advanced a non-physical theory of suggestion. Suggestion by whom? Perhaps by spirit intercourse. Rapidly, other spiritual interpretations of magnetism grew up to oppose the original physical theory. When the followers of Swedenborg (whom Modern Spiritualist leaders came to consider their father-figure) associated mesmeric trance-utterances with the voices of the spirits of the dead, anti-materialistic notions gained further strength. These conflicting interpretations confused the issue whenever Spiritualists tried to claim a long genealogy of scientific respectability while simultaneously disclaiming adherence to gross materialism. However self-defined, the strange fraternity of mesmerists and mediums was in a vulnerable position. Because of its common focus upon mind and spirit, it could be accused of or praised for being both a pseudo-religion and a pseudo-science.[2]

At first there was little apprehension over the devastating criticism to come. The 1840's and 1850's were bright years for those who hoped to communicate with the far worlds of discarnate consciousnesses. Worrisome problems of how natural laws governing the living and the dead could be set aside had their answer: no miracles or divine intervention were involved; the supernatural was the natural human way after all. With its winning appeal to bemused religiosity, intellectual respectability, and sentimentality—and a taste for show added for good measure—Modern Spiritualism was an immediate success in America.[3] It is easy to deduce why it was taken up by the uneducated and poorly-educated. But why was it—as first it was until enthusiasm began to peter out in the 1860's—looked upon with favor by men of some sensitivity of mind?

The lure held out by Modern Spiritualism to intelligent men on both sides of the Atlantic rested in its seemingly happy blend of a science of progressivism with an idealistic philosophy of spirit. By the first generation of the nineteenth century, many men—especially in America—were living outside the orthodox fold; that they no longer had the Calvinist or Anglican God to worship caused little concern. Man's right to question all things had been won from the long battle against authoritarian religions. Whatever unease remained lay in clinging remnants of belief in supernatural forces that seemed more than man's emancipated mind could control. Dissatisfaction also came to men who felt somehow cut off from greater realms of being by the insistent leveling process of secularism. Men of the type who might later become "soft Darwinists"—placing faith in the god-like refinement of man's inner qualities—desired a vision of how to transcend the mortal coil while remaining steadfastly human.[4] Many found that vision offered and fulfilled by Modern Spiritualism.

Alexis de Tocqueville had concluded in 1840 that Americans

felt real distaste for the impractical follies of supernatural phenomena. Notwithstanding this appraisal, Modern Spiritualism caught hold across America within a remarkably short time after the Fox sisters placated the ghost of a murdered peddler in the cellar of their upstate New York home in 1848. Within two years several reverends, a doctor, a general, a journalist, the poets Nathaniel Willis and William Cullen Bryant, and Fenimore Cooper and George Bancroft were gathered around a séance table in New York City. An article in the *New York Courier* of August 1, 1853 contained these impressive facts: a dozen newspapers and periodicals were devoted to promulgating spiritualism; more than one hundred publications on related topics had appeared, some reaching a circulation of more than ten thousand copies; a rising number of professional men said they "believed"— among them a Protestant bishop, a college president, members of Congress, foreign ambassadors, and Wisconsin's Governor Talmadge. In June of 1854 the first spiritualist organization, the Society for the Diffusion of Spiritual Knowlege, was founded in New York City. In 1857 Harvard expelled a student for practicing mediumship, in anxious reaction against a movement that welcomed such messages from the spirit world as "Orthodoxy does not matter over here." Harriet Beecher Stowe was soon converted, and in 1862 a message that Modern Spiritualism credited with saving the beleaguered Union was supposedly sent to Abraham Lincoln by Daniel Webster's spirit.

The quickness of assent granted to Modern Spiritualism had to pay its penalty; by the 1870's disenchantment came as swiftly as had success. Modern Spiritualism hurt its cause by insisting that its members depend upon a special priest-like group of mediums. Educated classes originally favorable to it withdrew their support as they noticed the ease by which these professional practitioners, who acted as intermediaries between the human and spirit worlds, could veer into fraud. Further, and stronger, reaction set in when Modern Spiritualism attempted to be more than an uplifting mental exercise. Once it exposed its own ambiguous nature by striving to usurp the privileges of both science and religion, it was in trouble. Men leaped to its attack, and others to its defense. The battle was on between those who set an intuitive spiritualistic vision of the universe against a rational, materialistic view.

Involved from its inception in this, one of the century's major controversies, Modern Spiritualism initially kept its bloodletting outside the church walls and the laboratory. This self-protective position was possible as long as it retained a strong sense of its two-fold appeal and allowed some men to come to it as a new and far-searching science and others to be content with it as a new and less-demanding religion. But there were men like Arthur Conan Doyle who wanted the moon—wished Modern Spiritualism to be a new religion fully sanctioned by the new sciences. "Nothing is secure until the religious basis is secure," Doyle stated for the spiritualists, "and that spiritualistic movement with which I am proud to be associated is the first attempt ever made in modern times to support faith by actual provable fact." [5] The ambitious, audacious scheme was disclosed. Spiritualism's intent was to manipulate science for its own fervent religious ends; it refused to let non-believers in the sciences take the upper hand in their desire to impose coolly intellectual questions. Modern Spiritualism had been safe from attack as long as it was content to be supernaturalism's champion in the market-place. When it began to make excessive claims for its importance, it lost its character with the orthodox as a poor but honest relation and also weakened its position with the scientists as a possible ally to rational inquiry by confusing "purely psychical experience with spiritual values." [6]

F. W. H. Myers, one of the founders of psychical research, proposed that the clear-eyed stare of reason, rather than the glazed glance of emotion, be brought to bear upon spiritualism;

if spiritualistic phenomena were checked out by scientifically controlled investigations, traditional faith and modern facts might be mutually upheld. Christianity was inadequate and so was "the nihilism of the brutes of the field." [7] In one of the best credos of the S.P.R., he later wrote,

. . . we must remember that our very *raison d'etre* is the extension of the scientific method, of intellectual virtues—of curiosity, candour, care, —into regions where many a current of old tradition, of heated emotion, even of pseudo-scientific prejudice, deflects the bark which should steer only towards the cold, unreachable pole of absolute truth. We must recognise that we have more in common with those who may criticise or attack our work with competent diligence than with those who may acclaim and exaggerate it without adding thereto any actual work of their own. We must experiment unweariedly; we must continue to demolish fiction as well as to accumulate truth; we must make no terms with any hollow mysticism, any half-conscious deceit. [8]

Up to a point Arthur Conan Doyle agreed with Myers. (He was ready to encourage the work of psychical researchers as long as they affirmed that séance phenomena originated in the spirit world and refrained from unpleasant suggestions that illicit practices were involved.) Doyle realized that intelligent men, forced to turn away from both materialism and orthodoxy, called "for proof and for knowledge." This, he said proudly, was what spiritualism alone supplied, "so that a science of religion may be built up, and man given a sure pathway amid the quagmire of the creeds." [9] According to Doyle, spiritualism had always been willing to honor science, but Myers and his colleagues were not so certain. As would-be scientists, they found unsettling evidence of sentimentality and intellectual irresponsibility in Modern Spiritualism. It would take more than the mediums' say-so to convince them that spiritualism sought to examine by scientifically verifiable means those tenets of inwardness and reality shared with Christianity and yet freed from its bonds.

At this impasse the Society for Psychical Research was born

out of necessity. It assumed as its concerns those of the Modern Spiritualists, while asserting its own methods of proof. Among the most immediate results was another look at what "inwardness" and "reality" might mean. With this reassessment emerged a new psychology—and, eventually, newly vitalized modes of literature.

In 1869 the Committee of the London Dialectical Society began research into spiritualist phenomenona. Two noted, and ennobled, scientists were hard at work at private investigations during the 1870's: Sir William Barrett, Professor of Physics in Dublin, and Sir William Crookes, who was intent on testing the touted powers of the medium D. D. Home. In 1876 Barrett's report on his investigations to the British Association led to the conference in 1882 at which the formation of the S.P.R. was first proposed. That same year the S.P.R. emerged under the hands of two classical scholars and a Cambridge philosopher (F. W. H. Myers, Edmund Gurney, and Henry Sidgwick), the physicist Barrett, and the interested amateur Frank Podmore. Their official intention was to investigate "various alleged phenomena apparently inexplicable by known laws of nature and commonly referred to by Spiritualists to the agency of extra-terrane intelligence, and by others to some unknown physical force." Sidgwick was chosen the first president of the Society, which soon attracted a number of men famous in the intellectual world: Sir Oliver Lodge, Richard Hodgson, J. H. Hyslop, Lord Rayleigh, and William James.[10] Later came Charles Richet, Bishop Boyd Carpenter, Henri Bergson, Gilbert Murray, Hans Driesch, Andrew Lang, Arthur Balfour, Tennyson, Ruskin, Charles L. Dodgson, J. A. Symonds, William Bateson, and Gladstone, who called psychical research "the most important work, which is being done in the world. By far the most important." [11] On the Continent such men as Binet, Janet, Freud, Jung, T. H. Flournoy, and Bernheim showed interest; leading members also participated in the International Congresses of Psychology of 1889, 1892, 1896, and 1900.

Crookes and Myers alone suggest the prestige the S.P.R. hoped to enjoy. From 1870 to 1874 Crookes had worked actively in psychical research in the belief that spiritualism might well prove a fraud. Then, in Doyle's words, he "came over" to full commitment to the phenomena he investigated. Coming over, he brought with him an impressive scientific pedigree to which he continued to add: the discovery of Thallium; the invention of the radiometer, the spinthariscope, and the Crookes tube; the presidency of the Royal Society, the Chemical Society, the Institution of Electrical Engineers, and the British Association; the foundation of *Chemical News;* the editorship of *Quarterly Journal of Science;* the Royal Gold Medal from the Royal Society, the medal of the French Academy of Science, the Davy Medal, the Sir Joseph Copely Medal, and the Order of Merit.

In connection with his work with the S.P.R., Myers—together with Gurney and Podmore—wrote the two volumes of *Phantasms of the Living,* which was cited as "undoubtedly an epoch-making work, in the strict sense that it laid the foundations of a new subject. . . ." [12] As the writer of the dramatic monologue "Saint Paul" in 1867 and *Science and a Future Life* in 1893 and *Human Personality and Its Survival of Bodily Death* (published in its unfinished state in 1903), Myers had moved from the vague literary expression of religious ideas to the earnest, and hopefully scientific, study of supernaturalism. By pointing out the workings of the subliminal, *Human Personality* gave its readers a foretaste of those theories of Freud, Jung, and William James that were still to be widely popularized. As Myers defined it, the subliminal was that large area below the threshold of consciousness where the abnormal (including hysteria, dreams, obsessions, and automatism) and the *super*normal lay—those powers which linked man with "a wider spiritual environment" and whose natural language was symbolic. [13]

Crookes and Myers represent the many men who came to believe in the possibility of genuine psychic manifestations. In discussing this cultural phenomenon, which was almost as strange as the phenomenon being investigated, Doyle stated happily, "Indeed, it is not too much to say that nearly all the bigger men, the men who showed signs of strong mentality apart from this particular subject, adopted the psychic explanation." To Doyle, these men "were all in different degrees on the side of the angels." [14] Angels perhaps, but fallen in the eyes of colleagues who considered any granting of serious attention to the subject laughable, if not despicable. One of their fellows wrote,

I remember, for example, that the first thing I ever heard about Sir William Crookes was that he *had* been a brilliant scientist, but that recently he had unfortunately gone off his head, and lapsed into spiritualism. . . . . Similar stories were circulated, no doubt from the highest scientific motives, about Harry Sidgwick and William James—in short about every prominent psychical researcher—to my certain knowledge. [15]

Nothing is more to the point than to examine the lives of two contemporaries of Henry James who became intimately involved with the work of the S.P.R. even at the cost of their reputations for sanity: his acquaintance Henry Sidgwick and his brother William. The reasons for these men's great expenditure of energy upon psychical research indicate what they hoped to gain from an examination of the human mind in possession of supernormal powers. In turn, one is better able to see what might repel and intrigue Henry James about the fields of choice offered by "mental science" and its object of inquiry.

Two Men's Concerns: Moral Systems and Open-Ended Facts

Henry Sidgwick, Knightbridge Professor of Moral Philosophy

at Cambridge and first president of the S.P.R., typifies the Victorian gentleman who, by the aid of his trained intelligence, tried to resolve the doubts that same intelligence imposed on his attempt. Sidgwick devoted the greater part of his life to an attempt to revive his lost faith in a morally-guided supernatural structure by logically, scientifically testing the presence of extra-human manifestations in this world. Although he managed to establish the genuineness of the supernatural to the satisfaction of others, his wife included, he never managed to satisfy himself. Yet he had to keep trying.

Sidgwick had to have hope there was a moral plan to the universe or moral action would be meaningless. Man—his kind of man—could not go it alone without the assurance that this world was matched by another world of pure moral truths. He felt a direct parallel existed between the attempt to make "an intellectually coherent system out of the data of sense-perception" and the attempt to achieve the same end by means of theism's data of moral intuitions.[16] Science, he concluded, needed the stability of a planned, supernaturalistically controlled universe, while morality needed the stability given by accepted religious beliefs.

The son of a clergyman and the cousin of E. W. Benson, who became Archbishop of Canterbury, Sidgwick was brought up an Anglican. He was soon, however, "engaged in a desperate internal struggle with the intellectual difficulties which the Christian religion, as then understood in England, presented to honest and instructed minds" (p. 87).[17] By 1869, at the age of thirty-one, Sidgwick decided he could not declare himself a convinced member of the Church of England. This cost him his fellowship and assistant tutorship at Trinity, but the college created a new lectureship in Moral Science that demanded no theological stand on his part and allowed him to pursue his studies uncommitted to any religious faith.

When he first came to Cambridge as a student in the 1850's,

Sidgwick joined the Ghost Society recently founded by Benson and others, but the ten year period from 1865 to 1875 marked his first serious investigations of Modern Spiritualism. At Cambridge he was private tutor to Myers, the one who finally urged him in 1873 to initiate a scientific program of inquiry into psychical phenomena.[18] Sidgwick was ready for such a suggestion. His reading in Lecky's *History of Rationalism* had led him to consider the evidence for miracles that Lecky had ignored and to insist that the miraculous be admitted as a real element in human experience. In his youth great stress had been placed upon the notion that doctrinal truths must be "proven" by evidence. Thus when Sidgwick came to the spiritualists' claim to miracles, his reason indicated that to accept one body of claims meant the acceptance of similar New Testament claims.

Firmly believing there was "something" in spirit-rappings and in religion, Sidgwick decided he must not allow reason to overestimate the possibility of chicanery among the spiritualists; he became one of the first to believe that scientific reason—the faculty most apt to deny supernaturalism—must be used to prove the presence of the supernatural for avowedly moral purposes.

Sidgwick's religious and philosophical position pushed him to the question whether men's minds turn them into "conscious automatons." If men make judgments on moral and ethical matters, how, then, can they be only machines? They are not; only science's single-mindedness makes them so by ignoring "the peripheral and the abnormal, the sense-data of dreams, of delirium, of persons under hypnosis, and so on" (p. 113). The next logical step was to consider the claims made by those who had had supernormal experience. For Sidgwick, "it was natural that, in desiring it, he should seek for evidence of it in the one corner in which it seemed to him that evidence might still conceivably be found" (p. 115)—in the dusky realms of the supernatural.

His was the right approach, Sidgwick felt certain, only he was not the right man for the job. In a diary entry of 1884 he wrote,

"I don't feel the least gift for making a legitimate hypothesis as to the causes of the phenomena, and I am too unobservant and unimaginative about physical events to be at all good at evaluating particular bits of evidence . . ." (p. 102). C. D. Broad disagreed: "the fact that Sidgwick, whose reputation for sanity, truthfulness, and fairness was well known to everyone who mattered in England, was at the head of the Society gave it an intellectual and moral status which was invaluable at the time" (p. 94). Broad concluded with acerbity,

It was hardly possible to maintain, without writing oneself down as an ass, that a society over which Sidgwick presided and in whose work he was actively interested consisted of knaves and fools concealing superstition under the cloak of scientific verbiage. Needless to say, this feat was not found to exceed the capacity of some critics. . . . (p. 94)

It would be difficult to write William James down as an ass. It is also difficult to ignore the wide-spread evidence that by 1882 he was an ardent supporter of Sidgwick's endeavors. When James had to face the query, "Is psychial research encouraging a return to superstition or is it the beginning of an effort to return to a lost sensibility?" he elected the second possibility.[19]

What the older religions and philosophies had been unable to give, William James hoped might be made manifest through the new science of psychial research. Always one to act having once come to a decision, James—with Myers and Gurney—was instrumental in setting up the American branch of the S.P.R. in 1884 (the year in which he had solidly arrived at his position of pluralism and anti-deterministic volition). From 1884 to 1889 he was a corresponding member of the British S.P.R. When the American branch joined the parent society in 1890 (the year he concluded his twelve-year stint on *Principles of Psychology*), he became a vice-president, an office he continued to hold until 1909 except for the term he served as president from 1894 to 1895. While president James also helped direct the American "Census of Hallucinations" conducted from 1889 to 1894 and published in the tenth volume of the *Proceedings of the Society for Psychical Research* —data he called "the first really scientific study of hallucinations in all its possible bearings, on the basis of a large mass of empirical material." Constantly, James made connections between the new psychology he was evolving and the need to study the psychical phenomena "leaking" into this world from the realm of the supernatural.[20]

It was a risky business, William James knew, this paying concentrated and publicized attention to phenomena which the fraudulent and gullible had taken for their own.[21] But through meticulous research, proof might yet be had of "*the presence*, in the midst of all the humbug, *of really supernormal knowledge*." [22] This knowledge might be drifting about in the universe in the form of a discarnate spirit-essence that craved to take possession of a receptive organism. By slipping into a human mind, such an essence might make possible the communication between the dead and the living. And where there is communication there is the chance for a gain of knowledge.

In a letter to his siter Alice, William James praised the way she had faced "the doom of nervous weakness." He assured her that

there's more in it than has ever been told to so-called science. These inhibitions, these split-up selves, all these new facts that are gradually coming to light about our organization, these enlargements of the self in trance, etc., are bringing me to turn for light in the direction of all sorts of despised spiritualistic and unscientific ideas. Father would find in me today a much more receptive listener—all *that* philosophy has got to be brought in.[23]

William was indeed receptive to "all *that* philosophy," but with a difference. The elder Henry James had attempted to stem irresponsible spiritualism with philosophy. His eldest son tried to meet the problem of superstition by means of a truly "radical empiricism." [24]

William James's particular interest has been analyzed in this way.

The relationship of mental healing, psychical research, and religion in James' attitude is a clear one. To him all of them were similar manifestations of vastly important and little-understood areas of the human mind and its powers, which must be investigated by any means at our disposal if progress in understanding was to be achieved. To his own consideration of all of them he brought his pragmatic philosophy and his insistence that a thing was not necessarily untrue simply because it conflicted with known principles of science. In psychic phenomena *something* happened even though it was still impossible to know exactly what or how.[25]

Indeed, "Everything conspired to make William James a pioneer in psychical research," but not necessarily one of its scientists.[26] To James it was science that was binding the minds of intelligent men. His mind, however fine (although of a different mesh from Henry's), and its processes, however interesting, were too haphazard to allow him to systematize fully his findings in the various fields of thought that engaged him. Perhaps as a result of his scientific lacks and certainly as part of his view of the universe as open-ended, James was a declared opponent of the status-quo mentality of the typical scientist. His "determination to investigate the margins and edges of all that is known" took him far beyond the boundaries considered safe by contemporary science; in his eagerness to know everything, he tested phenomena "which seemed to have some other than strictly materialistic and mechanistic causation" (pp. 3, 7).[27] His insistence that questions concerning telepathy or mind-survival were "just as reasonable as any other kind of question" and that such questions were "not to be decided *a priori*, or in deferential regard for authority, but by recourse to rigorous investigation" was not likely to make him the mascot of orthodox science (p. 14).[28]

How neatly William's definition of the pragmatist describes that other slightly raffish type who ventured into psychical research! The pragmatist turns away from abstraction and insufficiency, from verbal solutions, from crude *a priori* rationalizations, from fixed principles, closed systems, and pretended absolutes and origins.

He turns towards concreteness and adequacy, towards facts, towards action and towards power. That means the empiricist temper regnant and the rationalist temper sincerely given up. It means the open air and the possibilities of nature, as against dogma, artificiality, and the pretence of finality in truth.[29]

James was an intuitive thinker if ever there was one. Still it was *facts* he wished, even when working with matters that seemed to deny the place of fact in affirming the role of faith. Continually aware of the irony of the philosophical-religious overtones of his investigations, he observed, "This is anything but a theological age, as we all know; and so far as it permits itself to be theological at all, it is growing more and more to distrust all systems that aim at abstract metaphysics in dogma, or pretend to rigor in their terms." [30] But what was an intelligent man to make of the so-called religions of séances and science? "Are the much despised 'Spiritualism' and the 'Society for Psychical Research' to be the chosen instrument for an era of faith?" he questioned a friend in a letter of March 30, 1884. "It would surely be strange if they were; but if they were not, I see no other agency that can do the work." [31]

James refused to abdicate his capacity to reason simply to please his desire to believe. In reply to the same correspondent who now objected that the American branch of the S.P.R. seemed to be anti-spiritual, James tersely wrote early in 1885 that "what we want is not only truth, but evidence . . . . You'd better chip in, and not complicate matters by talking either of spiritualism or anti-spiritualism. 'Facts' are what are wanted." [32] Always facts.

In editing the papers related to spirit communications between

Dr. Richard Hodgson and Mrs. Leonora Piper, the Boston medium, James wrote,

I myself feel as if an external will to communicate were probably there, that is, I find myself doubting, in consequence of my whole acquaintance with that sphere of phenomena, that Mrs. Piper's dream-life, even equipped with "telepathic" powers, accounts for all the results found. But if asked whether the will to communicate be Hodgson's, or be some mere spirit-counterfeit of Hodgson, I remain uncertain and await more facts, facts which may not point clearly to a conclusion for fifty or a hundred years.[33]

   Although William James never received enough facts to convince him once and for all that any psychic phenomenon was uncontestably verifiable, he continued to stand up staunchly for psychical research as part of his obstinate battle against the locked minds of his contemporaries. Aware that many said "soft-headedness and idiotic credulity are the bond of sympathy in this Society, and general wonder-sickness its dynamic principle," he insisted that "were I asked to point to a scientific journal where hard-headedness and never-sleeping suspicion of sources of error might be seen in their full bloom, I think I should have to fall back on the Proceedings of the Society for Psychical Research." [34] "Vast, indeed, and difficult is the inquirer's prospect here," he later concluded,

and the most significant data for his purpose will probably be just these dingy little mediumistic facts which the Huxleyan minds of our time find so unworthy of their attention. But when was not the science of the future stirred to its conquering activities by the little rebellious exceptions to the science of the present? Hardly, as yet, has the surface of the facts called "psychic" begun to be scratched for scientific purposes. It is through following these facts, I am persuaded, that the greatest scientific conquests of the coming generation will be achieved. *Künh ist da Mühen, herrlich der Lohn!* [35]

   "Facts" were all important to William James, but the kind he understood best were those that blended wonder with reason. In his preface to *The Will to Believe,* he pointed out that "reason" is only one of "the various 'points of view' which the philosophers must distinguish in discussing the world." He cited another writer who had once commented, "Reason is but one item in the mystery; and behind the proudest consciousness that ever reigned, reason and wonder blushed face to face." James put the matter bluntly during the address he made in accepting the presidency of the S.P.R. "I am not ashamed to confess that in my own case, although my *judgment* remains deliberately suspended, my *feeling* toward the way in which the phenomena of physical mediumship should be approached has received from ghost and disturbance stories a distinctly charitable lurch." [36]

One of the most significant effects of William James's concern over psychical research was the path it showed him into the darker rooms of the mind. His friend Ralph Barton Perry observed that James's dislike of "orthodoxies, respectabilities, schematisms, unities, architectural symmetries" came from his feeling that their insistence upon normality missed the essential abnormal quality of man's being. [37] James tried to force his contemporaries—largely enamored of the thought of an orderly world—to confront oddity. He hoped concentrated study of abnormal phenomena would lead to a psychology deemed truly scientific because it included *all* human nature—the chaotic as well as the calm, the dark as well as the light. Perhaps by means of psychical research which overturned facts as traditionally defined, the facts of life might be revealed in all their power. It was psychical research and its allied science, abnormal psychology, that moved into areas men tended to close off in fear of what they might see there. It was psychical research that might show men what it really was to *be* in all completeness.

Henry James and the Powers of Consciousness

In 1851 Charles Kingsley somewhat gloomily observed that the new generation was straying from the parental paths of belief. He noted "the more thoughtful are wandering either towards Rome, towards sheer materialism, or towards an unchristian and unphilosophical spiritualism." [38] Today that great friend of scholars, hind-sight, indicates that, dead center in the nineteenth century, men had the choice of materialism or two ways to choose to side-step it. One could be a supernaturalist by means of traditional religion or through adherence to the new spiritualistic cults that had grown up in emotional reaction against both institutionalized creeds and the empirical temper. Within thirty years of Kingsley's pronouncement there was yet a third way to beat materialism at its own game: the new psychology that tried to superimpose science's tests upon wayward phenomena of spirits and psyche. [39]

Even while each battled materialism, religious orthodoxy and Modern Spiritualism were already at odds when the Society for Psychical Research entered the fray. Soon there were internecine wars among the waning orthodoxy who worshiped God's Spirit and held belief in man's immortal soul, the quasi-religious cult that worshiped man's spirit and believed in an immortal consciousness, and the quasi-science initiated to probe Spirit and spirits. This interplay, assumed in anything but a playful mood, spread confusion over the later half of the nineteenth century. One issue, however, remained clear. For most of those involved, whatever their motives and their aims, at stake was man's ability to control, to create, and to fulfill the possibilities of his own unique consciousness.

The Society for Psychical Research, only in part concerned with material of a specific religious or spiritualist flavor, divided its phenomena into two main bodies: physical and psychical. Within three years interest shifted from spirit-materialization to slate-writing; by 1894 the investigation of ghosts as evidence for survival waned, and the very real Mrs. Piper's entrée to Summerland was investigated instead. By 1908 the S.P.R. concluded that the physical phenomena detected at séances were fraudulent; they also reported that studies of psychical phenomena gave unquestionable demonstration of occasional telepathic communication between living persons without the aid of a known intermediary. It is, of course, what the S.P.R. had to say about psychical manifestations that is of importance in this survey.

The Society was not primarily interested in *things*, in tables, floating horns, and drifting rose petals; it was interested in human *minds*. The gadgetry that thickened the twilight air of the séance parlors was of note only as it demonstrated the activity of the Odyic force—was it natural or supernatural?—that imposed its will upon these objects. Only when the source and extent of that possibly non-materialistic power (alternately called spirit, mind, *psi*, or consciousness) was determined could it be used to connect natural and supernatural worlds: this was the goal of religion and the challenge of science.[40]

In 1891 Mark Twain's essay "Mental Telegraphy"—first written in 1878 and originally submitted to and rejected flatly by *North American Review* in the early 1880's—was finally, and willingly, granted publication by *Harper's Monthly*. Mark Twain printed a note with his essay that explained the odd fact of its much earlier date of composition. Exuberant over the "discovery" called "telegraphy" which he had made some seventeen years before, he commented,

It is the same thing around the outer edges of which the Psychical Society of England began to grope (and play with) four or five years ago, and which they named "Telepathy" . . . . And they have succeeded in doing, by their great credit and influence, what I could never have done—they have convinced the world that, mental telegraphy is not a jest, but a fact, and that it is a thing not rare, but exceedingly common. They have done our age a service—and a very great service, I think.[41]

Mark Twain noted that evidence for the same phenomena he had studied since the late 1860's had been assembled by the

"Psychical Society of England" during the 1880's. Such attention seemed to make legitimate an intellectual interest in the more outré powers of the mind. The society's prestige, however debased in some quarters, tended to turn matters "considered dangerous and incredible eight or ten years ago" into something "harmless and ordinary" by 1891; or so Twain concluded.

There were as many problems as possibilities, however. For one, how could consciousness, the unfathomable entity, be studied by a science based—as sciences thought they had to be—upon mechanistic ideas alien to the entire concept of spirit? In Henri Bergson's words to the S.P.R. in 1913, "the phenomena with which you are occupied are undeniably of the same kind as those which form the subject-matter of natural science, whilst the method you follow, and that you are obliged to follow, has often no relation with that of any of the sciences of nature." [42] For all their hopes, the founders of the S.P.R. knew that "the fundamental cause of the characteristic difficulty and controversy which attaches to psychical research is the fact that we are called upon to weigh one improbability against another." [43] It was improbable that sane, respectable witnesses should be lying or deceived; the occult events described by them were also improbable. One could hardly control the wayward actions of the mind long enough to examine its actions, especially the mind no longer attached to the body. Yet was it not in the direction of the unfathomable, the improbable, and the uncontrollable that the really meaningful answers to life seemed to lie? If the top of Sisyphus's hill were ever gained and held, before men's eyes would stretch an expanse of knowledge far greater than that possible to those who conceived of life in physical terms alone. But in the midst of these aspirations the sense of the absurd was all too present.

In 1900 Theodore Flournoy reported to his friend and fellow S.P.R. man, William James, concerning the hopes and the follies, and their mutual toppling, that had had dramatic enactment at the International Congress of Psychologists in Paris (in the same

year and at the same place Henry Adams received an overwhelming revelation of a very different kind of occult force).

The main part of the Congress was, I believe, the presentation of Spiritism in the form of several projects . . . which very much scandalized
the narrow-minded anatomophysiological group. . . . As for the *Institut
Psychique International*, that great humbug of the mystically minded will
have lived as long as roses or two-headed monsters live. It was solemnly
presented to the Congress in a dignified way by Ochorowicz, and supported by Richet; I waved my little censer for it too,—and, in the evening the Institut received sumptuously all the members of the Congress
in its own quarters, a superb apartment put at their disposal by some
opulent Russian prince. It was as glamourous as a soap bubble that is
about to burst. The next day, at the meeting of the organizing committee
which was to draw up the constitution and rules of the budding Institut,
they came to the conclusion . . . that it was necessary to postpone
everything until the Institut possessed a capital of from 300,000 to 500,-
000 francs—that is to say, as I see it, putting it off indefinitely. To sum
up, a firstclass funeral following a fairy baptism. Console yourself for
being unwillingly one of the god-fathers of this illustrious still-born
child by realizing that you are in good company; the final ridiculous
outcome of this colossal hoax is shared by so many accomplices that
there is just enough absurdity spurting on each member to allow us to
laugh ourselves silly over human stupidity! The Institut could live only
on misapprehension; it was dead as soon as people began to suspect it
a little. In the thought of the initiators, Yourievitch, Murray, etc. it was
a matter of a collective enterprise devoted to rigorous scientific study
of *spirito-occulto-supranormal* phenomena; but for that it was necessary
that at its head there should be leaders of indisputable scientific reputation such as Janet (and I had given it my support only on this strict
condition, as did many others)—and not people who are suspect (such
as Rochas, etc.). On the other hand, Janet consented to devote himself
to it only with the very fixed idea that it would not be concerned with
occultism, spiritism, etc. This contradiction in both internals and exter-
nals became evident through the discussion about the name, some members wishing Institut PSYCHIQUE, this word alone being capable of interesting the general public and adding money to the treasury of the
Institut—other members demanding the name Institut PSYCHO-
LOGIQUE, in order to stress a concern with psychological studies in

general, to the exclusion of the occult field. But the general public will never bring its offerings to an institution whose aim is not to satisfy the public curiosity on psychic, occult facts. "Uberhaupt," it is not through an institution created at one stroke, with fanfare and trumpets, that science progresses generally; and it needed the megalomanic naïveté of a slavic brain, over-excited by the atmosphere of Paris, to give birth to this grandiose dream of an establishment in Paris where, at the expense of all the nations, mediums coming from all four corners of the world would be hospitalized until the official experts in charge of investigating them could finally proclaim what is true and untrue about the mysteries of the after-world! "

It was Henri Bergson, philosopher of the intuitive, the time-flux, and the *élan vital*, who mused on what would have happened if modern science had evolved as a science of the mind. In the previously cited speech, presented when he assumed the presidency of the S.P.R. in 1913, Bergson pointed out that if science's tradition had been mental rather than physical, psychology would, by now, be far beyond physics; psychical research would stand as science's primary preoccupation, and men would be closer to life than to mechanics. In his conjectures Bergson saw this science totally devoted to that vital inward force that rules outward forms. If two centuries earlier men had only known they stood at the fork of the road leading in one direction toward the natural and the physical and in the other toward the supernatural and the mental, and had taken the latter turn, "We should have gone very far in what at present we call the unknown or the occult, but we should have known less of physics, chemistry, or mechanics, unless which is very probable, we should have come upon them by another road as we traveled round the occult."

Perhaps better to have no physics than no psychical knowledge. The first gave man the illusion of power over his world; the second would have given him power over himself.

It would be monstrous and inexplicable that we should be only what we appear to be, nothing but ourselves, whole and complete in ourselves, separated, isolated, circumscribed by our bodies, our consciousness, our birth, and our death. We become possible and probable only on the conditions that we project beyond ourselves on every side, and that we stretch in every direction throughout time and space.

The expansion of knowledge and the dignity of man as a creature of more than mere matter had, after all, been the common goal of most scientists—whether, like Roger Bacon, they sought it by means of studies in the supernatural, or, like Francis Bacon, by experiments in the natural.

Contention continued, nevertheless, even among the aspirants after the same expanded vision. In 1883 a correspondent wrote *Light*, the official Spiritualist publication, to ask, "What is the distinction between the Society for Psychical Research and the Central Association of Spiritualists?" *Light* promptly replied that the S.P.R.'s members "are busy with phenomena only, seeking evidence of their existence . . . . As a Society they are studying the mere bones and muscles, and have not yet penetrated to the heart and soul." [45]

There are indeed two ways of reading nature, as John Cardinal Newman once remarked: as a machine—a system to be studied with mere curiosity; or as a creation—a system to be studied with awe. Things (ghosts, for example) that are part of a spiritual world made by a Divine Creator can elicit awe for their beholders, but if the same things are viewed as mere parts of a mechanistic system they arouse only curiosity. Awe and curiosity; the desire to wonder and the urge to know: these reactions mark the difference between the way ghosts are looked at in a religious age committed to affirming faith and in an agnostic age committed to critical science. They mark the difference between the way Modern Spiritualism looked at ghosts and the way they said the S.P.R. looked at them.

Proof that showed occult manifestations as genuine was the one thing that would unite the contenders. On the happy day uncontestable proof came, there would be "nothing less than the opening of a new volume in Science, and the discovery of a whole new world of beings, unfamiliar to us and unrecognized by the normal senses, who yet under certain conditions are able to interact with matter and to produce by their activity and latent powers results beyond the ordinary capacity of man." [46] On that day, perhaps, Frederic Myers would have answered affirmatively what he called the most important question, "Is the Universe friendly?"

Alfred North Whitehead declared of the present state of religion and science, "We have here the two strongest general forces . . . which influence man, and they seem to be set one against the other—the force of our religious intuitions, and the force of our impulse to accurate observation and logical deduction." [47] Before such a reconciliation could be effected these questions had to be met: would science help to confirm or to deny the existence of spirit?—help to put man in touch with "latent powers" beyond the "ordinary capacity of man," or continue to deem him a thing in a universe of things?—help to expand his sense of reality to the width and breadth of consciousness, or contract it to the area of his eye's glance?

To many, answers to these questions once lay within the pages of the *Proceedings of the Society for Psychical Research*. Such answers were characterized by fragments, not wholes; analyses, not syntheses; scattered glimpses, not a controlling point-of-view. [48] Wholes, syntheses, and the point-of-view of a strong central consciousness are more likely to be found in the fiction of the age—in the novels of Henry James rather than in the prognostications of William James; in the work of the man who had stood at the edge of the controversy between religion and science, matter and mind—the man who had looked, listened, and made choices appropriate to his own concerns and had then gone off to write what it pleased him to write.

The cult of Modern Spiritualism and the Society for Psychical Research still function in the mid-twentieth century. Although each group is championed by some, ridiculed by others, and ignored by most, the questions they faced almost ninety years ago are still unanswered by their handful of *facts*. The fiction of Henry James exists too—also championed, ridiculed, or ignored. It is in his writings that the *drama* of the encounter of consciousnesses takes place. The powers of the mind (not of the material brain) gave James the kinds of metaphor he believed in. Consciousness worked for him as an approach to life, as a redefinition of reality, and as art. In the drama, rather than in the facts, as much meaning—if not more—might be found as ever the Modern Spiritualists or the S.P.R. had hoped for. For often the immediate and lasting expressions of what men might live by are neither philosophical, nor theological, nor scientific; they are literary.

Interest in Modern Spiritualism had produced no great art,[49] but the advent of psychical research reopened to writers of the supernatural tale the possibility of viewing the uncanny as an actual, if strange, form of reality.[50] Psychical research made two changes in the literary situation: first, it gave new definitions for what supernaturalism is—extending its dimensions and clarifying its qualities, thus making it, in a sense, new material altogether; secondly, it offered up these new definitions in a new form—the psychological case study of the so-called haunted or supernaturally-attuned consciousness.[51] What the artist would do with these changes was up to him.

A study published in 1917 announced that since 1882 the S.P.R. had had a "decided effect in stimulating ghostly stories." Because of its research there had been "more interest in the occult, more literature produced dealing with psychal powers than ever before in our history." [52] The prospect of what writers might gain from the triple crown of Modern Spiritualism, psychical research, and literature seemed limitless.

If one but grant the hypothesis of Spiritualism, what vistas open up for the novelist! . . . Intensely dramatic psychological material might be produced by the conflict resulting from the double or multiple personalities in one's own nature, according to spiritualistic ideas. There might be complicated crossings in love, wherein one would be jealous of his alter ego, and conflicting ambitions of exciting character. The struggle necessary for the model story might be intensely dramatic though altogether internal, between one's own selves. One finds himself so much more interesting in the light of such research than one has ever dreamed . . . . The personality of the "sensitives" alone would be fascinating material and the cosmic clashes of will possible under these conceived conditions suggest thrilling stories.

In looking back over the literary ghosts of the past, this conclusion was made:

The modern apparition is much more complex in personality than the crude early type, and shows much more variety. The up-to-date spook who has a chance to talk things over with William James, and knows the labyrinths of the human mind is much better adapted to inflict psychal terrors than the illiterate specter of the past.[53]

Henry James had more than one chance "to talk things over with William James";[54] he certainly knew many of the "labyrinths of the human mind"; his specters inflicted with "psychal terrors" were anything but "illiterate"; and there is ample proof that his path crossed that of the S.P.R. on several occasions.[55] But although James's interests were psychological, the ultimate testing point for him was whether the S.P.R. could supply his particular artistic needs.

H. G. Wells, sometimes friend and ultimately foe of Henry James, proclaimed the 1890's as "the Golden Age" of the English short story.[56] Of the three main kinds being turned out in great quantities (the realistic, the romantic, and the aesthetic tale), the romantic included such sub-types as the detective story, the science-fiction tale, the mock-fairy pieces of Max Beerbohm, and the tale of sentimental nostalgia, while the aesthetic school worked out fantasies detached from all but stylistic concerns or dove deep into the "unwholesome and morbid." [57] Onto this groundswell of artistic experimentation stepped Henry James, who has been associated with realism, romance, and aestheticism.

Eighteen ninety-one marks the beginning of a flow of stories from Henry James's mind which confounded those of his contemporaries who insisted that supernaturalistic materials were debased inspiration for literature. For almost fifteen years—the years of his artistic maturity—the stories appeared. Among them are "Sir Edmund Orme" (1891), "Sir Dominick Ferrand" (first published as "Jersey Villas"), "Nona Vincent," "The Private Life," and "Owen Wingrave" (1892), "The Altar of the Dead" (1895), "The Friends of the Friends" (published as "The Way It Came" in 1896), "The Turn of the Screw" (1898), "The Real Right Thing" (1899), "The Third Person," "The Great Good Place," and "Maud-Evelyn" (1900). Nineteen three brought forth "The Tone of Time" and "The Beast in the Jungle," and 1908 "The Jolly Corner," which preceded in publication, though not in date of inception, the never-completed occult novel, *The Sense of the Past*.[58]

In Chapter XIV of *Biographia Literaria* Samuel Taylor Coleridge remarked of the division of labor he and Wordsworth had decided upon for *The Lyrical Ballads*. Elected as the one to turn "to persons and characters supernatural, or at least romantic," he arrived at a definition for "poetic faith": that which is able "to transfer from our outward nature a human interest and a semblance of truth sufficient to procure for these shadows of imagination that willing suspension of disbelief for the moment. . . ." A century later Henry James, on his own terms, was still at the task of drawing forth "poetic faith" from "persons and characters supernatural, or at least romantic" about which no facts could ever be found sufficient to convince the gentlemen of the S.P.R.

One of the main purposes of this book will be to examine the ways in which Henry James merged the passions of Henry Sidgwick and his brother William, while altering them hugely, into his own impalpable probings of moralities and facts.[59] His literature of the expanded consciousness often shows slight resemblance to those stories by other writers dully and with mediocrity committed to the occult on its own demanding terms.[60] James discarded a great deal of what most concerned his contemporaries; he kept what he required—the sense of wonder, of potentiality, of extension, and of power—from his generation's intense involvement with the life of the consciousness.

CHAPTER II

Positive Renunciations

All for Art

William James eagerly grasped at whatever psychical research had to offer; in it he saw very real possibilities for his psychology. Henry James carefully abstained from adherence to psychical research or to the supernaturalistic fervors that had instigated that science; in them he saw very real threats for his art. But then Henry James seems to have often renounced more than he took: among the renounced things, what most men consider valuable. He renounced, his most sullen critics insist, life itself. For one thing alone—that urgency for which he gave up the rest—he held out his "passionate arms." This was his art, his *Bon*, which ran toward him "with its overwhelming reasons pleading/ All beautifully in Its breast. . . ." [1] Whatever was irrelevant or actively detrimental to his needs as a writer, he willingly did without, even the two ways into the art of supernaturalism most accessible to him: the way of religion and the way of science.

The two sources most immediate to his writing hand were his father's religio-philosophical system of supernaturalism and the occult cases being recorded by the S.P.R. Engaged by both possibilities, James examined them closely, noting his conclusions on the one in his memoirs and on the other in his critical prefaces. But almost from the start he renounced systems and cases as non-viable material for his fiction. The reasons for this particular

Big Renunciation Scene indicate precisely those elements he considered most essential for the writing of any fiction, supernaturalistic or not. These reasons also suggest that what might seem only a characteristically negative gesture on his part was—to James at least (and his views are a *donnée* it would be well to honor)—a positive gesture that further affirmed his kind of allegiance to his kind of art.

"Father's 'Ideas'"

The elder Henry James was a confirmed supernaturalist of a highly original kind. When he decided that neither Orthodoxy, Swedenborgianism, Emersonian Transcendentalism, nor Modern Spiritualism would do as a mode to reconcile man to his universe, he created his own religion of spirit in their stead.[2] Although the younger Henry James later insisted that his was "a total otherness of contemplation,"[3] the father's icons of philosophy and religion and the son's icons of art rested upon similar pedestals. The Jamesian religion, as well as the fiction of his son, laid great stress upon man's ability to be "something free and uncommitted." The vital importance of "inward consciousness," placed in "an intensity of relation to the actual," was the issue essential to father and son, as was "a passion" which "kept together [the] stream of thought, however transcendent and the stream of life, however humanized."

Almost everything was present in the father's ideas that might have urged their full acceptance by the younger James as a thrust toward the writing of conventional literary supernaturalism: everything except the two elements of drama and style. Lacking these, all else was naught. Henry would write William that he could "enjoy greatly the spirit, the feeling, and the manner" of their father's "whole system." But he added the parenthetical modifier, "full as this last is of things that displease me too. . . ."[4] The manner: that was the eye of the needle through which all things must be drawn before they could enter the kingdom of James's paradise of art. His father's expression was too thick a thread to pass; or rather, and even worse, it seemed no thread at all.

In his reminiscences of childhood James carefully tried to delineate the sense of void he had felt because he belonged to no church. James had not missed an authoritarian foundation for belief in God, an accepted plan for an ordered universe, clear-cut guidance for moral choice, comfort in time of grief, or a bulwark of dogma against evil. What he missed was the "fun" of a "line of diversion." Of what avail was it to be "so extremely religious" as his father's system insisted, if there was nothing "in the least classified or striking to show for it"? [5] James was quick to admit that his boyhood desire for a religion to call his own was based on his "love of the *exhibition* in general"—all that could fill his mind with "figures, faces, furniture, sounds, smells, and colours" and so provided "a positive little orgy of the senses and riot of the mind." [6]

According to his own metaphor, James realized he could easily have entered the temple of his father's beliefs, but he chose not to since the space there seemed too cramped, and, paradoxically, too empty. If a well-conducted religion offers the props of vivid sights and sounds, it also crowds one's life with people who enact a continual drama in front of backdrops the sensibility considers exciting. [7] How much more satisfying his father's system of supernaturalism would have been if James could have detected in it "a consciousness of Swedenborg that should have been graced at least with Swedenborgians. . . ." [8] What he wanted from religious belief—an expanding, populated landscape to fill his own expanding consciousness—he did not receive.

Potentialities of drama were not absent from his father's system, as James was aware. The psychic crisis that had led to the inception of Henry James, Senior's, beliefs (belief sired by terror) was drama of the first order, complete with a hideous haunting presence and an eerie sense of the abyss.[9] The son knew how *he* would have drummed up drama over the coming of Mrs. Chichester with the healing purple-bound volumes of Swedenborg in hand.

> . . . I felt how the *real* right thing for me would have been the hurrying drama of the original rush, the interview with the admirable Mrs. Chichester. . . . and then the return with the tokens of light, the splendid agitation as the light deepened, and the laying in of that majestic array of volumes which were to form afterward the purplest rim of his library's horizon and which I was thus capable, for my poor part, of finding valuable, in default of other values, as coloured properties in a fine fifth act.[10]

The father offered the "scant son," already "a novelist *en herbe*," the great gift of his ideas with their "interest and amusement and vividness." Latently dramatic as the ideas were, filled with "something very great and fine," "as valid as it was beautiful," they remained only abstractions. Not so the father's consciousness in the mind of his son. Just as Henry James worked out the Chichester affair in dramatic terms, he reported a remembered scene from his childhood as if it, too, were part of "a fine fifth act." Staging his description as if it were the scene in a play, he placed himself in the role of the small boy who clandestinely watches his father address an inner dialogue to the outer world of the "general human condition." All lay in actual silence, but "If one wanted drama *there* was drama, and of the most concrete and most immediately offered to one's view and one's suspense. . . ."

Drama was one of the two elements James demanded. The other was *style*. Style was nowhere to be had in his father's clotted system of supernaturalism.

> Was not the reason at bottom that I so suffered . . . under the impression of his style, which affected me as somehow too philosophic for life, and

at the same time too living, as I made out, for thought?—since I must weirdly have opined that by so much as you were individual, which meant personal, which meant monotonous, which meant limitedly allusive and verbally repetitive, by so much you were not literary or, so to speak, *largely* figurative. My father had terms, evidently strong, but in which I presumed to feel, with a shade of irritation, a certain narrowness of exclusion as to images otherwise—and oh, since it was a question of the pen, so multitudinously!—entertainable. Variety, variety—*that* sweet ideal, *that* straight contradiction of any dialectic, hummed for me all the while as a direct, if perverse and most unedified, effect of the parental concentration, with some of its consequent, though heedless, dissociations. I heard it, felt it, saw it, both shamefully enjoyed and shamefully denied it as form, though as form only. . . .

If James denied his father's private system of supernaturalism as holding no meaning for his art, he also denied the other more public, but just as shapeless, forms of religion available to him.

In a letter sent from New York on a November Sunday in 1863 to his friend Thomas Sergeant Perry, the twenty-year-old James revealed the frustrations his desire for "merriment" or "at least, contentment" received.[11] It was "a wet, nasty, black, horrid, damp—disgusting day." If he could only satisfy "one of the elementary cravings of mankind" by reading a novel, all would be well, but he knew he could "procure nothing approaching a Romance unless I go out in the rain and buy the Sunday Herald." James was determined not to go to church to relieve the monotony, since he had been twice, and disastrously, the previous Sunday: in the morning to a Presbyterian church to hear the minister his mother had attended as a girl, who "gave us hell," and in the evening to hear Mrs. Cora V. L. Hatch, whose audience was like his notion of the early Christians in the Catacombs, except that she asked for ten cents at the door and was presented by "a fat showman" who was probably "Mr. Chorus V. L. Hatch." By day's end, however, his self-determination was overthrown, and he went off to "a service held by the so-called 'congregation of the new dispensation'. . . ." An amusingly written letter by a bored and lonely young man stranded in a bleak Sabbath-city, it shows how religious services as various as Presbyterian, "new dispensation," and "early Christian Catacombs" gained James's attendance only by default. They offered their own kinds of drama, indeed, but unjoined to the proper kind of style. The missing novel, the much desired Romance, could alone have given him both.

Henry James did not care for what the Society for Psychical Research had done to the novel and the romance. The Society was the culprit that had caused "the marked sad drop in the general supply, and still more in the general quality" of the ghostly tale.

The good, the really effective and heart-shaking ghost-stories (roughly so to term them) appeared all to have been told, and neither new crop nor new type in any quarter awaited us. The new type indeed, the mere modern "psychical" case, washed clean of all queerness as by exposure to a flowing laboratory tap, and equipped with credentials vouching for this—the new type clearly promised little, for the more it was respectably certified the less it seemed of a nature to rouse the dear old sacred terror.[12]

How easy it was for James to reject the type of "the mere modern 'psychical' case" when he came to write his own most famous tale of the supernatural.

I had for instance simply to renounce all attempt to keep the kind and degree of impression I wished to produce on terms with the to-day so copious psychical record of cases of apparitions. Different signs and circumstances, in the reports, mark these cases; different things are done—though on the whole very little appears to be—by the persons appearing; the whole point is, however, that some things are never done at all: this negative quality is large—certain reserves and properties and immobilities consistently impose themselves. Recorded and attested "ghosts" are in other words as little expressive, as little dramatic, above all as little continuous and conscious and responsive, as is consistent with their taking the trouble—and immense trouble they find it, we gather—to appear at all. Wonderful and interesting therefore at a given moment, they are inconceivable figures in an *action*—and "The Turn of the Screw" was an action, desperately, or it was nothing. (pp. xix–xx) [13]

James chose to renounce "this negative quality" in order to gain the positive mark of "the dear old sacred terror." Ghostly fiction must be marked by "expressiveness," "responsiveness," and "action." That is, by drama. When he wrote his tale of ghosts at Bly, James had to decide between "having my apparitions correct and having my story 'good' "; between having "good ghosts"—which, "speaking by the book, make poor subjects" —and a "good" work of art; between going by the rules or making his own to go by; between being under the " 'outside' control" imposed by laboratory facts or giving "the imagination absolute freedom of hand" with "no pattern of the usual or the true or the terrible 'pleasant' (save always of course the high pleasantry of one's very form) to consort with" (p. xx).

There were other reasons why James believed that any form of scientific inspiration would deny him drama and style. Science often heaps up facts without accompanying them by that grace-giving sense of context and continuity that grants them significance.[14] Science also has a penchant for absolutism, and just as William James damned the absolute, so did Henry. Science wishes to control the basic messiness of reality by reducing it to order, while both Jameses pictured reality as open-ended, in flux, always dramatic.

There is further "the grim fact that 'science' takes no account of the soul, the principle we worry about," and makes "as naught" the "poor palpable, ponderable, probeable, laboratory-brain" in its sterile studies of telepathy.[15] James admitted that science was probably right in its view that men—"however nobly thinking and feeling creatures"—are "abjectly and inveterately shut up in our material organs." But as an artist who hon-

ored the style and sense of drama that the fully aware and continuing consciousness gives to life, James abhorred the flattening
effect that the S.P.R. seemed to impose.

Of the criticisms James placed upon the shoulders of scientists
of the psychic, one of the heaviest was this: they specified. The
large and courageous (as opposed to "the small and timid") value
ambiguities, those shadowy Eumenides that populate James's
ghostly tales with their indeterminate thickness of being.[16] Hints,
not facts, are what swell into fine fiction. "Redundancy," the
"free flowering of the actual," and "calculable regularity" are
what make up "the wrong, as opposed to the ideal right." [17]

Lastly, the methods utilized by the S.P.R. were destructive of
the premises on which the best ghostly tales are based: "that blest
faculty of wonder" and "the creation of alarm and suspense and
surprise and relief." [18] In the words of James's credo,

the question has ever been for me but of wondering and, with all achievable adroitness, of causing to wonder, so the whole fairy-tale side of life
has used, for its tug at my sensibility, a cord all its own. When we want
to wonder there's no such good ground for it as the wonderful. . . . (p.
xvii)

In this preface, one attached to the volume of the New York
Edition that contains several of his declared tales of the ghostly,
James stated that it is the revelation of "aboutness" that joins the
source of his art (the wondrous) and the emotional effect of his
art (the feeling of wonderment in the presence of the wondrous)
into a meaningful whole: "excited wonder must have a subject,
must face in a direction, must be, increasingly *about* something"
(p. xvi)—that something by which the artist is ultimately to be
judged. Wonder alone could be but an attempt "all at the horrific
itself." [19] But wonder that makes connections between the object
that engenders it and the person who feels it reveals if the artist
has anything of importance to say about "the horror of what [lies]

behind life," and proves his artistry by the way he chooses to disclose that horror.

James's preface to the volume containing "The Beast in the Jungle" further details the criterion upon which he rested his general renunciation of psychical research's implications for art. "Prodigies" keep their character "by looming through some other history—the indispensable history of somebody's *normal* relation to something. It's in such connexions as these that [ghosts] most interest, for what we are then mainly concerned with is their imputed and borrowed dignity. Intrinsic values they have none." James concluded,

The moving incident, the rare conjunction, whatever it be, doesn't make the story—in the sense that the story is our excitement, our amusement, our thrill and our suspense; the human emotion and the human attestation, the clustering human conditions we expect presented, only make it. The extraordinary is most extraordinary in that it happens to you and me, and it's of value (of value for others) but so far as visibly brought home to us.[20]

R. P. Blackmur has tried to distinguish between psychology (that form of "generalized science" used in the novel) and psyche (that form of "magic" used in incantatory poetry),[21] whereas James's distinctions are between the kind of psychology used in psychical research laboratories and that used in his fiction of the supernatural. Magic, however, was also on his side. Probably without knowing why, the lead article of that issue of *The Bookman* devoted to a survey of contemporary supernatural literature agreed.

It is worth noticing that those who claim to have received visions from "the other side of the moon" have rarely ventured into the region of the supernatural story. Sir Arthur Conan Doyle's efforts in this direction will not bear comparison with the work he wrote before his spiritualist experiences. . . . The ghost seen, the voice heard seem indeed to be less satisfying as a spur to artistic creation than the ghost believed in and imagined. No spiritualist has equalled the horror of Henry James's "The Turn of the Screw". . . .[22]

The ghost given credentials and seen is less satisfying than the ghost believed in as art and imagined. This, roughly, is the difference between what is demanded by the man of systematic thought and the man of imagination. There have been poets who have tried to write as philosophers, and psychologists who have attempted to be poets. But James would never do in a dual role as both systematizer and as artist (for all that Quentin Anderson has to say on the subject of James's supposed Swedenborgianism). The reasons for James's singleness of purpose (and personality) are perhaps these: art gave James what he needed, and because his father's systems and the S.P.R.'s cases lacked the drama and style of art, their methods were renounced.

James did not, however, renounce the material explored by both the systems and the cases. When he paused to evaluate whether he might do greater things as a writer of adventure tales or as a fictionalist of the supernatural, he chose the latter,

because the spirit engaged with the forces of violence interests me most when I can think of it as engaged most deeply, most finely and most "subtly" (precious term!) For then it is that, as with the longest and firmest prongs of consciousness, I grasp and hold the throbbing subject; *there* it is above all that I find the steady light of the picture.[23]

Therein lies the drama and the possibilities for style that James took as his in the creation of the tale of the supernatural.

Both the psychical researcher and the artist pride themselves on possessing "the observant and recording and interpreting mind." But while the researcher asks of it an "authentic" report, the artist demands a report that is "authentic," "really interesting," and "beautiful." [24] A brief look at certain analogies set up between these two types of men of penetrating vision can help define what James repudiated in psychical research and what he made out as its possibilities if used on his own terms and for his own aims.

In his 1914 statement concerning the development of his ghost novel, *The Sense of the Past*, James recalled that he had considered the original idea "as matter for possible experiment"—one whose interest and difficulties both inspired him as he "groped [his] way into it, a certain number of steps over the threshold, as it were, after a somewhat loose and speculative, perhaps also somewhat sceptical, fashion." [25] James the artist moves tentatively like his hero Ralph Pendrel through the door into the ghostly rooms of the London townhouse; moves also like a well-trained psychical researcher determined to test the veracity of reports that a house is haunted.

The narrator of James's 1901 novel, *The Sacred Fount*, also expressed the problem faced by psychical researchers and artists alike.

I don't know why—it was a sense instinctive and unreasoned, but I felt from the first that if I was on the scene of something ultimate I had better waste neither my wonder nor my wisdom. . . . I was just conscious, vaguely, of being on the track of a law, a law that would fit, that would strike me as governing the delicate phenomena—delicate though so marked—that my imagination found itself playing with.[26]

This is the man who insists that he feels his way toward a truth by means of the mode of psychic sensitivity that is also the very thing he is trying to learn more about. If he is an S.P.R. man, the truth he uncovers cannot be proven to the satisfaction of his fellows in the "regular" fields of science—those who define evidence in empirical terms. If he is an artist, the truths he uncovers about the mind's invisible essences must be proved intuitively "on the pulse" of his readers. The conscientious psychical researcher is distraught that his truths will not be taken as facts; forced onto the defensive by his own tenuous position, he attempts reconciliation with his critics by attesting to a clinical, analytic, unbeautiful approach to consciousness.[27] The artist is delighted that the same truths can only be felt. By its insistence on facts the world of science may be rejecting a great discovery. By its considered disregard of facts the world of art is richer by its acceptance of the artist's disclosures. Or so the Jamesian artist, *manqué* or not, likes to argue.

Note the remainder of the passage from *The Sacred Fount*. Here the would-be artist goes far beyond the psychical researcher in "creating" from what he sees; he commits the outrageous act of manipulation of clues by fitting them to his own vision. "A part of the amusement they yielded came, I daresay, from my exaggerating them—grouping them into a larger mystery (and thereby a larger 'law') than the facts, as observed, yet warranted; but that is the common fault of minds for which the vision of life is an obsession."

Since he exaggerates the facts for the amusement of it, and tidies things up under the permission of a "larger" law, this Jamesian character, sensitive as he is in tracking down the laws that underlie "delicate phenomena," would never do as an investigator for the S.P.R. He goes too far, even as the psychical researcher goes too far in the eyes of conventional scientists. (Whether he goes too far for Henry James himself—not as amusement-seeker, but as law-maker—will be discussed later.)

There is yet another critical difference that causes the Jamesian artist to deviate from the methods of the researcher: the question of the need for maintaining psychical distance from one's material. Following is the description of the man who devotes his life to the study of consciousness, one who has effaced his personality in order to make himself properly detached and objective. This man is no longer

a living, breathing man with a life of his own; he has become what we may call an abstract spectator. . . . Such a personality is not a real man. . . . He has put aside all interests, all living attitudes, and all the varied manifoldness of his concrete life, and has converted himself into a mere onlooker, whose whole aim is to understand the ways in which things are linked together. . . . [He] finally comes to abstract from the activity of the knowing subject itself. . . . This mere abstract knower, who has detached himself from every personal characteristic, attitude, and interest, who simply watches the processes of Nature and registers them, is a useful creature for many purposes, but he can scarcely be taken as a complete and adequate representative of what consciousness, or self-consciousness in the fullness of its concrete being, means.[28]

Anti-Jacobites will see this as a telling portrait of Henry James. In fact, it was written to characterize the man of science of the kind James repudiated. To James, the scientist as spectator of the consciousness renounced involvement with drama and style in order *to register facts of life*. To James, the artist as spectator of the consciousness renounced whatever denied drama and style in order *to create fables of life*. Further, take note of what the two men view as spectators. What the scientist-psychical researcher looks at is the datum; his material does not pretend to be other than facts. The Jamesian artist's datum is symbolic; it is a sign that stands for something at a transcendent remove from the facts.

If the scientist is a spectator in a laboratory, the artist is a spectator in a theatre. In his *Notes of a Son and Brother* James implied the artist is a man in the audience detached from the action on stage. Yet he maintains close relationship with the figures on that stage; like Lambert Strether, he might well have imaged himself as one who "sees and understands, and he has . . . almost like a gaping spectator at a thrilling play, to *see* himself see and understand."[29] The artist allies himself with the world of the theatrical, with that world's use of mummery, make-believe, and mountebankery—the histrionic world from which science tries to disengage itself as it buries humiliating memories of alchemists, patent-medicine men, and séance mediums.

At his least self-deceiving, the Jamesian artist is free to live in the best of the several worlds implicated with the occult. Wherever he finds amusement and interest, he makes metaphoric alliances with charlatan mediums or probing S.P.R. men. Whenever they are merely dull, stupid, and uncomprehending of the larger realities of life, he denounces them both.

CHAPTER III

Fairy, Fantaisie, *or Psychical?*

Genres, Sub-Types, and Themes

It has been rightly noted that total precision in attributing genre designations to individual works of nineteenth-century fiction is often impossible; it is not even necessary.[1] When faced with the large number of those tales written by Henry James over the course of fifty years that do not readily fall into any specific area, much common-sense and more than a little arbitrariness of labeling is called for. James himself spoke of these stories as *fantaisies*, fairy-tales, romances, ghost stories, usually without bothering to explain himself further. Some sixteen stories and one novel offer themselves for consideration. All may generally (very generally) be called fiction of the fantastic; present are those elements of the bizarre, the whimsical, or the grotesque, drawn together into that ingenious design by which the fantastic is defined. Under this inclusive type, there are several discernible sub-types. Even here, the boundaries are blurred by overlapping qualities and mutually-possessed themes that forbid a strict sealing off of one from another. Despite "the generic instability" that has also been attributed to the Gothic,[2] there is still some rhyme and reason to their various kinds.

"Ghost story" may be applied to those fictions in which apparitions appear (or are thought to appear). Within this category rest "Sir Edmund Orme," "The Friends of the Friends," "The

Ghostly Rental," "The Turn of the Screw," "The Real Right Thing," "The Third Person," "The Jolly Corner," "Owen Wingrave," and *The Sense of the Past.*

The terms "supernatural" and "occult" add further stories to the canon. The first term refers to powers that lie beyond the norm, while the latter stresses the hidden qualities of knowledge or influence that extend past the range of ordinary understanding. In either instance, as literary types they are used by James in reference to human powers or knowledge alone. They are extraordinary, all the same; they tend to shake up prosaic attitudes toward "natural" possibilities. Within this range are "The Tone of Time," "Nona Vincent," "The Private Life," and "The Last of the Valerii." "The Altar of the Dead" and "The Beast in the Jungle" form yet another, very special Jamesian niche within the fantastic that defies traditional sub-categorization; in each, a man and a woman seek meaning in terms of inner lives so hidden from the daylight view and yet so powerful in their shaping influences that their stories may be rightly called variations on the "occult."

"Psychical" tales by James are few in number but notable. "Professor Fargo" and "Maud-Evelyn" illustrate contemporary interest in the activities of the mind apart from the body. Transposition of the self in time and place draw in "The Great Good Place," *The Sense of the Past,* and "The Private Life," as well as "The Turn of the Screw." Self-haunting and psychic vampirism play strong roles in many of the already mentioned stories, as they do in certain works—*The Sacred Fount, The Portrait of a Lady, The Wings of the Dove*—that have no direct connection with James's fiction of the fantastic, the supernatural, or the ghostly.

Taken in itself, this genre-juggling is of little value. The burden of this book is to reveal what is vital in James's ventures off the main path of realism as traditionally defined for the novel. How these sub-types and thematic variations work and why James wished them to work in their particular, often peculiar

ways, is the real issue. At this point, two simple admonitions will
be reiterated. First, "supernaturalism" as used by James pertains
to that which is *human* (no divine presence is implied); it mani-
fests qualities that are generally hidden (occult) to the empirical
eye and that are above and beyond (super-, supra-, preter-, and
trans-) so-called, normal powers. (Where these human powers
came from originally and what larger powers endow them are
matters for consideration James managed to avoid.) Second,
James was supremely an eclectic and a pragmatist of art. He
would use any tradition, genre, idea, germ, clue, motif, if he felt
it would work for him—if it would metamorphose into something right and real under his hand. No theoretical purist, however attentive to his craft, he was shameless in filching whatever
caught his fancy and inspired his imagination—especially if it
helped him create "the really effective" tale, which was "about"
something of importance to human life.

It is almost impossible to make out the uses to which James
put what he called variously "the fairy-tale side of life" and his
"little fantasies" without a notion of how he phrased answers to
that basic question asked by the artist, What is reality? Once we
see how he assessed the supposed divisions between the fancy and
the imagination, the romance and the novel, in light of the reality
question, and how he assimilated these conventional responses,
then the ways in which he went beyond these pat dualisms to
form a new kind of realism based upon "the great extension" of
consciousness become apparent.

Two Worlds and The Rope Between

In 1885 James wrote a friend, "*Life* seems to mean moral and
intellectual and spiritual life, and not the everlasting vulgar chapters of accidents, the dead rattle and rumble, which rise from the
mere surface of things." [3] "I don't think I really do know what
you mean by 'materializing tendencies,'" James wrote in 1889

to the students of the Deerfield Summer School, who breathlessly waited to learn his last word on the art of the novel, "any more than I should by 'spiritualizing' or 'etherealizing.' There are no tendencies worth anything but *to see the actual or the imaginative, which is just as visible,* and to paint it." He concluded, "I have only two little words for the matter remotely approaching to rule or doctrine; one is *life* and the other *freedom*." [4] (My italics.) The sense of life that rumbles over the surface of things was readily available in the accepted tradition of literary realism; and it was easy enough for James to turn to that growing interest in life unmarked by "vulgar" chapters which the current fiction of George Eliot offered. But where did he have to look for freedom? The 1907 preface to *The American* speaks clearly to this quest, which had begun for him a generation earlier.

In his preface James immediately discloses what the romantic is not. It does not arise from the idea of facing physical dangers more intense in degree than those constantly encountered in real life, or from the inclusion of exotic props and characters (since even those unknowns turn into knowns through experience). Freedom alone truly marks the romantic: "the free play of so much unchallenged instinct" and "the exercise of one's *whole* faculty" that leads to "the happiest season of surrender," "the season of images so free and confident and ready. . . ." [5]

As James next points out—in a tone that separates him from those of whom he speaks—, the freedom gained is like that enjoyed by "artless schoolboys" who can "brush questions aside and disport themselves . . . in all the ecstasy of the ignorance attending them" (ibid.). The adult knows only too well what responsibility, lack of ignorance, and controlled ecstasy necessitates: that mixture of slightly weary wisdom that knows it is better off being here, not back there in the innocence of childhood, while yet feeling nostalgia for that full freedom that can never again be had.

The totally romantic view frees one: it is wonderful, and dangerous. The romantic disregards answers to questions it does not even know exist. The romantic shakes loose from "the inconvenience of a *related,* a measurable state," which the statisticians of life value highly. The romantic releases experience into something "disengaged, disembroiled, disencumbered, exempt from the conditions" that usually "drag upon it," "uncontrolled by our general sense of 'the way things happen' " (pp. xvii-xviii).

James pictured the balloon—the rope severed that usually attaches it to earth—to image what is beautiful and irresponsible, desirable and destructive. Without concealing his admiration, James pointed to the writer who, "for the fun of it," "insidiously" cuts the cable "without our detecting him" because "our particular sense of the way [things] don't happen" has been "skilfully and successfully drugged" (p. xviii). Of course, everyone knows it is wrong to let the awareness of what is real be destroyed by opiates. Then why does James reveal glee over the thought of applying these drugs "with tact" so that "the way things don't happen may be artfully made to pass for the ways things do"? (p. xviii). Whose side is he on anyway? Trickster that he is, and admirer of others' tricks, James is on the side of truth(s). Any truths sighted from the balloon are as valuable as those seen on the ground, since "the imaginative . . . is just as visible" as "the actual." Just as visible if one is placed at a vantage point to see them both, to compare and to contrast, and to merge them into an understood whole.

The real presents "the things we cannot possibly *not* know, sooner or later, in one way or another." It is what we see close up, by empirical data and immediate contact. The romantic

stands, on the other hand, for the things that, with all the facilities in the world, all the wealth and all the courage and all the wit and all the adventure, we never *can* directly know; the things that can reach us only through the beautiful circuit and subterfuge of our thought and our desire. (p. xvi)

What we learn by means of the romantic is imaged by the labyrinth ("the beautiful circuit and subterfuge"), which is also the description of the process by which we come to know it. The best way to beat the puzzle of a maze is to fly above it and look down; then we can see the entrances and the single, saving exit.

Life lived continuously in a balloon is impossible; practical considerations forbid it. Richard Poirier notes how often James tried to mediate between the forces of air and ground in his comedies in order to escape the self-limiting vision of either realm.[6] Comedy, indeed, requires a perfect balancing act, as does fiction based on ironic reports of manners. But there are certain kinds of writing served best by the panoramic, free-floating view of the romantic. One kind is that of the purely pleasurable fantasy; another is that of the amusing tale of superhuman powers. Both give the writer the "general privilege" of the "creative passion," the chance of "living in so large a light" (pp. xiii-xiv). Is, then, the excursion by balloon at best merely a harmless holiday for the poor, tired businessman or artist, when it is not, at its worst, a potentially dangerous outing? (As when Freud speaks of the powers of *ars poetica* to overcome the distaste over egotistical fantasies, so that "by changes and disguises," by "bribes" of "a purely formal, that is, aesthetic, pleasure," we are placed in "a position in which we can enjoy our day-dreams without reproach or shame." [7]) Or does the balloon ascent, rightly handled, place one in the line of indirection where one comes to sense what can never be directly known? Does this elevated vision take one sufficiently above "the mere surface of things" and toward the "moral and intellectual and spiritual life"?

As Poe, another balloon man, noted of C. A. Dupin's all-seeing mind, the large overlying letters that sprawl across the face of a map—missed by most—are made out easily by the perfected vision of the true artist: he who sees truly, while others see only partially, thus fantastically. By "thought and desire," we see what we could not see if set lower down on the horizon. What is seen from this high vantage point has its own value to the artist, but it is not an eccentric, hermetic, useless vision for all this.[8] "He values it, all sublimely and perhaps a little fatuously, for itself —as the great extension, great beyond all others, of experience and of consciousness" (p. xiii).

The Ambassadors represented to James his most successful novel. It is often cited as the supreme example of the new realism toward which all James's fiction tended. James wrote the following to describe Lambert Strether's life of the consciousness: "Nothing is manageable, nothing final—nothing, above all for poor Strether, natural"; indeed, much in the processes of inner experience gives him "almost a sense of the uncanny." [9]

James's account of how *The Ambassadors* originated in his mind presses home the way the fantastic and the occult are associated with his definition of the creative process, as well as the life of the mind he sought to portray. Out of the "fact" of a comment by William Dean Howells came the imagined scene of Gloriani's garden and the fictitious figure of Strether; both were then placed against the background of the artist's vision. A "more fantastic and more moveable shadow" than Howells's own real flesh could ever be, Strether was projected upon James's mind ("the white sheet suspended for the figures of a child's magic-lantern") as his hero went about "the delightful" business "of looking for the unseen and the occult. . . ." [10]

James had another hero—his favorite of all, the Man of the Imagination—who looks much like Strether and turns out to be James himself. Such a man was rightly to figure in all James's fictions, whether they are labeled as romance or novel, once James was able to track down this illusive gentleman. James noted that the occasion had been "a long-sought" one. "The personal history, as it were, of an imagination, a lively one of course, in a given and favourable case, had always struck me as a task that a teller of tales might rejoice in. . . ." [11] Once found, the Man of Imagination would be known by "the play of strong imaginative passion, passion strong enough to *be*, for its subject or victim, the very interest of life . . ." (ibid.). James realized such a person existed to serve, not the fancy that dissociates itself from life, but the imagination that joins with life. Still, such a good man is hard to find unless one knows where to look.

James's search and his success form parallels not only to Lambert Strether's own "delightful" business "of looking for the unseen and the occult," but to the quests entered upon by Spencer Brydon and Ralph Pendrel of "The Jolly Corner" and *The Sense of the Past*; to quests entered, indeed, by the best of the heroes of James's tales of the supernatural, who encounter their own saving doubles and merge with them.

It happened for me that he *was* belatedly to come, but that he was to turn up then in a shape of one of those residual substitutes that engage doubting eyes the day after the fair. He had been with me all the while, and only too obscurely and intimately—I had not found him in the market as an exhibited or *offered* value. I had in a word to draw him forth from within rather than meet him in the world before me, the more convenient sphere of the objective, and to make him objective, in short, had to turn nothing less than myself inside out. What was *I* thus, within and essentially, what had I ever been and could I ever be but a man of imagination at the active pitch . . . ? (pp. 370–371)

Upon the base of the realistic assessment of the inner life, James placed the romantic metaphors for the discoveries made in that realm. This was the achievement he came to eventually. First, he had to discover the error of locating the real and the romantic in the external world alone.

As a young writer James admitted he knew nothing of American business life, what "the hovering disembodied critical spirit"

of the usual American reviewer considered *the* reality. Seeking
what he did know directly, James turned to novels of the international scene. He was instantly accused of "sneaking attempts to
substitute the American romantic for the American real" and of
creating figures who "muffled" themselves "in the lightest, finest,
vaguest tissue of romance and put twenty questions by." [12]
Damned if he did work with the American scene, and damned
if he did not, James continued to move at cross-purposes to his
reviewers' definitions. Rather than "brush questions aside," like
the "artless schoolboys" of his preface, James clung to those
questions raised by "the tragedies in life that arrest my attention
more than the other things and say more to my imagination"
than to "readers who don't really know the world and who don't
measure the merit of a novel by its correspondence to the
same." [13] By the time he wrote the preface to *The American* thirty
years after the fact of the novel, he affirmed that his sense of the
rightness of the real had been correct (as opposed to simplistic
definitions of "romance" and "reality"); what had been lacking
within the book itself was the full understanding of where his
particular kind of reality was to be found. That is, *The American*
of 1877 placed James part way toward his eventual discovery of
a style and vision that extends, rather than retracts to the level
of, say, the Bellegardes; what the novel did not yet know about
itself, the preface later revealed, and it took a balloon ascension
to do it.

The preface to *The American* indicates how the romantic can
be assimilated into the "realistic" novel by the man who possesses
the hard nerves of both a pragmatist and a devoted artist. The
preface to the volume that contains such stories as "The Altar
of the Dead," "The Beast in the Jungle," "Owen Wingrave,"
"The Friends of the Friends," "Sir Edmund Orme," and "The
Jolly Corner"—the bulk of his avowedly ghostly tales—further
comments on the direct ways in which the tradition of literary

supernaturalism furnishes life and freedom by means of "the great extension."

Wonder and amusement are found in abundance in "the whole fairy-tale side of life," he wrote.[14] It cannot be ignored that the fairy-tale is one side of life; it must necessarily be taken into account by anyone's full assessment of all possible sides.[15] The writer of the fairy-tale deals in "the unmeasured strange" and finds peril and strength in its possibilities for being either silly or charming. The silly is best avoided, "the wide strong wing" of amusement and wonder most easily spread, and neatness of effect best achieved "by hugging close the 'supernatural' "—especially the ghostly, "the most possible form of the fairy-tale" (pp. xv, xvii).

Since the supernatural springs from "some communicated closeness of truth," the responsible artist who makes it his "basis of vision" may well be able to answer "the questions we would put" (p. xviii). Some of those questions may, "by the very nature of the case, be unanswerable," but one can still hope for "the greatest number of questions answered, the greatest appearances of truth conveyed" (pp. xviii-xix). Notice how often this matter of questions that *must* be faced and answered has come into the discussion; here, and twice in the preface to *The American*. Even if he felt his art acted counter to any certainty of answers, he insisted on viewing life as the right questions to be asked. This responsibility is what James's Man of Imagination promises; whatever fantasies, fairy-tales, or ghost stories he tells, they will not be irresponsible, answer-evading fancies.

To turn to the wonderful does not deny reality, but a mistaken denial of the unknown can betray the nature of life. The careful connection of the unknown with the everyday—of the supernatural with the natural—is what promises the larger sense of reality. "The moving accident, the rare conjunction, whatever it be, doesn't make the story," James wrote when trying to show why "The Jolly Corner" is more realistic than any pirate or detective story.

. . . the human emotion and the human attestation, the clustering human conditions we expect presented, only make it. The extraordinary is most extraordinary in that it happens to you and me, and it's of value (of value for others) but so far as visibly brought home to us. (p. xx).[16]

It was part of James's task to lodge the extraordinary within the human consciousness, not outside it.[17] It was also his, perhaps more vital, task to bring home the notion that the extraordinary must be given full credence in "realistic" renditions of human life.

"The Great Extension"

When the reviewer, R. Ellis Roberts approached the posthumously published *The Ivory Tower* and *The Sense of the Past* in 1917, he thought perhaps to find in "the late, the final James" the same kind of allegiance to literary realism for which the early James was noted. "Every one must praise James . . . the later James . . . but need we read him?" Roberts asked, and then decided it was difficult even to offer praise. "I have felt for some time that Henry James was retreating further and further into himself; that he was viewing his characters not as they were, nor even reflected in a mirror; but he drew them from the reflections of photographs in a mirror. The more remote, the more difficult, the less human . . . all that was appealing to him." [18]

In light of James's last two novels Roberts believed he found in their author a man who fled from his age backward in time; one who had withdrawn from humankind and had turned his back upon any mature involvement with reality in order to play irresponsibly like a clever child. For James at the end "worked to baffle rather than create. Difficulties appealed to him not that he could solve, or show by the inability to solve that they had their own meaning, but just as difficulties. What was in origin an art became a game . . . the worst of all games, a game of skill . . ." (p. 107).

Originally, Roberts mused, James's sense of reality was close to that of Richardson and Flaubert. As long as it remained solidly in that literary tradition, James's was a good, a meaningful art. Then came the unsettling change from verisimilitude to revelation.

James, in his later work, abandons verisimilitude altogether. Now the fantastic, the mystic, the expressionist may abandon verisimilitude safely; they do not want to produce illusion; they want to force a revelation. But if your observant novelist, or student of moods and manners forsakes verisimilitude, he is put in a awkward case: he has to support his truth and his illusion on nothing but his bare word, so to speak. (p. 108).

No wonder the man was baffled. He was caught up by the labels he had pasted upon James and thus could not recognize in him an artist of revelaton. He realized that "the fantastic, the mystic, the expressionist" might forgo verisimilitude with impunity, but to him James *had been* an "observant novelist, or student of moods and manners"; therefore, James *must* continue to be judged in those terms.

A far more perceptive comment had been made fourteen years earlier by William Dean Howells (one obviously overlooked by others at the time). In 1903 Howells called attention to the fact that

a whole order of literature has arisen, calling itself psychological, as realism called itself scientific, and dealing with life on its mystical side. This, in fact, now includes what is best known in fiction, and it is not less evident in Tolstoy, in Gorky, in Ibsen, in Björnsen, in Hauptmann, and in Mr. Henry James, than in Maeterlinck himself.

Himself long the defender of rationalism and the earthly, Howells concluded, "We have indeed, in our best fiction, gone back to mysticism, if indeed we were not always there in our best fiction, and the riddle of the painful earth is again engaging us with the old fascination." [19]

The matter of where James had been heading in his late work is not answered completely either by Howells's awareness of James's "mystical" qualities or by Roberts's misapplied appellations of the artist of revelation and the artist of verisimilitude. Certainly a strong clue is offered by their remarks, however, confirmed, at least in part, by *The Sense of the Past* itself. What Roberts witnessed was the birth of a new form of realism, however unrecognized or unwelcomed. Incomplete, flawed, *The Sense of the Past* is an example of hard labor at best, and, at worst, of a birth as monstrous as a two-headed child. However, we now— half a century later—ought to be able to see the novel for what it attempted: the revelation of the expanded consciousness that redefines fact as intuitive awareness, occult moral vision, and transcending spirit.[20] It is, in its way, a partial fulfillment of the manifesto James had made public thirty years earlier in "The Art of Fiction." "It goes without saying that you will not write a good novel unless you possess a sense of reality; but it will be difficult to give you a recipe for calling that sense into being. Humanity is immense, and reality has a myriad forms. . . ." [21]

In 1884 James was still following standard formulas when he wrote, also in "The Art of Fiction," that art is the "power to guess the unseen from the seen, to trace the implications of things, to judge the whole piece by the pattern. . . ." By 1905 he had long been deducing the unseen from the unseen as well and finding wholes even greater than the pattern, thus irritating his brother William no end. With barely suppressed sarcasm, Henry replied to a critique William submitted on *The Golden Bowl* that even if it sent him to "a dishonoured grave," he would one day write the book William desired based "on that two-and-two-make-four system on which all the awful truck that surrounds us is produced. . . ." [22]

James's future adherence to non-arithmetical fictional formulas is detectable as early as 1886. In the early 1880's he had taken a kind of Masonic vow to support literary realism as instituted and defined by William Dean Howells. By 1886 James continued to honor Howells's consuming "love of the common, the immediate, the familiar and vulgar elements of life," [23] but he had come to question whether the good, greying, dean-like Howells saw all there was to see. [24]

James realized that Howells held "that in proportion as we move into the rare and strange we become vague and arbitrary; that truth of representation, in a word, can be achieved only so long as it is in our power to test and measure it." He judiciously characterized Howells as "looking askance at exceptions and perversities and superiorities, at surprising and incongruous phenomena in general." But what marvels of literature might not be made up out of wily exceptions, tricky perversities, and transcending superiorities? Was not the exclusion of the unnatural and the supernatural, on the insistence that it did not exist, an arbitrary denial of the artist's rights of exploration? Carefully, calmly James objected to Howells's self-limiting proposals. "One must have seen a great deal before one concludes; the world is very large, and life is a mixture of many things; she by no means eschews the strange, and often risks combinations and effects that make one rub one's eyes."

With the fairness that usually marked his appraisals of Howells, James added, "Nevertheless, Mr. Howells' standpoint is an excellent one for seeing a large part of the truth. . . ." A large part, yet there was more, since Howells's was a standpoint which remained earth-bound. By the next year James knew he would never be satisfied if he went on with Howells. He wrote

William in 1887 that he continued to "deplore" Howells in the role of literary critic. "He talks from too small a point of view. . . . Any *genre* is good which has life. . . ." [25] As he was coming to recognize, this criterion spread itself out over the world of his regular fiction, as well as subsuming the genres involved with the fantastic, the supernatural, the gothic, and the ghostly.

In 1876 Roderick Hudson observed that "the more the mind takes in, the more it has space for." In 1909 Max Beerbohm noted of James:

To read (say) "The Golden Bowl" or "The Wings of the Dove" is like taking a long walk uphill, panting and perspiring and almost of a mind to turn back, until, when you look back and down, the country is magically beneath your gaze, as you never saw it yet; so that you toil on gladly up the heights, for the larger prospects that will be waiting for you. [26]

The expanded vision became appropriate to all James's works; his avowed supernatural fiction simply made the upward journey easier since it provided its own quick balloon ascension into the world of "blest wonder."

Men who try to take larger views of life often test the possibilities for expansiveness offered by religion (that which rises above human consciousness toward the divine source), or the subconscious (that which probes beneath human consciousness), or the romantic (that which frees itself from consciousness altogether). James's ruminations and final choices in each of these areas are apparent and important. We have looked at his opinion of the romantic; remaining are James's attitudes toward the possibilities for extension of religion and the subconscious.

R. P. Blackmur once characterized James as "an example of what happens to a religious man when institutionalized religion is taken away." [27] James made his art fill the place left void by his indifference to conventional belief. Many men have traded religious belief for art; James made a religion of art and an art of supernaturalism as well, and rested both upon his particular notion of the expansive powers of consciousness and the positioning overlook they could give him.[28]

James often placed discussion of the aesthetics of consciousness within a context of religious concerns, or, in reverse, sometimes spoke of art in spiritual terms. As an agnostic James did not *know*, but he did believe in "souls" and "spirit." Of course, he defined these words as "consciousness"—that human state of being which has nothing to do with abstractions of divinity. But even where he, like his brother William, pressed consciousness toward psychic explanations, divorcing it from theological interpretations, Henry often retained the metaphoric language of conventional belief.

A passage in *Notes of a Son and Brother* makes it clear that as a young man James thought the influence upon him of the Reverend Willam C. Leverett was slight compared to that of the painter William Hunt.[29] Rather than religion, it was art, early and late, that gave him a sense of extension. In 1910 he expressed in a significant phrase his belief that art gave him "the consecrated 'interest' of consciousness [that] so peoples and animates and extends and transforms itself; it so gives me the chance to take, on behalf of my personality, these inordinate intellectual and irresponsible liberties with the idea of things." [30] It was "above all as an artist" that he appreciated

this beautiful and enjoyable independence of thought and more especially this assault of the boundlessly multiplied personal relation (my own), which carries me beyond even any "profoundest" observation of this world whatever, and any mortal adventure, and refers me to realizations I am condemned as yet but to dream of.

If the religion of art acted to expand James's own sense of life, the art of supernaturalism served him in solving certain problems besetting the secular writer of unbounded human consciousness: problems of how to objectify supernormal influences, nebulous appearances, and ambiguous realities; how to present the link between the *mundus sensibilis* and the *mundus intelligibilis:* how to make external inner terrors and revelations; how to dramatize what is seen in juxtaposition with what is signified.

As contrast and comparison, note how the seventeenth and eighteenth centuries turned to debates over the definition of "extension," for when it came time for James to declare himself, his "science of the soul" would cause him to attribute it to that which possesses no material substance—the human consciousness.

In the 1640's the Cambridge Platonist Henry More and René Descartes engaged in correspondence concerning their differing views of the nature of the universe, God, and the soul. They returned repeatedly to the question of "extension." [31] Descartes insisted that only material bodies possess this quality, not the soul or mind. Henry More affirmed that, however immaterial, the soul—even God's—possesses extension in order to exist in the world; extension is not to be equated with matter since spirit must be included within its definition. Descartes countered with the argument that an extended entity is something we can imagine ("be it an *ens rationis* or a real thing"), but that souls, minds, God can only touch our understanding; extension requires substance and substance is matter.

During the eighteenth century, extension was increasingly thought of as independent of bodily solidity, while matter was itself spiritualized by means of the notion of immensity. [32] From Locke to Grove and from Addison to John Langhorne and John Baillie, aestheticians of the mind developed definitions in light of the Sublime in their need for a concept of unlimited human knowledge. The previous desire to leap away from earth in order to find divine sources of revelation was replaced by an effort to discover the source of awe here and now, not to do away with awe's magnifications altogether.

The controversies of the seventeenth century could never concern Henry James. He might have been intrigued by one point alone: that it was mind that possessed "the great extension" while matter had nothing to do with the question. As for the eighteenth century's whirl of debate, on three counts alone James's "great extension" would never coincide with "the aesthetics of the infinite." That century took its delight in immensity without form or symmetry; it was an immensity that comes into men's imaginations via the unconscious; it came by means of a mechanistic piling up of sensations. These attributes of formlessness, unconsciousness, and mechanistic promiscuity would be enough to make James look askance, even if all other differences of philosophy, psychology, and aesthetics separating the two centuries were overlooked. Further, the eighteenth century—which tended to separate the "beautiful" from the "sublime"—honored the latter most, especially when enjoyed apart in fine solitude. James had no need of sublimity; he acted in the name of "the *beautiful* report" of human relationships made possible by the shared sense of "the great extension" as defined by late nineteenth-century psychology and his own discoveries in the art of fiction.

Robert J. Reilly's article on "Henry James and the Morality of Fiction" covers important ground in this matter, with the analogies it finds between Henry James's moral beliefs and William James's concern over "human awareness of the multiplicity of the qualities of 'the divine.' " [33] Reilly points up the subjective quality of Jamesian religious life, which allows all angles of vision and grants validity to all religious feelings. With his stress, however, on the brothers' delight in "the always fascinating individual case" in a "world in which no moral act is uninteresting, or untypical, or unimportant," Reilly projects a notion of moral relativism or authorial indifference which is more like the Joycean artist-creator paring his nails impervious to the consequences of his characters' actions; it is at odds with my view (excellently stated by Dorothea Krook[34]) that Henry James's characters "all mind passionately what is morally right even when what they in fact do is morally wrong. . . ." Perhaps James's own notations contained in *French Poets and Novelists* [35] are closer yet to the mark; in one place he associates the "moral" with a "deeply sympathetic sense of the wonderful complexity of our souls"; in another he also insists that "the whole thinking man is one" and we dare not, in our love, leave out "the moral element" from one's complex "appreciation of an artistic total." Morally flexible, lover of multiplicity, foe of outmoded definitions of right and wrong behavior, and one of the most compassionate of modern writers, James is, however, a writer who wrote with passion about a vision of goodness whose dominating wholeness must never be reduced to the merely pleasurable, unique particle. (He creates this sense of wholeness in his works of fiction, not just in passing in his journals and letters; there is often the sense that his fiction contains a totality of vision lacking in his personal statements because of the public quality and artistic rendering they possess in that form alone.)

If James did not see the positive moral pattern in its entirety from the vantage point of his angle of expanded vision, then he saw nothing. Some interpreters of James would have it this way,[36] but I continue to concur with Dorothea Krook that James managed as well as a man can to see whole and to see meaning in that whole. Nothingness and negation and chaos are included in that vision, since without these qualities he would cheat on the complexity that must contain all within it even while connecting the parts into *something*—something positive and ordered—by the very power of the moral vision that resists the notion that the presence of the opposite of virtue cancels it as a fact of life. These are assertions as yet; they are still to be proved by an examination of James's fiction—in this instance his art of the supernatural, his most immediate response to the urge to expand life to its totality, not contract it to zero.

It was, characteristically, the conscious mind in which James most interested himself. In this James's fiction differs in kind from many novels encountered today, just as it presented a new face from the earlier literature of the unconsciously received sublime. Tales about psychic manifestations now turn readily to the subliminal levels of the human mind. Irrationality, insanity, and surrealistic babblings furnish the stuff for modern ghost stories of guilt, terror, and uncanny perceptions. In his study *Stream of Consciousness in The Modern Novel,* Robert Humphrey refuses to separate consciousness from subconsciousness and pre-consciousness. To Humphrey and other recent students of the subject, consciousness' range is vertical (non-awareness rising through multiple layers toward full awareness), as well as horizontal (dull awareness at the left, shading all the way toward acute awareness at the far right).[37] Most of us tend to ignore Freud as a "strong exponent of reason and of the practical values of the daylight world of consciousness" in favor of Freud as lord of the deeply-layered twilight zones of the mind.[38] The inclusion of these vertical layers seems literature's gain and psychology's hope.

Unalloyed pleasure over the contemplation of multiple layers of consciousness was not necessarily felt by James's contemporaries. James Iverach, the compiler for Hastings' *Encyclopaedia* for the entry under "Consciousness" took umbrage with the notions held by William James and William Sandys. To Iverach there was no hope that psychology or science could turn to this buried layer "for the principles of rational explanation." The unconscious "must remain a negative conception" quite outside the scope of psychological investigation. It is better left out there, untouched, since the "effects of this doctrine of the sub-conscious self on psychology, ethics, and theology are so far-reaching, and to us so disastrous" because a doctrine which offers no certainties to reinforce the "truth, reality, and necessity" that make man civilized.[39]

Reasons that alarmed conventional moralists like Iverach need not have deterred an artist like Henry James. Evidence of unconscious and pre-conscious motivations are certainly present in James's writing (and, according to Freudian critics galore, in James's own psyche).[40] But James usually chose not to make the subconscious the realm of his fictional plots, or to hand over its modes of expression to his characters. Wherever the subconscious appears James hastens to show it in the process of being brought up to the level of consciousness; this movement from the hidden (the art of the occult) to the revealed (the art of revelation) becomes structural, an intrinsic part of plot and theme through stress on the coming to awareness of an initiated mind; or the reverse situation receives his attention, as when the more benighted characters act out their inability to know, truly, what they are all so consciously about. In either instance, the author is working on the readers' conscious awareness of what the characters' consciousnesses are bringing to the light (whether their light and ours, or ours alone).

Max Beerbohm's famous cartoon shows James's beady eyes fixed upon two clandestine pairs of shoes resting outside a bedroom door. This characterizes an altogether conscious mind at work. We are not told of what James might have been aware if he had examined those shoes while in the throes of nightmare, while struggling through delirium, or while touching the raw edges of insanity. The consciousness James presents fictionally is horizontal in Humphrey's terms, not vertical; it is inclusive, rather than the overly exclusive concentration given by the fiction that purports to account for men's subconscious instincts alone.

James made his attitudes on this matter clear when he described the very scene that Beerbohm would depict in his car-

Ashmolean Museum, Oxford

Mr. Henry James

toon. In an essay on D'Annunzio written in 1904, James criticized that fiction which separated physical passion from the whole act of living; to him the result was empty, partial, modified of truth and beauty. Where *passione* looms large, James felt "that by the operation of a singular law no place speedily appears to be left for anything else." [41] Such a self-enclosing art is

> [s]hut out from the rest of life, shut out from all fruition and assimilation [and] has no more dignity than—to use a homely image—the boots or shoes that we see, in the corridors of promiscuous hotels, standing often in double pairs, at the doors of rooms. Detached and unassociated these clusters of objects present, however obtruded, no importance.

It will be what "the participants do with their agitation, in short, or even what it does with them, *that* is the stuff of poetry. . . ." But passion—vertical instincts unrelated to people consciously aware of the quality of their responsiveness to life's horizontal range—has "neither duration, nor propagation, nor common kindness, nor common consistency, with other relations, common congruity with the rest of life."

The Two "Marriages"

James's amanuensis, Theodora Bosanquet, did more than type. She watched, made notes, and came to conclusions. One such was that James contracted two "marriages" with Romance and Experience (translation: romanticism and realism). Another conclusion was that he tried to merge the marriages into a single union.[42] This sounds either like the bigamy perpetrated by a lecher or an exemplary lover's attempt at total reconciliation. It also sounds as if James were acting like an unwitting Hegelian or Coleridgean. Perhaps that is what he was, in his yearning after extension.

James delighted—often overly much—in the dramatic interplay that results from ambiguities, ambivalences, contradictions, and paradoxes. An artist devoted to opposites tends to fragment life by seeing it as multiples, but the novelist of synthesis gathers everything into a ball composed of tied-together snippets. Just as the fairy-tale wanderer (or the Whitmanian spider) throws a ball of filaments far ahead of him and then follows after its seemingly accidental course, moving along its unraveled length, whose end he retains in his hand, James tried to extend his consciousness into the world in order to wander after it, attached by it both to that world and to the central self. "Till the world is an unpeopled void," he wrote in 1904, "there will be an image in the mirror." [43]

Hegel noted the conflict between the dual aspects of the consciousness when the changing and individual opposed the changeless and universal. In the end, he believed, consciousness resolves its antagonisms and recognizes its oneness. James also noted the cross-purposes worked by "the precious element of contrast and antithesis"; he, too, sought a way to make contradictions "somehow hang together." [44] When this happens, they are not merely the sum of their parts; the newly evolved form suggests "a tissue of implications, extensions, and connections in the central set of relationships. . . ." [45] Connections may only add together what is already present, but implications and extensions reach far beyond what is solidly seen.

A bigamist is a man who lives in two places. As a result he sometimes contradicts himself as he moves from wife to wife. A writer who is both romanticist and realist—however much he merges the two into a single union—is also found unexpectedly in strange places, speaking in outrageous contradictions. James was an agnostic, a humanist, and a part-time realist in the conventional sense; this mortal coil was the empirically-observed place he made one of his worlds. James was a romancer in an unobtrusively tethered balloon that went aloft into the rarefied air of consciousness; that realm of the supernatural and the occultly psychological was his other world by which he could gain a clearer view of the primary world, not lose sight of it altogether. [46]

Since the terms and values of each world tend to differ—though not necessarily to cancel one another—James's dual com-

mitments sometimes sent him in opposite directions. He went
to far places, declaring that if he were not "carrying the field of
consciousness further and further, making it lose itself in the
ineffable, he shouldn't in the least feel himself an artist." [47] To
live in two worlds makes a man a mystic in a very special sense,
as Howells had correctly observed. Erich Auerbach's remarks on
the particular kind of mystical-realism found in the writings of
the ancient Hebrews give yet another clue to the kind of dual-
purpose realist and romanticist James was. However "chosen"
a person he may have felt himself, James was, of course, no
Hebrew; he felt in no way bound by any belief, Gentile or not,
in the Divine Absolute. Yet there is something arrestingly similar in the view of reality held by James and the writers of the
Old Testament.[48] Here is Auerbach describing the manner in
which the story of Abraham and Isaac is told; it is remarkably
like the manner of the later novels of James.

. . . the externalization of only so much of the phenomena as is necessary for the purpose of the narrative, all else left in obscurity; the deci-
sive points of the narrative alone are emphasized, what lies between is
nonexistent; time and place are undefined and call for interpretation;
thoughts and feeling remain unexpressed, are only suggested by the
silence and the fragmentary speeches; the whole, permeated with the
most unrelieved suspense and directed toward a single goal (and to that
extent far more of a unity) remains mysterious and "fraught with background." (pp. 11–12)

To the Hebrews, God's influence acted like the sense of the
human psyche to James; each power "reaches so deeply into the
everyday that the two realms of the sublime and the everyday
are not only actually unseparated but basically inseparable" (pp.
22–23). To both James and the Hebrews the total story was to
be placed in a context

which often removed the thing told very far from its sensory base, in
that the reader or listener was forced to turn his attention away from
the sensory occurrence and toward its meaning. This implied the danger

that the visual element of the occurrences might succumb under the dense textures of meanings. (p. 48)

In the writings of the Hebrews reality was found in the hand of God and truth in God's absolutes; in the writing of James, reality rested in the consciousness of men and truth in the flux of non-absolutes. In either instance, the search for reality and truth turned these men toward the supernatural experiences of the human heart.

Finally, there is William James's moment of awareness of what his brother was attempting in his fiction. One of the tales, he wrote to Henry,

makes me think that I may have partly misunderstood your aim heretofore, and that one of the objects you have had in view has been to give an impression like that we often get of people in life: Their orbits come out of space and lay themselves for a short time along of ours, and then off they whirl again into the unknown, leaving us with little more than an impression of their reality and a feeling of baffled curiosity as to the mystery of the beginning and end of their being, and of the intimate character of that segment of it which we have seen. . . . You seem to acknowledge that you can't exhaust any character's feelings or thoughts by an articulate displaying of them. You shrink from the attempt to drag them all reeking and dripping and raw upon the stage, which most writers make and fail in. You expressly restrict yourself, accordingly, to showing a few external acts and speeches, and by the magic of your art making the reader *feel* back of these the existence of a body of being of which these are casual features. *You wish to suggest a mysterious fulness* which you do not lead the reader through.[49] [My italics in the final sentence.]

The James of the early works offers realism defined as predominantly social and external; the James of the middle and later works offers himself as the not too distant kin of the romanticism of Coleridge and Carlyle, Hawthorne and Melville, as well as to the realism of Mark Twain and Howells. James rests within the

Great Tradition of the British nineteenth century; he also rides the continuing wave of the American Romance Tradition. Through him the twentieth century gained one suggestion of how to achieve the best of two possible literary worlds; in him we see adumbrated F. Scott Fitzgerald's remark that "the test of a first-rate intelligence is the ability to hold two opposed ideas in the mind at the same time, and still retain the ability to function." From within the consciousness emerge freeing fantasy and directing imagination. From outside press the contingent contexts through which the consciousness perceives; out there wait the materials that the consciousness will absorb into the subjective before projecting them outward again in the form of objectively realized metaphors for life. If realism has of late changed its definitions into something new, so has romanticism. The type of the new realism and the type of the new romanticism converge to engender a new view of reality. Henry James, celibate in life, is one of its progenitors.

Part Two

LITERARY CONTINUITIES

CHAPTER IV

The Vampire Breed

A Young Man's Fancy

As a narrative tradition the supernatural precedes the years of Modern Spiritualism and the S.P.R. by almost as many centuries as did Old Spiritualism. The man who wishes to tell tales about the stranger sides of human experience may call upon the private musings of either fancy or imagination; he may also look back over the ancient holdings of fiction about ghosts, demons, and other occult presences and then pull them forward into his own time to shape them as he will. To write a story about ghosts or vampires, he does not need to consult the pages of the *PSPR* or current gossip about mediumistic doings; nor need he depend upon his mind alone. There is the simple fact of literary imaginings, copious in both quantity and time-span, about things that go bump in the night. Further, the matter of whether he believes in the supernatural is beside the point; his belief in its efficacy for his art is foremost.

From boyhood Henry James thrived on the Continental and British literature of the ghostly: the gothic romance, the lore of the vampire, and the convention of the revenge ghost. He grew up reading the scarifying tales of Dickens, Le Fanu, Wilkie Collins, Balzac, Hoffmann, Edgar Allan Poe, and *Blackwood's;* in this pleasant occupation he differed little from most young men of the nineteenth century. The main deviation from the norm is that James stopped merely reading other men's ghost stories and, at certain marked periods during a long writing career, attempted to create his own body of supernatural fiction.

Around 1861 the youthful James (eighteen at the time) translated Prosper Mérimée's "La Vénus d'Ille" at the urging of his friend John La Farge. The rejection of the story by an unspecified journal failed to alter James's pleasure in working with this eerie tale; it had set him to "fluttering deliciously—quite as if with a sacred terror. . . ." [1] Significantly, among James's first published pieces of fiction were several patterned after the ghostly ilk either in their use of details or the fabric of their being; the first decades of his writing apprenticeship added even more. Seven stories— "The Story of a Year" (1865), "The Romance of Certain Old Clothes" and "DeGrey: A Romance" (both of 1868), "A Passionate Pilgrim" (1871), "Professor Fargo" and "The Last of the Valerii" (both of 1874), and "The Ghostly Rental" of 1876—indicate the influence that a romantic literature of the gothic and the ghostly had exerted upon the receptive mind of an impressionable young reader.

Of this early group of tales "The Romance of Certain Old Clothes," "DeGrey," "Professor Fargo," and "The Last of the Valerii" are similar in their portrayal of the destructive forces of the possessive will. Since no question of belief in the actual presence of non-human forces was present to confuse the issue, James was free to treat that matter literally or metaphorically in terms recognizably descriptive of what we know as the vampire factor.

It is obvious that at first James worked with the vampire motif merely to intrigue others and give pleasure to himself. As his considerations of the nature of human will deepened, and as his realization of its powerful potentialities for good or ill took on strong moral coloring, his portrayal of the vampire moved from its ancient source in the Fancy to that of the Imagination; it changed from the act of setting down small *amusettes* to the act of creating larger truths of human relationships.

"Spiritual Snatching"

If the nineteenth century provided its readers with a continuing, often banal, sometimes innovative fictional portrayal of the vampire, it also wove the intellectual background against which the problematic issue of *will* was laid. Some of its threads were inherited; many were loomed on the spot by James's contemporaries. Some he used specifically in his tales of the supernatural; many made up the whole pattern of that carpet he used throughout his House of Fiction.

The possession by the self of what is not the self was a major sin in the tradition James inherited, whether drawn from Nathaniel Hawthorne's abhorrence of the desecration of the sanctity of the human heart or his father's denunciation of "spiritual snatching." [2] It was a sin that seemed to wax, not wane, in strength as the century lengthened.

It is characteristic of James's century that the question of the sanctity of self increasingly merged with the issue of power. Power could be viewed as a natural, physical quality under control by science. Or it could be defined as a non-physical "supernatural" force resident both in and outside man's consciousness; if this, then it was to be investigated and brought under control by such quasi-religions as Modern Spiritualism or the new sciences of psychology and psychical research. Once the nature of power was rightly defined, the larger question remained: would this power be used for weal or woe?

A number of men of James's generation—none more vocal than his brother William—affirmed their belief that the psychical powers of the human will were a splendid and potent means by which man might control his world without falsely dominating it. Whether it was Schopenhauer's Will to Live, Nietzsche's theory of the Superman, Samuel Butler's Creative Evolution, George Bernard Shaw's Life Force, or Henri Bergson's *élan vital*, the powers of consciousness might make man a match for the gods, if not replacing them altogether. With barely suppressed exuberance, a psychical researcher wrote,

The human will evokes energies which act upon Matter. Until now this action has been of a mechanical nature and through the use and control of the physical forces. . . . But there now begins to be apparent a further development of powers latent in man's psychical constitution, —powers capable on the one hand of being controlled by the acts of Will and Imagination, and able on the other hand to affect material conditions without the aid of the physical organism or of any mechanical appliance. . . .[3]

In gloomy contradiction to this highly confident attitude, the hero of one of the best sellers of 1908, *The Witching Hour*, looked inward and "found himself standing on the threshold of a world unknown—in the presence of a power, a knowledge of which he believed would explain all that had been mysterious and baleful in his life." Then revealing that he had perhaps read *Moby-Dick* and *The Dynasts*, he mused that

there was a force at work with an intent as definite as the purpose of an artistic weaver . . . —a force throwing its willing, unconscious, frightened, reluctant, or rebellious shuttles through the warp of time. . . . In the hands of these forces it seemed to Brookfield that he himself and all his friends and acquaintances were but puppets.[4]

However, by the novel's end the same man comes to the belief that certain persons to whom fate gives psychic force of will as a strange gift could put their occultly obtained knowledge to highly moral use. These forces would lose their vitality if their possessors ever tried to pervert them to evil ends; but used with decency they would be limitless in their potency.

In Henry James's fiction the question is not so easily answered. Will is an ambivalent force. There is will that comes on the wings of knowledge as embodied by Milly Theale and will as sheer gall in the instance of Mona Brigstock. There is characteristic American will that wells up in the ample bosom of Mrs. Newsome, the metallic breasts of Madame Merle, or the quiet, somewhat flat chest of Maggie Verver, and there is the vital will that Lambert Strether's good conscience uses to fight against the suspect ends sought by the personal powers of Chad Newsome. Sometimes the battle of the right seems to be won, as when Maggie Verver's awakened will (which comes swiftly upon intuitively derived knowledge) manages to dash Charlotte Stant's age-old wisdom and concerted efforts. Sometimes the worldly battle is lost by the good, as when the cleverly stupid Mona with her monomaniacal will thwarts the fine and vulnerable intelligence of Fleda Vetch (who does, however, have enough power to will Owen Gereth to act as she feels he must and so, perhaps, wins after all).[5]

Alerted by the fact that James wrote a number of vampire stories, some readers question whether James did not use the theme oftener than he was aware. James recognized that psychic vampirism informed such fiction as "Poor Richard," "DeGrey," and *The Sacred Fount,* but what about much of the rest of his writing? Isn't it also about persons (usually females) who devour the selves of others? Is not vampirism the blood-brand that ought to be stamped upon what is most unhealthy in James's fiction? Are not Alice Staverton, May Bartram, Milly Theale, Maggie Verver, Miriam Booth, Isabel Archer, and others soul-suckers of the men whose wills come under their spell? Sympathetic as Leon Edel is to James, does he not insist upon the fear James felt in his own relations with women, a fear that, consciously or not, marks all his love stories?[6]

It has been noted that Alexander Pope's use of supernatural machinery in "The Rape of the Lock" represents Pope's "attempt to do justice to the intricacies of the feminine mind. For, in spite of Pope's amusement at the irrationality of that mind, Pope acknowledges its beauty and its power." [7] This illuminating remark concerning Pope's attitude about the female psyche casts no slur upon the poet's celibacy and intimates nothing about his possible misogyny; it takes for granted Pope's ability to write about women's relationships with men with amusement, perceptivity, wit, and sufficient mental balance.

When certain critics approach the similar matter of James's attitudes concerning his women-in-love such calm deserts them. According to their view (which carefully draws upon biographical data and psychologizing conjectures concerning James's sexual inadequacies and fears), James's women choose to love the men they do (and the men choose to love in return) because they know such loves cannot be fulfilled normally, because they know one or the other partner in the affair must be destroyed. That is, May Bartram wants to be denied a normal relationship with John Marcher in order that she may dominate his consciousness rather than enjoy his body and in this way possess him more completely; Maggie Verver "forgives" the Prince in order to render his maleness subservient to her self-righteous womanhood.

That James used and reused the theme of vampirism to dramatize male-female relationships goes without question. That his men and women rarely work their way through to any kind of physical consummation of their psychically-felt, gothically-haunted love is a fact almost redundant of proof. Central to much of James's fiction are those renunciatory gestures, hypersensitivity of scruple, and fastidiousness of physical tastes that offer what looks like an easy way out of binding relationships.

It is tempting to set up equations between James's private ideas concerning women (if we could know what they were) and the way those ideas carry over into his fiction (if we had any way of gauging what he did or did not intend). (It is just as tempting to make sweeping statements conjecturing why many love stories written by men have heroines whose lips are more than a little rimmed with their lovers' blood: Hester Prynne, Eustacia Vye, Zuleika Dobson, Lady Brett, Sister Carrie, Nicole Warren, and Thea Fenchel are only a few examples.) But the larger question is whether these Jamesian advances and retreats are to be reduced to the simplification that sees *all* James's men or women—who pause (and pause and pause, by means of the sly syntax with its sense of timelessness) to consider whether they will or they won't —as masochistic combatants in the Sex War who hate where they pretend to love, who devour where they pretend to give, who negate where they pretend to affirm. Ought we rather to consider whether James was trying to work out the terrible intricacies of the love felt between highly-refined consciousnesses, with our answers somehow including all the possibilities of repressive neuroses and expansive insights.

Perhaps James sensed that tensions sustained between the sexes are as necessary as those that place our universe on the rack. William Blake said Reason (which he named "the Devourer") could only exist by constantly measuring Energy ("the Prolific"). Life must be consumed by death, just as death is swallowed by life; the waves must have the shore to ravage, as the shore must have the sea into which to drift its sands. Constant reciprocity was the answer the Romantics found; balancing compensation was what the Transcendentalists suggested; the need of the Other's freedom both to create and to destroy one's Being was one of Jean-Paul Sartre's conclusions. James is certainly no confirmed Romantic, Transcendentalist, or Existentialist in his view of life, but he inherited—and anticipated—a number of their implications of the way love's will-power acts.

We need not go further into the matter; it is necessary only to continue to recognize the closeness between the specific topic of James's manipulation of consciousness by means of metaphors drawn from the "supernatural" and the general problem of his attitudes toward men and women in love. I can only hope that what is said here may be of some aid in reassessing how right love and consciousness are at their best in the Jamesian worlds. This may also serve to mark the movement taken toward the abyss when that love and consciousness turn into "the fury of intention" that lashes through tales of gothic stress and strain, of vampire threat, and of psychic sensitivity that knows not wisely but too well.

Perhaps because James was torn between his personal views and those he chose to act by as an artist,[8] he paid particular heed to stories based on the terrible effects that the will-to-know and the will-by-knowing have upon their victims. In his notebooks he reminded himself that he ought to use

the idea of the *hypnotization* of a weak character by a stronger, by a stronger will, so that the former accepts a certain absolute view of itself, takes itself from the point of view of another mind, etc., and then, by the death of the dominant person, finds itself confronted with the strange problem of liberty.[9]

James's concern over the man who takes upon himself the personality he sees projected by another's view of him, and is thus enslaved by that assumed role, is very like Sartre's concern for the Existential Man. For Sartre and James all those who are Other than the Self threaten that self, "for their look, their deliberate stare from the outside, reduces the one gazed upon into a thing." James would not agree with Sartre that one finds one's freedom by remaining within an eternally alien encasement of Self, but he, too, abhorred the Medusa-glance of the evil eye that stuns the living consciousness into a stone form, rendering it a thing at the mercy of the wicked enchanter.

According to one's whim, metaphors of enchantment and occult possession may be applied to philosophical considerations of will-possession; but questions put by professional thinkers concerning the effects of knowledge and will must be dramatized when used by professional story-tellers. Folk tales about vampires have long shown great aplomb in manipulating the material it takes Sartre seven hundred pages to cover in *Being and Nothingness.* Especially successful are those stories about will that show what it is like to have For-Itself vampiristically suck in the subjectivity of the Other, the In-Itself that is you.

Favored by many nineteenth-century writers, and the type that engaged the talents of James to a significant extent, is the vampire-like creature that takes possession of the soul of the living person and, by drawing forth its force, causes the victim to waste away.[10] Just as many aspects of supernaturalism, previously philosophical and theological in form, assumed a psychological form over the century's course, vampire literature altered along similar lines. Occasionally there were hold-overs from the older tradition; stories were still told that depicted darkly beautiful females with blood-smeared lips who fed physically upon depleted victims. The "new supernaturalism," however, portrayed baleful but quite human "sponges" that drew away strength, thoughts, and souls of others in recognizably psychological terms. One of the first pieces James wrote, "*The Romance of Certain Old Clothes,*" is a conventional story drawn from the old demonic school of physical vampirism, but it was the this-worldly vampire's driving desire to know and to will all that the mature James sought to dramatize most often and far more effectively. Fiction that specifically concerns itself with vampire-psychology is highly important as a way into any understanding of James's general handling of the theme of power-struggles between human wills.

If the mood of vampirism is present in James's fiction wherever wills clash, psychical vampirism as a definitely worked-out metaphor for the excesses of *doing* as well as *being* appears in a specific set of his stories. Two of them, taken together with a novel by

Hawthorne and one by Howells, make a striking collection. Closely related in theme and matched in many details of character and plot, *The Blithedale Romance* of 1852, "Professor Fargo" of 1874, *The Undiscovered Country* of 1880, and *The Bostonians* of 1886 act as a brief index to what took place within one particular and favored literary tradition as it redefined the terms of mesmerism and "mental science." Thirty-four years separate the satiric social realism of Hawthorne's romance (with its context of the blasted vision of Utopian reform near Boston) and the satiric social realism of James's novel (revolving around the decay of transcendentalist dreams in Boston); fifteen years later we are in the twentieth century with *The Sacred Fount* of 1901. This fifty-year span marks the path from Blithedale to Newmarch taken by James's awareness of what he might make of a merger of an old literary tradition, a new psychology attentive to psychic powers, and his own continuing, and heightened, concern over human relationships.

There is a scene in *The Blithedale Romance* that adumbrates Howells and James; it mirrors both the Boston séance held at the Boyntons' (at which Howells's heroine Egeria acts at the behest of her father's hypnotizing commands) and Miss Birdseye's social gathering in Boston (at which Verena Tarrant appears to speak "inspirationally" in response to her father's mesmerizing hands). In Hawthorne's version Miles Coverdale describes the odd-lot of Bostonians filled with "mystic sensuality" who have come to witness the marvels performed by the Veiled Lady. On questioning "a pale man in blue spectacles," Coverdale is told "stranger stories than ever were written in a romance." He is informed of "instances of the miraculous power of one human being over the will and passions of another," and of the ways in which a wizard may take human character—"but soft wax in his hands"—and "mould it" into "guilt, or virtue" as "he should see fit." [11] With "horror and disgust" Coverdale listens to these statements, which intimate "the individual soul was virtually annihilated," but he is a pryer in his own right.[12] He is a pryer pried upon by a stronger force—a woman's, naturally.

When Coverdale comes under the influence of the dark lady, Zenobia, he senses that her "sphere, I imagine, impressed itself powerfully on mine, and transformed me, during this period of my weakness, into something like a mesmerical clairvoyant" (p. 57). Zenobia exerts her dominance over Priscilla the Veiled Lady as well as Coverdale, but it is the will-proud Hollingsworth whom she desires sexually. As is traditional in stories about vampires, whether told conventionally or with strong psychological slanting, clear sexual connotations are given to the struggle for mastery of the uncomprehending innocent. Direct connections between sexual domination and mesmeric control are made in *The Blithedale Romance* when Westervelt (that decayed Mephistopheles) comes to reclaim Zenobia, who had once been his, even while he attempts to draw the "sensitive" Priscilla under his power. Eventually the contest of wills is waged among Zenobia, Westervelt, and Hollingsworth to see who can win Priscilla. Hollingsworth emerges the rescuing hero, but one who finds himself drained of vitality and virility by the not-so-helpless Priscilla once Zenobia has gone to her death—the dark vampire figure disturbingly replaced by its blond counterpart.

In James's early story, "Professor Fargo," an itinerant mesmerist gains control over the soul and body of the daughter of an idealistic mathematician who fights in vain against Fargo's "magnetic" sexual powers. This seldom-read story (and no wonder, since it is not well written) throws further light over those Hawthornian attitudes toward spiritualism-cum-mesmerism that James continued to share in the 1870's. It also looks forward toward the views James and Howells soon presented more fully in *The Bostonians* and *The Undiscovered Country*.[13]

The narrator, a commercial traveler, finds himself stranded in a rural American village. Desperately seeking entertainment, he

sees a handbill announcing a performance to be given that evening in the town hall.[14]

A MESSAGE FROM THE SPIRIT WORLD

THE HIGHER MATHEMATICS MADE EASY TO
LADIES AND CHILDREN
A NEW REVELATION! A NEW SCIENCE!

GREAT MORAL AND SCIENTIFIC COMBINATION
PROFESSOR FARGO, THE INFALLIBLE WAKING MEDIUM AND
MAGICIAN, CLAIRVOYANT, PROPHET, AND SEER!
COLONEL GIFFORD, THE FAMOUS LIGHTNING CALCULATOR
AND MATHEMATICAL REFORMER!

The narrator soon encounters Fargo, a fleshly, sensual man
with reddish hair and beard, and impudent eyes that pretend to
carry on the visionary tradition of Ezekiel and Jeremiah but are
nearer in kind to "consummate Yankee shrewdness" (p. 262).[15]
Because of his obviously fradulent nature, Fargo interests the
narrator, a sceptic where matters of spirit messages are concerned.

That afternoon the narrator leafs through a copy of *Don Quixote*
in the tavern parlor before going out to wander in boredom
through the village graveyard. There he notices Fargo in "conversation" with a pretty deaf-and-dumb girl, one of those "who
are obliged to listen, as one may say, with their eyes," who must
use intuition rather than the senses (p. 266). That evening during
Fargo's performance he sees the girl on the stage with her father,
Colonel Gifford, who is "Don Quixote in the flesh."

Fargo's "miracles were exclusively miracles of rhetoric," the
narrator recalls. "He discoursed upon the earth life and the summer land, and related surprising anecdotes of his intimacy with
the inhabitants of the latter region; but to my disappointment,
the evening passed away without his really bringing us face to
face with a ghost" (p. 269). The achievements of the Colonel and

his daughter, who do rapid mathematical calculations in their heads, are more valid. Later the narrator talks with Gifford and finds him an honest visionary. Through science, Gifford plans to save the world, which cannot hope to be redeemed by spiritualistic chicanery. Although willing to travel in the company of a fraud like Fargo in "the attempt to *bribe* people to listen to wholesome truths" (p. 278), he complains about the necessity to couple pure science with mongrel spiritualism as an appeal to "a desperately weak-witted generation" (p. 279).

At this point the story is a mildly comic view of the way strange bedfellows lie together, the one out to illumine the truths of "the ripe, sweet fruit of true science" by means of amusement, the other to gain lucre by means of fraudulently feeding the public "intellectually, on poisoned garbage" (p. 283). It is a little parable of the eternal incompatibility of science and spirituality. But then Fargo challenges Gifford to a more serious contest: a duel of wills. Fargo says he can prove with "facts" (which Gifford as a scientist insists upon) that he has the power of "spiritual magnetism." In his case factual proof involves an outward act, a public experiencing of that power. Fargo turns to the men standing nearby and boasts with drunken braggadocio that

"it's not my peculiar influence with the departed that I chiefly value; for, after all, you know, a ghost is but a ghost . . . . You can't touch it, half the time you can't see it. If it happens to be the spirit of a pretty girl, you know, this makes you kind of mad. The great thing now is to be able to exercise a mysterious influence over living organisms." (p. 286)

How is it done?

"You can do it with your eye, you can do it with your voice, you can do it with certain motions of your hand . . . . [Y]ou can do it with nothing at all by just setting your mind on it. That is, of course, some people can do it; not very many—certain rich, powerful sympathetic natures that you now and then come across . . . . All you can say is that it's just magnetism, and that you've either got it or you haven't got it

. . . . It's a free gift . . . . Some folks call it animal magnetism, but I call it spiritual magnetism." (Ibid.)

At this Gifford publicly denounces Fargo.

"I speak in the name of science. Science recognizes no such thing as 'spiritual magnetism'; no such thing as mysterious fascination; no such thing as spirit-rappings and ghost-raising. . . . I have it on my conscience to assure you that no intelligent man, woman, or child need fear to be made to do anything against his own will by the supernatural operation of the will of Professor Fargo." (p. 287)

At this moment the Colonel has no notion over whose will Fargo plans to gain control. It soon appears that it is his daughter's spirit, and body, Fargo desires. In the story's final scene Fargo gambles everything on his ability to entice the girl's will, and wins. Before the father's horrified gaze, Fargo makes "a triumphant escape" with her out of the lecture hall (p. 298). The bereaved father goes mad, and the mesmerist and the girl he has won are never heard of again.

Spiritualism in conflict with science was one of the main patterns of the nineteenth century. Here science is defeated, but what science! Blindly confident in its reliance on conceptual reason; quixotically ignorant of one side of humankind. Here spiritualism is victorious, but what spiritualism! Vulgar, sordid, opportunistic, preying upon innocence (which learns to delight in its own corruption) by means of those psychical-sexual influences that an unscrupulous mind exerts upon weaker wills.

In William Dean Howells's *The Undiscovered Country* of 1880, Dr. Boynton makes his limp-souled daughter Egeria "the passive instrument" of his mesmeric will; his powers are devoted solely "to her development as a medium of communication with the other world." [16] When he observes, " 'I have seen her change from a creature of robust, terrestrial tendencies to a being of moods almost as ethereal as those of the spirits with which it has been my struggle to associate her' " (p. 180), he seems incapable of realizing what fate he has imposed upon her. " 'You have accustomed all your life to my controlling influence, my magnetic force,' " he tells her, " 'by which you have seen, heard, touched, tasted, spoken, whatever I willed' " (pp. 69–70).

That he has the right to master his daughter's psyche seems reasonable to Boynton. His one fear is that a strong counter-force (such as he says the sceptical Ford exerts) might pull Egeria's will over to the side of those who doubt spirit essences, and so wipe out the progress father and daughter have made toward a full knowledge of transcendental life. Before he dies, however, the terrible realization of what he has done comes over Boynton. He exclaims to Ford, " 'I seized upon a simple, loving nature, good and sweet in its earthliness, and sacred in it, and alienated it from all its possible happiness to the uses of my ambition. I have played the vampire!' " (pp. 318–319).

For all her helplessness Egeria Boynton herself proves vampirish. At one point she falls gravely ill. As she recovers it appears she has lost her clairvoyant powers, but in return she gains physical health. Increasing "normality" marks the cessation of those occult powers that had made her an unhappy creature estranged from the human world. Gaining in the strengths of this world, she becomes younger and more vigorous; simultaneously her father ages and weakens. He is drained as she blooms; he becomes the sacred fount from which she now drinks.

Meanwhile Ford has fallen in love with the girl. In Howells's version of the inevitable romantic obstacle that separates boy from girl, Egeria fears Ford because she superstitiously believes he has placed a supernatural spell upon her. He makes matters worse by telling her lightly that " 'we all control one another in the absurdest way' " (p. 323). Having known all too well what it means to be controlled by one man's occult powers, Egeria has no desire to be controlled by yet another's. Eventually she understands that the spell which lies upon her is that of human love, and that she loves not because of an imposed spell but because a spell has grown up as the result of her love. This is the only "control" Ford imposes; the only "will" at work is her own when she chooses to return his love. The binding power that was presented as partially occult in *The Blithedale Romance*, and depicted as sexual attraction alone in "Professor Fargo," is fully defined the *The Undiscovered Country* as love, that mutual absorption of human consciousnesses. The supernatural mesmerism used almost allegorically in Hawthorne's rendition has become, in Howells's novel, a metaphor for the natural assault of the affections.

Olive Chancellor of James's *The Bostonians* is fascinated by the "inspirational speaker," Verena Tarrant. She admits "the girl had moved her as she had never been moved, and the power to do that, from whatever source it came, was a force that one must admire." [17]

Drawn by the enchanting power of Verena's strange personality, Olive starts to impose the power of her own being to win her goal: the merger of two souls into one. This spiritual union is what Ford desired of Egeria Boynton; it is what the repressed Boston lady wishes of the bright-haired girl to whom she takes such an obsessional fancy. Unconsciously Lesbian as it may be, Olive's desire is a powerful one, which allows nothing to stand in its way; certainly not Verena's father, who is merely a cheap mesmerist with a shoddy male magnetism that is no match for Olive's moral earnestness. [18]

Mrs. Farrinder, another "mental" speaker, foretells Basil Ransom's antagonistic influence, but whereas she welcomes challenges made to her will, Olive fears them. Olive wants to make Verena "an immense power for good," while Ransom sees Verena as becoming simply an "immense power for quackery" under Olive's sponsorship (p. 95). It is over this issue that Olive and Ransom first begin to battle. When he has lost the initial rounds in the generalized contest for truth, Ransom's interest becomes increasingly personal. He begins to see Verena as "a touching, ingenuous victim, unconscious of the pernicious forces which were hurrying her to her ruin" (p. 247). " 'It isn't *you*, the least in the world,' " Ransom tells Verena, " 'but an inflated little figure (very remarkable in its way too), whom you have invented and set on its feet, pulling strings, behind it, to make it move and speak, while you try to conceal and efface yourself there' " (p. 336).

Notwithstanding Ransom's warnings, Verena cannot help herself where Olive is concerned. "By this time Verena had learned how peculiarly her friend was constituted, how nervous and serious she was, how personal, how exclusive, what a force of will she had, what a concentration of purpose" (p. 78). Verena willingly (because will-less) submits to Olive's influence. "The fine web of authority, of dependence, that her strenuous companion had woven about her, was now as dense as a suit of golden mail . . ." (p. 167). The web tightens because Verena's own attitude has been perverted into a liking of her subjugation. "Her share in the union of the two young women was no longer passive, purely appreciative; it was passionate, too, and it put forth a beautiful energy" (p. 168).

James made adroit use of the nomenclature of vampirism —both traditional in its stress on enchantments[19] and contemporary in his references to psychic pressures—to make clear what the sucking in of Verena's spirit entails. Olive "wanted to enter into her life" (p. 83). Verena was "now completely under her influence"; cunningly "the touch of Olive's tone worked a spell . . ." (pp. 137–138). Olive "now perceived that when spirit meets spirit there must either be mutual absorption or a sharp concussion" (p. 162). She achieves the desired effect by drawing Verena "completely under the charm" (p. 167). "To Olive it appeared that just this partnership of their two minds—each of them, by itself, lacking an important group of facets—made an organi⁄

whole . . ." (p. 156). "Together, in short, they would be complete, they would have everything, and together they would triumph" (p. 157). James even picks up that bit of stage business used between Zenobia and Priscilla in *The Blithedale Romance;* on leaving a party, Olive "prepared to throw a fold of her mantle, as she had once before, over her young friend" (p. 153). This gesture of symbolic enfolding will occur yet again before the struggle over Verena comes to its heated climax.

If two consciousnesses are to merge at the expense of one, a kind of spiritual murder must first take place. This is what Ransom strives to prevent. No longer merely trying to lure Verena away from a tawdry career, but to win her from a perverse love, he arrives at Marmion "to take possession of Verena Tarrant" (p. 348). When Verena learns why Ransom has come, she is distressed that rescue is necessary, especially when she realizes the spell *he* casts is that of a man's demanding love. "Why Basil Ransom had been deputed by fate to exercise this spell was more than she could say—poor Verena, who up to so lately had flattered herself that she had a wizard's wand in her pocket" (p. 385). With yet another "force she had never felt before . . . pushing her to please herself, poor Verena lived in these days in a state of moral tension—with a sense of being strained and aching . . ." (p. 386).[20] She loves Ransom but has not the strength to escape to him. Like Coleridge's Geraldine and Christabel, Olive and Verena sway to and fro under the spell of the strange passion that envelops them, but Verena has no sainted mother in Mrs. Selah Tarrant to whose spirit she might turn for saving supernatural aid.

The night Verena is to appear at a Boston lecture hall Ransom makes up his mind to act. "The vision of wresting her from the mighty multitude set him off again, to stride through the population that would fight for her" (p. 428). Arriving at the hall, he finds Verena's waiting room guarded by a policeman placed there by the wary Olive in hopes that the power of civil law can

prevent Ransom from imposing the power of his vital will.
Momentarily deterred, Ransom refuses to budge from the spot.
He senses that behind the locked door Verena "would know in
a moment, by quick intuition, that he was there, and that she was
only praying to be rescued, to be saved" (p. 433). Verena appears,
her face "full of suffering" (p. 439). Quickly others gather and
an open tug-of-war commences. Caught among the many emotions felt within her receptive consciousness, Verena

> trembled with nervous passion, there were sobs and supplications in her
> voice, and Ransom felt himself flushing with pure pity for her pain—her
> inevitable agony. But at the same moment he had another perception,
> which brushed aside remorse; he saw that he could do what he wanted,
> that she begged him, with all her being, to spare her, but that so long
> as he should protest she was submissive, helpless . . . . [The] spell upon
> her—thanks to which he should still be able to rescue her—had been
> the knowledge that he was near. (pp. 440–441)

Suddenly Olive throws herself "between them with a force
that made the girl relinquish her grasp of Ransom's hand" and
pleads that he allow Verena an hour to appear on the lecture
platform. As possessive as ever Olive has been, he replies, " 'She's
mine or she isn't, and if she is mine, she's all mine!' " (p. 442).
The struggle proceeds. Then Ransom "perceived, tossed upon
a chair, a long, furred cloak, which he caught up and, before
[Verena] could resist, threw over her" (p. 446). One last onslaught
upon Verena's person is made when her mother "hurled herself
upon her," but the girl, "struggling to free herself," gives her
hand to Ransom and goes into the night with him under the
urgency of his physical and psychic force (pp. 446–447).

James does not end his story with the traditional promise that
the heroine and the hero will live happily ever after. "But though
she was glad, [Ransom] presently discovered that, beneath her
hood, she was in tears. It is to be feared that with the union, so
far from brilliant, into which she was about to enter, these were

not the last she was destined to shed" (p. 449). The fairy-tale maiden endowed at birth with powers of white magic has been wrested away from the pathetic witch of black magical powers by the man of superior will, one whose love, the reader fears, will itself be spirit-quenching. As for James, he had moved from mesmeric vampirism used as the topical focus of a minor tale, "Professor Fargo," to a concentrated view of psychic assault, grounding the plot of a major novel upon a massive metaphor for will.

Fifteen years after *The Bostonians* James's *The Sacred Fount* was published. William Dean Howells slyly said he knew what the story was really about,[21] but most of us tend to agree with John Henry Raleigh that "One could easily go insane trying to ascertain what has happened" in the novel.[22] However, numerous articles and a book have been written at the risk of just such insanity (in the same perverse way that one takes on the self-destroying task of musing over "The Turn of the Screw"). The concern here, however, is specifically with James's use of the vampire-motif rather than with the novel's entire range of meaning. As Jean Franz Blackall has noted of other critics, this reading will "deal only with those portions . . . which most satisfactorily sustain" this chapter's immediate interests.[23]

Arriving with his curiosity already aflame, the narrator of *The Sacred Fount* promptly dedicates himself to verifying his theory about the soul-suckers at loose on the lovely grounds of the English countryhouse, Newmarch. Is not the sacred fount of life being drunk in greedy gulps by Long and Mrs. Brissenden, who grow younger and lustier as, simultaneously, Mrs. Server and Brissenden grow older, more feeble? The narrator's immediate attention centers around the drawers at the well of the victims' consciousnesses. The reader soon asks the larger question whether the man who searches them out is not also a compulsive imbiber.[24]

Certainly there are moments when the narrator has scruples.
To a fellow-guest whose aid he has enlisted, he remarks,

"We ought to remember," I pursued, even at the risk of showing as too
sententious, "that success in such an inquiry may perhaps be more
embarrassing than failure. To nose about for a relation that a lady has
her reason for keeping secret—"
    "Is made not only quiet inoffensive, I hold"—he immediately took me
up—"but positively honourable, by being confined to psychologic evidence."
    I wondered a little. "Honourable to whom?"
    "Why, to the investigator. Resting on the *kind* of signs that the game
takes account of when fairly played—resting on psychologic signs alone,
it's a high application of intelligence. What's ignoble is the detective and
the keyhole." [25]

The narrator is reassured that a "psychologic" investigation
carried on by the amateur out of love for pure knowledge is of
no harm (in distinction from the professional detective, who is
lowered to the level of paid voyeurist). However, he soon takes
"a lively resolve to get rid of my ridiculous obsession. It was
absurd to have consented to such immersion, intellectually speaking, in the affairs of other people" (p. 89). His brief resolution
wavers and falls before his proud sense that *he* can succeed where
all others fail because of what he calls "My extraordinary interest
in my fellow-creatures. I have more than most men. I've never
really seen anyone with half so much. That breeds observation,
and observation breeds ideas" (p. 147).
    Although the narrator does not realize he could be charged
with psychic vampirism, he is aware of this attribute in others
and of its effects on its victims. Gazing upon Mrs. Server, he
notes,

I saw as I had never seen before what consuming passion can make of
the marked mortal on whom, with a fixed beak and claws, it has settled
as on a prey. She reminded me of a sponge wrung dry and with fine

pores agape. Voiced and scraped of everything, her shell was merely crushable. (pp. 135–136)

If this sight was not horrifying enough, worse was the fact "brought home" that "the abasement could be conscious. That was Mrs. Server's tragedy, that her consciousness survived—survived with a force that made it struggle and dissemble. This consciousness was all her secret—it was at any rate all mine" (p. 136). A vampire's victim does not ordinarily know she is being consumed, but Mrs. Server does. Still more terrible, she is the prey of two vampires: the person she loves and the man who watches her with such avidity.

The narrator had carefully tutored Mrs. Briss in the ways of "psychologic" investigators, but he comes to sense her "fatuity and cruelty." Besides "eating poor Briss up inch by inch" (p. 71), the time comes when she, the pupil, begins to drain her teacher of his own force. As she tells him, " 'You *made* me sublime. You found me dense. You've affected me quite as Mrs. Server has affected Mr. Long. I don't pretend I show it,' she added, 'quite as much as he does.' " The narrator can only reply, " 'Because that would entail *my* showing it as much as, by contention, *she* does? Well, I confess,' I declared, 'I do feel remarkably like that pair of lips. I feel drained—I feel dry!' " (p. 81). Dry as the bones that have been thrown down the shaft of the sacred fount of his being, desecrating it.

Not only is the narrator losing a portion of his consciousness to Mrs. Brissenden, he sees that Long is also against him. Wanting only to live, the two fight side by side to keep free of him. He knows "that as it was I who had arrested, who had spoiled their unconsciousness, so it was natural they should fight against me for a possible life in the state I had given them instead. I had spoiled their unconsciousness, I had destroyed it, and it was consciousness alone that could make them effectively cruel" (p. 295). Seizing the weapon he had held against them, they turn back their sharp-edged sensibilities upon him. The knower is known, the devourer devoured, as in the time-honored tradition of Jacobean revenge tragedies, in which everyone sins and everyone is destroyed.[26]

The Sacred Fount in 1901: fifty years had passed since Miles Coverdale in *The Blithedale Romance* found it as dangerous to peer as to be peered upon. In Hawthorne's time the old folk-theme of vampirism was no longer crudely represented as physical depletion alone. But from the years of Hawthorne's maturity to the first years of the twentieth century further sophistications continued to change the writer's approach to matters of psychic vampirism. This change is marked by the implied metaphors and the phrases used to describe that part of a man's being he most fears to have taken from him by human powers stronger than his own.

The Blithedale Romance: theft of *souls* in a secularized version of the age-old combat between the forces of damnation and salvation, of Devil and God. "Professor Fargo": irrational personal magnetism winning over scientific *mind*, fraud triumphant over truth, sexual mastery and the corruption of innocence by Yankee shrewdness. *The Undiscovered Country:* attempted deprivation of another's *humanness* by an imposed will that tries to make transcendent what longs to be earthly. *The Bostonians:* desire to annihilate *personality* in order to turn the victim into a mechanized puppet. *The Sacred Fount:* the destruction of the previous equilibrium between unconsciousness and *self-consciousness*, with all secrets dragged forth into the fierce light of knowing.

Soul, mind, humanness, personality, and self-consciousness: these are different words for what is essentially that intangible, unnameable quality which gives man his sense of unique existence. The words implied differ because the three men who dramatized the struggles involving that constant wrote out of an increasingly secular vision. Where vampires once were said to endanger men's bodies by sucking away blood, the source of physical life, they were then shown as stealing what is even more essential—that inner, non-material substance called "soul" as a hold-over from more religious times, subsequently named by "mind," "personality," "self-consciousness"—words more expressive of the secularized psychology of the age.

The vampire theme is an important one in literature. It can be used to dramatize struggles central to man's existence—between himself and other humans; between himself and the non-human forces of the universe; between qualities at odds within his own nature. It is small wonder that Henry James did much with a theme that got at the core of his unfaltering concern with human consciousness, knowledge, power, and will. Through activating the possibilities offered by the leavings of contemporary spiritualism and psychical research, James could—with drama and style—show that characters who lack awareness of their humanness prove not to be gods but vampires, and that for every vampire a stake awaits at the crossroads.

CHAPTER V

The Ghostly Encounter

"The Others"

The earliest of James's supernatural tales follow the lead of the vampire tradition. This attention—which concentrates upon the psychological effects of spiritual rapacity by evoking contemporary attitudes toward "mental science"—fits an apt chronological pattern. The years of James's reading and writing apprenticeships match the years well before the founding of the S.P.R., when to speak topically of the uncanny meant making implied associations between Mesmerism, Modern Spiritualism, and vampirism. When James began to write stories about ghostly appearances, however, the time-sequence reflects a somewhat later interest. His fictional ghosts—what he called "the Others"—start to appear immediately before and after the investigations made by the S.P.R. The facts of Mesmerism's hey-day in the 1840's were eventually assimilated by James's fictive treatment of will-possession in the 1860's and after; the founding of the S.P.R. in the 1880's was far more swiftly followed up by James's use of ghosts. No direct influence needs be asserted, but the impulses abroad in the land make the relation between the social facts and the fictional dramatizations more than mere historical coincidence.

Even as James countered dull, inactive, case-ghosts "washed clean of all queerness as by exposure to a flowing laboratory tap" with ghosts of his own creation that retained the more dramatic flavor of the pre-nineteenth-century type, his ghosts are yet "modern" in their setting. They fit decoratively into the atmosphere of country-houses and sea-resorts of the time period James labeled as now; they are ghosts recognizably of the latter half of the nineteenth century, not placed at a far remove of time and scene. Of a piece (however odd a presence they intrude) with James's general social realism, they stand ready to develop into one of his major themes: that coming-to-awareness that pervades the greater part of his fiction.

Eventually James came to place increased stress upon the dramatic discovery by his living characters that theirs is the terrible power of haunting: that it is not primarily the power of "the Others" that drives them toward the experience of mystery by which James defined "knowledge." Indeed, by the time James made his most subtle use of the supernatural in the 1890's and 1900's, this was his reigning theme. James's often masterly treatment of the psychological effects of self-haunting, one which carried him far beyond the inherited conventions of the ghost-story, will be dealt with in the next chapter. At this point it is necessary to follow him through nearly a quarter of a century: from "The Ghostly Rental" to "The Turn of the Screw" by way of "Sir Edmund Orme." Along the way one can mark the discoveries that moved James from *amusettes* to serious variations on the theme of the coming-to-awareness of life's full range of meaning. This movement could come about once James gained a deeper awareness of the meaning of style. Sophistication of theme alone was insufficient; style ultimately became the nature of the meaning.

The Pre-S.P.R. Man

Because it is youthful, flawed, and charged with certain promises of fulfillments to come, "The Ghostly Rental" of 1876 is a good example of the kind of supernaturally-tinged tale James was fond of reading and writing just before he gave himself up to the cause of social realism in the 1880's. It indicates that, by the end of his first decade of apprenticeship, the young James had changed from a romantic indulgence in the ghostly tradition that marked and marred "The Romance of Certain Old Clothes" and "DeGrey: A Romance." It shows him in a mood (also sketched out in "Professor Fargo") more critical, more playful, and ultimately more fruitful for his later work in the genre. Here he is seen following the Dupinesque mode that plays off allegiance to the intellect and the intuition, rather than the emotionally heightened mode of the Poesque grotesque that unapologetically attempts to assault the soul.[1]

The story is related by a young ministerial student who, by reading Dr. Channing as a Harvard undergraduate, has acquired a "theology of a greatful [*sic*] and succulent savor; it seemed to offer one the rose of faith delightfully stripped of its thorns." [2] (Some hint, at least, of mature Jamesian wit appears in this tale.) His consciousness freed by this watered-down orthodoxy from dogmatism and the need to accommodate mysteries, the bright young man is ready for whatever intellectual excitement comes his way. Sounding much like the young James and his cousin Bob Temple sallying forth to enjoy an evening among the spiritualists [3]—far merrier of mood than the earnest scientists of the yet-unborn S.P.R.—the student declares, "My eyes and I were on excellent terms; they were indefatigable observers of all wayside incidents, and so long as they were amused I was contented. It is, indeed, owing to their inquisitive habits that I come into possession of this remarkable story" (p. 106).

Once in possession of the details, the student shares them with a crippled maiden lady who, though immobile in her parlor, prides herself on knowing everything because she uses her eyes to the utmost. " 'Observe closely enough,' she once said, 'and it doesn't matter where you are. . . . Shut me up in a dark closet and I will observe after a while, that some places in it are darker than others' " (p. 119).[4] As the "quintessence of pure reason" (ibid.), Miss Deborah's is the kind of mind that has been at work ever since the Age of Reason. " 'Well, sir,' " she often asked, " 'what is the latest monstrosity in Biblical criticism?' "—for she "used to pretend to be horrified at the rationalistic tendency of the age. But she was an inexorable little philosopher, and I am convinced that she was a keener rationalist than any of us . . ." (p. 118).

As prideful rationalists, both Miss Deborah and the divinity student are recognizably members of the first half of the nineteenth century; with confidence they rely upon those powers of observation many of their generation thought would answer whatever questions might arise—even those concerning the supernatural. However, such assured reliance upon empirical observation was already proving difficult to retain in a world "in which everything happens" and where rationalists would soon be caught "intellectually unprepared." [5]

The mere sight of a house that strikes the student as "spiritually blighted" sets him on the trail toward the fanciful details of the tale the old sea captain tells him. The house arouses an inward terror that gives the student pleasure, but he is, at first, untouched by what shakes the soul of the haunted captain. The old man, having once wronged his daughter, is doomed to pay the homage of his guilt to her merciless ghost each time it hands gold to him in ghostly rental of the family home. The student stands by, "explicitly cultivating cheerful views of the supernatural" (p. 108); the captain staggers under his knowledge of what terror actually is; the reader lingers, a little intrigued, a little bored, and not at all affected.

The student's emotional stasis does not continue for long (even if the reader's does). Eager to learn all things for himself, he hastens forward toward the experience of terror which he (and James, even then) realizes is one way a man can experience a sense of life. Curiosity becomes an inspiration to him and risk a quality to be cultivated, and so the student becomes one of the first in the long line of Jamesian Nosy Parkers who take the path of knowledge either to consciousness' heaven or hell.

Inside the haunted house the student sees a dark blur standing at the head of the staircase that materializes into the ghostly figure of a woman in black. At that moment, to the surprise of his confidently analytic mind, he discovers that the vague suggestiveness of terror that comes over him far exceeds the evidence of his eyes; the facts simply do not explain the intensity of his feelings. He is driven to "poeticize" what he feels. Calling it "Dread, with a capital letter" (p. 130), he falls back upon the allegorical method that solaces by somehow distancing emotion in the process of intellectualizing it.

Later the student learns that the ghost is no ghost but the very much alive daughter, who has been deceiving her father in revenge for his earlier treatment. The unsettling thought remains, however, that "Dread" had had the uncommon power to make him stand immobile. Whatever "natural explanation" is accepted, the student admits the uncanny qualities of the psychological effects he experienced.

Was not this paralyzation of my powers in itself a supernatural influence? Not necessarily, perhaps, for a sham ghost that one accepted might do as much execution as a real ghost. But why had I so easily accepted the sable phantom that waved its hand? Why had it so impressed itself? (p. 132)

Why? Knowledge sought through ratiocination and empiricism alone was insufficient to give an answer to questions of the kind F. W. H. Myers, Sigmund Freud, William James, and Carl Jung would soon attempt to confront by other methods.

James early came upon the intuited truth that—whatever serves to disprove ghosts—the evidence for occurrences of psychological haunting cannot be easily dismissed. His handling of the theme indicates both the weaknesses current in 1876 and his later strengths. To choose to deal so carefully with "spiritual blight" shows him taking two strides forward in his adaptation of the fictional tradition of ghostliness. It is the story's ending —with the special twist that facile purveyors of the supernatural particularly relish—that shows James taking one step backward into triteness. This twist is intruded when the captain's living daughter suddenly sees the actual ghost of her father, who has just died, and realizes that it is she who will now be haunted, who will be punished for her sin of deception just as she had punished him for his sin of wrath. What James had begun as an artistically successful depiction of inward haunting becomes a trivializing insistence upon having a stock exterior ghost as well. It is not because a "real" ghost appears that this story fails. Artistic lumpishness enters because an arbitrary demand is made upon the reader suddenly to switch attitudes about the narrated events without previous preparation, because the ghost is added for no good reason other than to shock, and because James loses confidence in his own insights into how he might make the supernatural tale work for him.

The later James would avoid the gaucherie that mars the ending of "The Ghostly Rental." He would also move toward an understanding of possibilities only implied in that story. The student had tried to come to awareness by means of ratiocination but had been blocked from its attainment by certain psychological effects of hauntedness. Later James would discover that full awareness can be gained *by means of* the haunted consciousness (itself a vital adjunct to psychic sensitivity). He would uncover these truths: the failure to know does not come because one is haunted, nor does the success of knowing come in spite of hauntedness; rather, awareness may be attained through the saving effects of "the sacred terror."

The Revenge Ghost of Brighton

"Sir Edmund Orme" was written in 1891, the first story by James in the strictly ghostly genre to appear after that stimulating decade during which the S.P.R. was founded. Fifteen years of commitment to social realism separate it from "The Ghostly Rental," James's last attempt at the full-fledged tale of a ghostly encounter.

One mellow commonplace day in Brighton the narrator of "Sir Edmund Orme" meets a girl, with whom he quickly falls in love, and her ghost-haunted mother. From the onset he senses that mother and daughter are indissolubly linked; "each had the other so on her mind"; each holds there is "something 'awfully strange' " about the other; each has the seeds of coquetry. And coquettes, the mother says with emphasis, are "always punished"; they are "bad." [6] Why the mother, so white of face she seems almost an "apparition," is vehement on this point the hero soon finds out. She is under the surveillance of the dead. It is not the kindly eye of her deceased husband that is fixed upon her, but the accusing eyes of the man, long dead, who once loved her, who had been frivolously rejected by her, and who now seeks revenge upon her.

Charlotte Marden, the daughter, says to the narrator, " 'She looks as if she were waiting for the doctor, dear mamma. . . . Perhaps *you're* the doctor; do you think you are?' " "It appeared in the event that I had some healing power," he thinks to himself (p. 145). Eventually he does heal the mother's sense of guilt and lay her ghost, but he has to undergo an initiation before he can become such a sachem. He must first make himself worthy of seeing the dead and able to understand love's generosity. [7]

Mrs. Marden tells him "she had distinct intuitions." What most surprises him is "that some of these uncanny promptings were connected with myself" (p. 147). With all the force of her psychic powers, she makes "an intense appeal" to him for aid, but aid for what he does not yet know (p. 148). Yet he realizes some "mystic initiation is in store" for him. "From the first of her seeing me she had been sure there were things I shouldn't escape knowing." He admits he is somewhat frightened by her intimations, but "I wondered more than I shuddered" (p. 149).

Almost immediately he sees what Mrs. Marden predicts: the ghost of her former suitor, Sir Edmund Orme. Together with Mrs. Marden, the hero is "the only person in the world" who is able to see an apparition "invisible to the others." But if Orme appears as her curse, why then is the hero "to share so questionable a boon?" (p. 152). Because he loves with a love that seeks to give, not merely to possess. His ability to see is the proof of the quality of his love; it is what distinguishes him from the covey of admirers whom Charlotte has attracted to her side, and what binds him to the woman whose savior he will be through the healing power of his good love.

Orme is a "revenge ghost" in the high old style of overly-romantic men who take their lives when spurned in love and then come back to make the culprits writhe. He wants to make Mrs. Marden suffer for what she did to him; he can do this by gripping her with the fear that her daughter may yet come to see his ghost. As a ghost he knows he is a terror to the living; to force his presence upon others will be his mode of revenge upon women ungenerous in love, whether mother or daughter.

This wretched mother was to pay, in suffering, for the suffering she had inflicted, and as the disposition to trifle with an honest man's just expectations might crop up again, to [the narrator's] detriment, in the child, the latter young person was to be studied and watched, so that *she* might be made to suffer should she do an equal wrong. . . . [If] she should be caught, that is to say, in some breach of faith or some heartless act, her eyes would on the spot, by the insidious logic, be opened suddenly and unpitiedly to the "perfect presence," which she would then have to work as she could into her conception of a young lady's universe. (p. 168) [8]

Here, then, is the ghostly situation: the haunting apparition, the haunted woman, and the young man who loves a girl, herself blindly unconscious of the psychological sense of guilt her mother possesses and she herself risks. Psychic vision is the curse of the woman who has done wrong, the gift of the man who loves rightly, and the possibility for terror of the girl if she does not honor that man's love. But will the "good" vision of the hero intervene and counteract the haunting vision of the mother and prevent the "bad" unblinding of the daughter? The closer Orme hovers, the closer the hero feels to Charlotte, and the closer the mother is to them all—the four enmeshed in a strong psychic bond.

"The way to save her was to love her" (p. 162). When the hero tells Charlotte he loves her, Orme's ghost disappears from his side. But in the midst of a lovely evening, the ghost suddenly reappears. This time Charlotte sees someone. The vital question is whether, with sudden Blakean vision, she *really* sees what this figure of the silent gentleman in evening clothes actually *is*.[9]

Events move rapidly. The hero lunges toward the figure, but Orme vanishes. Mrs. Marden faints, is ill, is dying. The hero is sent for. The mother wishes Charlotte to give her love to him. Experiencing a sense of coercion, Charlotte hesitates. He cries to her, " 'Ah if you would let me show you *how* good I can be!' " (p. 172). Charlotte gives him her hand; then, it seems, at last she sees Orme, who leans over the couch where her mother lies. (Experience and knowledge are too important in James's scheme to remain repressed by innocence and ignorance, however comforting.) She cries out, her cry mingling with "another sound, the wail of one of the lost." "But," the hero recalls, "I had already sprung toward the creature I loved, to cover her, to veil her face, and she had as passionately thrown herself into my arms" (ibid.).[10] The two embrace with the fullness of love, then move apart to find Mrs. Marden dead and Orme's ghostly presence vanished.

At this point the old manuscript that contained the inner tale ends with the ambiguities characteristic of most good ghost stories and James's practiced mode of presentation. "Was the sound I heard when Chartie shrieked—the other and still more tragic sound I mean—the despairing cry of the poor lady's death-shock or the articulate sob (it was alike a waft from a great storm) of the exorcised and pacified spirit? Possibly the latter, for that was mercifully the last of Sir Edmund Orme" (p. 173).

And so the hero, through the power of his disinterested generosity, his ability to progress through the stages of increasing psychic vision, and the depth of his love, is able to break the spell of terror and win his lady. She is saved from her mother's dread fate, and they marry, to live happily ever after—until she dies in childbirth a year later. There are indeed mysteries, James implies, in the very act of common human life and death that require no ghosts to make them terrible in their inexplicableness. It is by just such a throw-away as the story's opening sentences that James shows he is at home in either world, since strangeness exists by daytime or night, is shaped in supernatural forms like Orme which can be made to vanish or in natural facts like death which cannot.

The Berkeleian Ghosts at Bly

Checking the impulse to drive right past the front gates of Bly out of the desire to offer the world of Jamesian criticism the gift of the absence of yet another look at "The Turn of the Screw," I shall turn into that drive and face those impossible questions that loom at its far end. My three-fold concerns will be presented in an ascending order of significance: an evaluation of why the criticism of this story has reached a certain point in the long debate; an argument for James's having most likely intended to use real ghosts; the matter of the story's telling, which makes the issue of the apparitions' reality (while certainly not irrelevant) of less crucial moment than the style and the structuring of the experience undergone by its participants.

To take on the task of reading over the criticism that has accumulated over the years might at first seem a numbing bore, but it really is not. Actually, it is pleasant and reassuring to see the wit and intelligence that has always been present in part in "the 'Screw' tradition" and that looks to be on the increase. Whenever Edmund Wilson spoke out from the Far Left, whether in 1934, 1938, 1948, or 1959, he articulated the best of the anti-ghost, pro-Freudian position; just so, Robert Heilman's articles of 1947 and 1948 were splendid examples of the Far Right pro-ghost, pro-religious reading.[11] Yes, there was a lengthy period of aridity and repetitiousness when the stress lay upon the governess's ill-health or became overly hortatory in defense of her saintliness. But critical bloom has been restored by the sun and air let in once that impasse was cracked open. There has been Dorothea Krook to right the absolutist excesses of both Wilson and Heilman, and Mark Spilka to bring the Freudians and the Purists into line.[12] To offset the crankly bores (whose monotony can be skimmed over quickly enough) there remain just enough eccentrics to give readers self-indulgent amusement and sober self-critical pause.[13] The most cheering fact is the new turn away from a wholly thematic emphasis toward the way the story works; it is in the direction of the stylistics of *how* (which build responsibly upon insights already gained by the years of debate over *what* the story means) that much of the best, most provocative new criticism moves.[14] Crucial matters of epistomology, morality, and metaphysics can hardly be dismissed now that we are on the other side of *The Ordeal of Consciousness in Henry James* (and *Jamesian Ambiguity and The Sacred Fount*). We can hardly not see the story's duality of interpretations consciously imposed by its well-placed ambiguities.[15] Well instructed in these matters, we can now discover the effects "The Turn of the Screw" has upon us as participant-readers; we move together with the governess and the children, as hugely implicated and just as driven as they, through the strange events at Bly. Shallow issues of reality-and-appearance carted in from outside the story fall away at the assault the story makes upon anything that would deny the particular Berkeleian sense of being as *esse est percipi* and the particular Jamesian sense that life remains inexplicable to the perception.[16]

The story Henry James played closest to his chest—the one he placed most centrally within the enchanted circle of supernaturalism—is the story most stubbornly resisted for being what it is. Initially, the interpretations—whether pre-Freudian or post-Freudian, mythic or Christian, allegorical or sociological in bent—concentrated on two major questions. Are the ghosts real or is the governess hallucinating when she says she sees Peter Quint and Miss Jessel?[17] From these questions come their companions: is the story to be taken seriously or to be treated as a clever but trifling hoax? The criticism of "The Turn of the Screw" was long nailed to the plank of "Is it real?" (therefore, serious) or "Is it illusion?" (therefore, frivolous).

James's contemporaries thought "The Turn of the Screw" was about real ghosts in the good old-fashioned tradition; to most the governess was a beleagured maiden set in dire peril. It has been a long time since readers have been content with this impression. As superstition disappears in the daily lives of those who read James, so does their ability to consider the possibility that the ghosts they know do not exist in the world could exist in the pages of a story. Naturally, this is meant as a high compliment to James—just as one is offered to Shakespeare whenever someone says, "Of course, Hamlet was mad; there was no ghost of his father, because Shakespeare's was a *modern* mind." It is logical, if unwise, for modern, intellectually responsible readers to insist that James as a modern, intellectually responsible man could not have intended the apparitions to be real.[18] According to this syllogism, if it is obvious to us there could be no ghosts, but the governess asserted she saw them, the only conclusion is that she "saw" them through the eyes of an hallucinated imagination. And people who hallucinate are mad.

Yet James wrote the story so that it may be taken as possessing ghosts seen by anyone capable of seeing them because they are there. "The Turn of the Screw" ought at least to be considered in context with the rest of James's work in its genre. In story after story James used real apparitions for his haunted characters to see. There is no reason to believe he suddenly turned fastidious in 1898; not with "The Jolly Corner" and *The Sense of the Past* still to come. At the time James wrote the bulk of his supernatural tales, people wanted ghosts; taken straight or explained scientifically, but not necessarily "explained away" as Mrs. Radcliffe had done to the detriment of the artistic atmosphere of her fiction. As a professional carefully eyeing his market, James understood the commercial need for the delightful sense of hackle-raising horror that ghosts provided his readers; like those who first heard Douglas read the governess's manuscript, he saw this story as "gruesome, as on Christmas eve in an old house a strange tale should essentially be. . . ."[19] Further, James had respect for the effects he could obtain by dramatizing the dead in confrontation with the living; he did not feel the need to apologize whenever he decided to use real ghosts.[20]

James's major concern was that his apparitions make good art, not the kind of authenticity the S.P.R. formulated in its records.[21] James wrote of Quint and Miss Jessel, "They would be agents in fact; there would be laid on them the dire duty of causing the situation to reek with the air of Evil." To measure their effect and to observe their success as active participants, he maintained, "was exactly my central idea." His idea was that they not be " 'ghosts' at all, as we know the ghost, but goblins, elves, imps, demons as loosely constructed as those in the old trials for witchcraft; if not, more pleasingly, fairies of the legendary order, wooing their victims forth to see them dance under the moon." [22] Ghosts "as we now know" them meant the static types found in S.P.R. case studies; haunting presences in the story-teller's tradition of the supernatural were precisely what James wanted for "The Turn of the Screw." [23]

James at first seems to have been pleased with his efforts. It had been easy "simply to renounce all attempts to keep the kind and degree of impression I wished to produce on terms with the today so copious psychical record of cases of apparitions." [24] As for the more difficult problems of cajoling his readers, he thought he had mastered them. By writing "Screw" in the vein of the traditional ghost-story he would evade the "particular challenge" thrown at him by critics of *The Aspern Papers,* who noted that Jeffrey Aspern was supposed to be "real" while none of the rest of the characters were. In contrast, James asserted confidently, everyone in "Screw" was "of a kind." The governess, Mrs. Grose, the children, the ghosts—all were equally real (or unreal, however one wishes to define characters in a fiction) and thus were "the very kind . . . least apt to be baited by earnest criticism . . ." (p. xiv).[25]

James thought he had liberated himself from the facts both S.P.R. men and literary critics, equally "earnest," demand.

The thing had for me the immense merit of allowing the imagination absolute freedom of hand, of inviting it to act on a perfectly clear field, with no "outside" control involved, no pattern of the usual or the true or the terrible "pleasant" (save always of course the high pleasantry of one's very form) to consort with. (p. xvi) [26]

In his mind the form of the ghost story stirred many responses, was therefore interesting, was therefore a success, "a perfect example of an exercise of the imagination unassisted, unassociated—playing the game, making the score . . . off its own bat" (ibid.). Alas, this self-confidence was diminished by the time he set down his preface to the New York Edition. Artistic satisfaction had been disturbed by the story's reception; it "shook" his "artistic" and "ironic heart" "almost to breaking" to realize the public wanted the very thing he had renounced (p. xviii). James had written his story under one set of rules; his readers too often wished to play another game under another set of rules.[27]

If James felt certain delayed pangs of apprehension over the way his ghosts were being received, he also experienced anxiety over the governess. He had been concerned only with what she said she observed.[28] He wanted to keep "crystalline her record of so many intense anomalies and obscurities—by which I don't of course mean her explanation of them, a different matter . . ." (p. xix). What we have here is James typically standing against a black or white position; he clearly implies that there are several ways to assess why the governess saw what she saw if one wants such explanations, as he did not. If one is eager to make absolute conclusions based upon the partial evidence the governess provides, what can one end with but that she is mad or she is sane? To James it was not the mere choice of insanity or sanity; his was rather the artistic decision to provide ghosts to be seen by people whether those people are mad or not, and whatever their mad or sane explanations for seeing what they do.[29]

Two points are brought up constantly by critics in their attempts to prove that the governess is insane or at least highly unreliable: she is in error in certain of her statements, and no one besides the governess sees the apparitions. As for the first indictment, if sanity is the accolade given those who never make a mistake of judgment or contradict themselves in what they report, who, then, is sane?[30] The second indictment is one that James (and the S.P.R.) thoroughly exploded. One of the aspects of the ghostly that most intrigued James, and one that he made frequent use of in his ghost stories, was the way apparitions tend to appear only to that rare person sensitive enough, imaginative enough, to be capable of seeing the ghostly. The kind, good, but gross Mrs. Grose never sees Quint or Miss Jessel, nor do any of the other servants. The fact that no one other than the governess sees them is no more proof that they do not exist than that they do; nothing is proven one way or the other to the satisfaction of those who insist upon facts. But in the tradition of the ghostly tale, as well as in the light of the contemporary scientific investigations being lavished upon ghost-appearances, the role of the governess as solitary perceiver falls into place with numerous other such accounts.[31]

Far more important than the tradition is the question of what effects James gains by having ghosts admitted as possible presences, and most likely, as probable ones. James's story is a record of what the governess said she experienced.[32] In "her anxieties and inductions" and the effects her emotions have upon others lies the drama the artist desires, of a kind not found in an S.P.R. record of factual explanation.[33] James was less interested in "her relation to her own nature" than in her relations to the uncle, Mrs. Grose, the children, and the apparitions (p. xix). We are used to thinking of James's characters as concerned only with their inner sensibilities; we sometimes forget how strongly James insisted upon them as being taken in dramatic reciprocity with others—thinking, acting, being *in a situation*. James recognized that the "fairy-tale" type tends, by its nature, to simplify, to pull in and intensify its effects. The effect he strove for was one of great concentration: that of a young woman pitted against her external antagonists. Since what she battles also includes the inner forces of her own nature, those forces are given the forms of persons she can see and confront—Quint and Miles, Miss Jessel and Flora.

In 1898 James wrote, "My bogey-tale dealt with things so hideous that I felt that to save it all it needed some infusion of beauty or prettiness. . . ."[34] Nine years earlier Walter Pater had written of the desire of "the romantic spirit" for "a beauty born of unlikely elements, by a profound alchemy, by a difficult initiation, by the charm which wrings it even out of terrible things; and a trace of distortion, of the grotesque, may perhaps linger, as an additional element of expression, about its ultimate grace. . . ." [35] This desire for the intensity that arises from the beauty of terror was held by Coleridge, Keats, Pater, and James alike. Because of James's hothouse concentration upon the terrible, beautiful events a "hard gem-like flame" of intensity is achieved. [36] It is an intensity that stands outside the minds of the living in the ghostly forms of Quint and Miss Jessel and thus reflects the horrors lying deep within the consciousness—the horrors thus doubled, the intensity screwed to the tightest notch.

In his preface to "The Turn of the Screw" James insisted that he had "but clung to an ideal of faultlessness," that he had planned his "excursion into chaos" as "a piece of ingenuity pure and simple, of cold artistic calculation, an *amusette* to catch those not easily caught (the 'fun' of the capture of the merely witless being ever but small), the jaded, the disillusioned, the fastidious." There was "not an inch of expatiation," James remarked; "my values are positively all blanks save so far as an excited horror, a promoted pity, a created expertness . . . proceed to read into them more or less fantastic figures." [37] Manfred Mackenzie in his delightfully written if—in my judgment—wrong-headed article, is disturbed by the tale's lack of meaning. His proof is "the overwhelming concern in the Preface . . . with the *hows* of suggestion: the whys, those limited deplorable presentable instances, were to be avoided with all cunning." [38]

It is my intention to dwell upon these "*hows* of suggestion." Not because I feel, with Mackenzie, that there are no discernible *whys*, but because I believe the story's howness ought to be the way one comes to that whyness. [39] In 1890 William James's *Principles of Psychology* had begun to reveal to its audience (somewhat more limited than that for his brother's tale of 1898) that reality is whatever "stings" our interest; the stinging takes place when we can have "belief" in what we experience as a "state of consciousness" and a set of "circumstances." Belief is much more than mere thought and the reception of ideas; it is what we turn to "with a will" because we can enter into practical relations with it.[40] It is on these terms, I suggest, that we can best make our way through the "stinging" reality of Bly; by letting it guide our responses,[41] we may respond as the Jameses intended men to respond to "the whole lived-world"—by a full relationship of Thought to Object, rather than a self-imprisoning reliance upon Thought alone.

In "The Turn of the Screw" the wholeness of relationship pivots around the governess's duplication of her inner fears by the outer figures she confronts. Unadmitted to herself, the governess's infatuation for the absent uncle repeats itself symbolically before her eyes in the persons of Quint and Miles, Miss Jessel and Flora. The living children and the dead servants are, all four, *Doppelgänger* ghosts mirroring her own desires.[42] Thus everyone at Bly, living or dead (except Mrs. Grose, who is relegated to the role of "the listener") is made part of the governess's experience of the tale—what William James called the "sticky," the "warm" aspects of our Self as it exists "out there" in the world before us.[43] Ghosts and children will be those selves that first give the ego its sense of elated release and then move in to check, to criticize, and to torment.[44] No wonder James was more interested in portraying the governess's relationship to "the Others" since they are in effect her own nature. It is less ambiguous and more dramatic to chart what she is according to what the Others do and are than to assess her by what she seems to be in and of herself alone.

The absent uncle and the present Quint are the same "type" (with little Miles in training to duplicate the master-mold), while the governess and Miss Jessel (and Flora in the just opening bud) have too much in common for comfort. The governess refuses to see how alike the two men's natures are. To her who has seen him but twice the uncle is a marvel; to her who has seen him but once Quint is a "horror," a "hound," a "low wretch." [45] To her he was "our employer's late clever good-looking 'own' man; impudent, assured, spoiled, depraved" (p. 477). Although she accepts Mrs. Grose's implications about Quint's character with her "full vision" and realizes he did "what he wished" with women, she refuses to bring that vision to bear consistently upon her master's character—for whom Quint was his "own" man. Misled by her romanticizing, she is unable to turn momentary insights concerning their likenesses into a full indictment; she cannot admit that if Quint is no gentleman in class status, neither is the uncle one in the moral sense. " '*She* was a lady,' " Mrs. Grose has said of Miss Jessel, while Quint was not a gentleman; even while the governess knows she is a lady, she refuses to name the uncle as no gentleman.

Miles is his uncle in miniature. On first sight of him the governess is enraptured by his "indescribable little air of knowing nothing in the world but love" (p. 452). If Miles inspires love, it is questionable if he is capable of feeling it. He is "almost impersonal and certainly quite unpunishable"; he had, "as it were, nothing to call even an infinitesimal history" (p. 459). Who is it who has no past and no history because he has never shared experiences with another? Who is "impersonal and certainly quite unpunishable"? Who has "never for a second suffered"? (p. 459). It is that creature to whom the governess likens Miles when she says, "he was therefore an angel" (p. 460). Miles is, indeed, hardly human in his lack of shared sympathy, a past, and vulnerability to pain. He is that irresponsible, indifferent supernatural being it is death for a mortal to love. [46]

Miles wears waistcoats like his uncle's (as Quint does; stolen ones). "Turned out for Sunday by his uncle's tailor . . . Miles' whole title to independence, the rights of his sex and situation" were full upon him (p. 506). In the face of such self-approval and charm the governess thinks, "Oh but I felt helpless! I have kept to this day the heartbreaking little idea of how he seemed to know that and to play with it" (p. 507). The uncle had known how taken she was with him, and—playing on this emotion—had persuaded her to accept the position with its strange conditions. When the governess learns that Miles had insulted Mrs. Grose, she asks, " 'And you forgave him that?' " " 'Wouldn't *you?*' " Mrs. Grose replies. " 'Oh yes!' " the heart-entangled governess admits (p. 483).

Males such as the uncle and Miles are forgiven everything by sentimental young women, even while they indignantly condemn someone like Quint who is simply the uncle on a lower social scale and Miles in an older, more experienced form. The uncle is far away and Miles is but a child, so she is "safe" from them at the same time she can enjoy thoughts of their charm. Quint is near at hand, and so the evil potential of the same irresponsible sexual magnetism that characterizes the three males in the governess's life is all too threatening.

If she condemns Quint for being what he is (as she refuses to condemn the uncle or Miles), the governess condemns Miss Jessel (and her miniature, little Flora) for having submitted to that same devastating charm. She finds she cannot help but identify herself with the last governess. The apparition of that wretched woman brings her revulsion because it is herself as she yet might be recognized before the world. Coming to the head of the stairs, the living governess finds the woman in a pose of deep sorrow. Able to stare off Quint, she cannot face her predecessor, who is the more terrible of the two ghosts—because symbolically herself. When she returns from church the governess again encounters "the most horrible of women." She images her as "my vile predecessor" and names her " 'You terrible miserable woman!' " —one "dishonoured and tragic" with "her haggard beauty and her unutterable woe" (p. 511).[47] At this moment the governess decides she must stay on at Bly to fight back against the two ghostly figures and the corrupted children, who represent what stands in her romance-filled mind for the unfulfilled relationship between the absent uncle and herself.

James liked to work with parallel constructions, pairing couples as in *What Maisie Knew* and *The Golden Bowl.* "The Turn of the Screw"—pervaded by "play" imagery—presents the governess sensing, although not admitting, that she is one of the participants in a frightening "play-within-a-play." [48] She must enact the double role of herself as a living person and as the apparitional Miss Jessel, while Miles is the stand-in for both his uncle and Quint. Each level of relationship, real or imagined, occurring in past or present; each action of betrayal and frustrated love; each duplication of consciousness: all turn the screw tighter upon her.

The battle for Flora's soul lost, the governess hopes she may now exorcise Quint's ghost and save Miles and herself (not realizing that Flora's defeat adumbrates her own). Mrs. Grose banished, the stage is cleared. The drama is soon to end with the most dramatic of conflicts: the insidious encroachment of one human consciousness upon another (a struggle once seen as the devil's infiltration of the human soul). In her assumed sacerdotal role as hearer of confessions (the act in which the guilt-ridden reveal all they know of themselves, the act that the MS Douglas holds declares the governess has had to do to bring herself some peace), she will strive to end the intrusion of Quint's consciousness upon Miles's by intruding her own. "Mightn't one," she asks, "to reach his mind, risk the stretch of a stiff arm across his character?" (p. 540). Hers is the infiltration she ought to resist, not Quint's; it is the spell of her symbolic infatuation she must break, not one held over the living by the dead.[49] Note that Miss Jessel's ghost is no longer seen; it is as if it has now merged into the governess's inflamed consciousness.

Unaided,[50] she attempts to win the battle for Miles's soul and her own without the weapon of sufficient self-knowledge. Pridefully confident that she is strong enough, clever and brave enough, the governess watches Miles's self-assurance collapse "that gave the very distance of his fall in the world" (p. 547). She is ecstatic at having won a victory over the will of the nephew, whose power of personality has unwittingly symbolized to her all that has kept her under the absent uncle's domination and in fear of Quint. "They are in my ears still, his supreme surrender of the name and his tribute to my devotion. 'What does he matter now, my own?—what will he *ever* matter? *I* have you.' " Then comes "the stroke of the loss I was so proud of" as Miles utters "the cry of a creature hurled over an abyss . . ." (p. 550). With her triumphant joy in bending the fatal power of the "master" to her own will, the governess brings Miles's consciousness to its end and blights her own for its lifetime.

" 'Of course we've the others,' " Miles mentions to the governess as they wait alone in the great house that final night. " 'Yet even though we have them . . . they don't much count, do they?' " (p. 541). Whether he speaks of the house's servants or its ghosts, Miles is correct. In each of James's tales of the supernatural the conflict that counts is fought out between one living being and another living being. James's ghosts personify the latent evil of the world (primal, social, or whatever) that finds its hiding place within the living, not an abstract, dismissable evil that vanishes when the dead return to their other-worldly dwelling place. It is the governess—though able to "see" the ghosts because of the fineness of her imagination—who is morally blind to the fact that by the perverted quality of that imagination she gives them their potency. Until she came to Bly the dead seemed not to have appeared; her zeal affords their evil its continued effectiveness even after their deaths. The evil found at Bly is given in almost Berkeleian terms: evil, however real and lasting, is *not* until it is seen, and the evil at Bly was not seen (thus passive) until the governess came to realize it and then pressed on obsessively to lay her own ghosts.[51]

Henry Adams found the power of the unconscious, impersonal Dynamo one of the most frightening phenomena of his age. Henry James found the power of the Virgin governess who tried to impose her conscious, personal will upon those around her perhaps the most terrifying phenomenon of all, especially since the same young woman—marked by beauty of poise and balance—acts as "a stave against chaos, real, subjective, or imagined."[52]

This is one of the terrible facts of the story: we are not permitted the relief of damning her; we may not rest with an Everlasting Yea or Nay, nor at the Center of Indifference. So well did James carry out his task of intensity that, while we view apart the terror of the governess, we simultaneously share her terror. James said of his tale that there is "no eligible *absolute* of the wrong."[53] Opposed to such absolutes, the open-ended universe of the story tips its horrors out of the final paragraph. We are in the grasp of the governess, as is Miles's lifeless body, helpless but to go where she takes us—away from any comforting memory of the cozy opening paragraphs of the story, away from the complacent company gathered around the Christmastide fire.[54] We are snatched beyond the explaining reach of Douglas and of the narrator, who had tried to "frame" the tale tidily, reassuringly, with that rationalistic convention that tells us this is merely an old tale drawn from a locked-away manuscript. We leave all security behind and are swept into the immediate fever that envelops those who both see ghosts and become ghosts.[55]

In his essay of 1919 entitled "The 'Uncanny'," written five years before Edna Kenton's viewing of "The Turn of the Screw" appeared, Sigmund Freud had these remarks to make about the use by literature of those fears that well up from repressed infantile complexes or surmounted belief in animistic powers. In real life, Freud contended, the psychologist can distinguish between fears repressed and surmounted; however, "the realm of phantasy depends for its very existence on the fact that its content is not submitted to the reality-testing faculty." [56] The story-teller has great license in his attempt to draw upon our fears of the uncanny: "he can select his world of representation so that it either coincides with the realities we are familiar with or departs from them in what particulars he pleases. We accept his ruling in every case" (ibid.).

According to Freud the artist "can increase his effect and multiply it far beyond what could happen in reality, by bringing about events which never or very rarely happen in fact. He takes advantage, as it were, of our supposedly surmounted superstitiousness; he deceives us into thinking that he is giving us the sober truths, and then after all oversteps the bounds of possibility" (p. 405). The story-teller, who "has a peculiarly directive influence over us," must act to place us in "states of mind" that arouse our "expectations," even while he dams up our emotions (p. 406).

The artist constantly risks our "dissatisfaction, a kind of grudge against the attempted deceit" (p. 405). To "escape our rising vexation and at the same time to improve his chances of success," he must keep us ignorant "for a long time about the precise nature of the conditions he has selected for the world he writes about," or else he must "cunningly and ingeniously avoid any definite information on the point at all throughout the book" (pp. 405–406). If he succeeds, he has taken us through the experience of those *thoughts* about hovering animistic powers that we as members of modern civilization believed we had left behind, and of those *feelings*, complexes, that we as adults insisted we had passed beyond. We learn, to our terror and our delight, that we have been made children again, both in terms of human history and in our own life-span. Time reversed, as children—innocent and corrupt—we are placed once more in the hands of our governess-story-teller, sainted and demonic; we are shown the apparitions of all our former "teachers" who have instructed our hearts in the ways of experience.

Coming-to-Awareness

"The Ghostly Rental" is a near failure and "Sir Edmund Orme" a pleasantly effective mediocrity. "The Turn of the Screw" is generally conceded to be a masterly achievement after its own kind. I shall here include reference to *The Portrait of a Lady* (whose connection with the Jamesian supernatural tradition is detailed more fully in Chapter 8). The quality of these four works is discernibly different. Since they are autonomous pieces of fiction they must stand or fall on their own. One shrinks from a rough-shod grouping in the name of tracing a common theme or mode of craft. (A perverse law springs into play when critics try to force disparate works into a single pattern to illustrate what most interests them; in the leveling act of noting similarities, the best examples of art tend to be debased rather than the worst pieces being raised up.) Yet certain significant likenesses, parallels, and deviations wait to be pointed out among them, and so the critical risk will be taken.

Coming-to-awareness is a pattern that instructs the movement of a story's telling as well as what it is about. It is both the method and the thematic thrust. From first to last in James's writing career there is discernible a definite commitment to what happens within a selected consciousness as it moves, or refuses to move, or moves "too late" from lack of awareness through refinements of knowledge to some kind of comprehension. The young student of "The Ghostly Rental," Isabel Archer, and the lover of "Sir Edmund Orme" are surprised by the world opening up to reveal events unanticipated by their original innocent vision. Each in his or her way, and to varying degrees, experiences

something about the possibility of terror. Complacency of un-
tested vision is upset in "The Ghostly Rental" and *The Portrait
of a Lady.* The governess of Bly also experiences strange things,
but, in her case, they were not complete surprises to her; she had
already met them in her romantic imagination before encountering them as ghostly presences. However, the meetings do not
lead her to self-knowledge. Rather, she seems to move deeper and
deeper into the deceptions of her own desires. (The fact that the
governess later writes out her memory of the events at Bly and,
years afterward, hands the MS to Douglas is an indication that
her emotions recollected in tranquillity may have finally brought
her to awareness. However, reference to these details come only
at the head of the long tale; once Douglas starts reading the MS,
what the governess may have become after the events drops from
view. By the end of the story, all is swept away but the terrible,
destructive fact of her moral blindness and the pity it elicits.)

The ghosts in the first three stories act as the catalysts to
self-knowledge on the part of the main characters; in "The Turn
of the Screw" the ghosts of Quint and Miss Jessel are there to
show *us* what the governess is, what she ought to be able to realize
about her deepest nature, and what she refuses to admit she is.
The "ghost" in "The Ghostly Rental" that pricks the callow
student to his limited self-examination is not a real ghost. (The
supposedly genuine apparition intruded later into the story is not
only a major flaw in the narrative, it leaves no mark upon the
young man's consciousness.) By making the ghost-encounters
"real" in "Sir Edmund Orme" and "The Turn of the Screw,"
James follows a hallowed and effective literary tradition, one
earlier than the conventions of Mrs. Radcliffe and Horace Walpole, which presented ghost presences only to explain them away
at the end. The ghost of Gardencourt is far and away the most
subtle mutation of the inherited traditions. It can be viewed as
a mere, but masterful, metaphor for what Isabel thinks she wants
to encounter in life, since it serves expertly to show her as having

ironically attained full knowledge once it finally "appears" to her. The veridical hallucination that comes to Isabel at the moment of Ralph Touchett's death need not be read as an actual ghost appearance; it can remain a finely handled poetic truth that measures Isabel's deepest point of awareness. It may, of course, be taken as "real." Either way, the surrounding texture of the novel's realities is not damaged and the reader's sensibilities not shocked.

Finally, there is the matter of love and revenge. Experience alone does not lead to full awareness; it could stamp on one's consciousness a still ingrowing, isolating egotism. Life as relationship is a requirement in the James canon; love (generosity of spirit) becomes the one possible way out of enclosing, flawed experience toward an expanding, perfected awareness. The daughter who pretends to be an accusing apparition in "The Ghostly Rental" has chosen to act in revenge against the father who once thwarted her love; the "real" ghost of the father appears, in turn, to punish the daughter for her unfilial actions. The ghost of "Sir Edmund Orme" desires to revenge himself upon the woman who slighted his love by posing himself as a threat to her daughter if she, too, slights the importance of loving; he can only be exorcised by the young man who loves truly and by the girl's capacity to love him in return. Love without revenge marks Ralph Touchett, the good ghost of Gardencourt; therefore, he can leave something valuable behind, not simply offer relief by his disappearance. The situation in "The Turn of the Screw," as in all matters concerning this difficult tale, is much more complex. Love as an emotion is intensely felt in the story, but in its several forms (often mutually intertwined): as possessive, self-indulgent, and destructive; as well-intentioned and sacrificial; as sophisticated sexuality; as shallow innocent response. In "The Ghostly Rental" and "Sir Edmund Orme," where motives of revenge are at work, they are at least enacted in the name of retribution against those who have sinned against love. The governess, however, and the ghosts at Bly work out a pattern of sin, punishment, and self-hatred that tends to efface whatever knowledge of self true loving might offer.

Simply put (perhaps too simply), coming-to-awareness by means of the ability rightly to love is a quintessential Jamesian theme; its coin-opposite is the failure to know the full extent of one's consciousness (and thus what life portends) because of the rejection of love. The presence of love does not promise victory in overcoming the often implacable facts of existence; the nature of evil is not overthrown merely by the gracious powers of love. But a life without its knowledge has no knowledge of self; the result is a character who is victimized totally or is a rampaging victimizer in his own right.

In James's tales of the ghostly encounter ghosts connote states of being in the narrative iconography. Whether they stand as actual presences or as manipulated metaphors for consciousness, James uses them as "agents of an action"—that which is the central drama of his fiction—to drive, lure, coerce, or win the living from innocence to self-comprehension, and to a comprehension shared, suffered, and perhaps capable of saving.

CHAPTER VI

The Self-Haunted

Self-Haunting

Boon—the writer-character H. G. Wells created as the sac from which his own stored-up venom might be released against Henry James's theories of fiction—presents a ghost story in parody of the Jamesian mode. Boon's complaint is that annoyed readers can never make out whether James is insisting there are actual ghosts in the country house of one Mr. Blandish, or whether he is telling a legend about a past ghost, or dramatizing psychic foreboding, or offering the stuff of dreams. All one can make out from this "James story" is that the characters *sense* something eerie in their midst.[1] Wells was correct in judging that James's supernatural fiction depends for its effect upon the oppressive feeling of unspecified terror over the "something that is there." What Wells failed to detect was that most often the malaise of hauntedness rises from the bog of the characters' own dank selves. What he failed to appreciate was the new psychological gothicism evolving out of James's manipulation of the traditions of literary supernaturalism.

James had to find something to respect, as well as something that allured, in the fair body of supernatural material before he could urge it to yield its possibilities of expression. He could accord respect to the drama and style of the consciousness that presses to know all about itself, even at the risk of becoming its own most terrifying, or most saving, ghost.

As exampled by "The Hound of Heaven" or *The Hound of the Baskervilles*, self-haunting was a ruling theme in late nineteenth-century literature. As men drew away from theological super-naturalism, visible ghosts, once viewed as spirits of the dead enrolled in the legions of the damned, were explained as hallucinatory manifestations of inner guilts. The source of ghosts, it was now said, was men's minds, not the Devil's guile.[2]

Whatever the source of self-hauntedness—human or diabolic—the psychology of fear and the tradition of the supernatural were kept closely joined, both in the popular mind and the literary consciousness. Indeed, terror over what can suddenly spring out of the un-jolly corners of one's own self seems always to have been essential to the tragic mode, based as it is "on the assumption that there are in nature and in the psyche occult, uncontrollable forces able to madden or destroy the mind." [3]

Poets, philosophers, and psychologists came to realize that the finer and more sensitive the mind the more danger that it may go awry. Psychical research reached the conclusion that "We should not expect to find multiple personality in a guinea-pig or suppressed complexes in an amoeba; a mind must be fairly highly developed before it can go wrong in an interesting and instructive way." [4] Furthermore, the longer men such as Francis Galton (cousin of Charles Darwin), Freud, Jung, and William James studied the matter, and the more novelists such as Conrad, Howells, and Henry James exploited it in their fiction, the fewer differences they detected between sanity and insanity. Sanity was only a tableland, "small in area, with unfenced precipices on every side, over any one of which we may fall." [5]

Thirdly, nineteenth-century examination of the question revealed that one of the most profound reasons for the terror felt by the modern man was his inability to perceive precisely what haunted him. *Angst* this feeling came to be labeled by the philosophers, *malaise* it was called by Henry James—the sensation that sweeps over one haunted by the world, that comes as one haunts oneself, or, perhaps worst of all, as one becomes the haunter of others.

The lively literary possibilities of the man confronted by his *Doppelgänger* were used with great awareness by German romanticists early in the century. "Scientific" explanations commonly replaced this vivid term by the century's end. Psychologists held that current studies in the

phenomena of so-called dissociation of personality tend already in this direction: there is one mind, but two or more Egos are implanted upon it, knowing about one another's content as if they were strangers. . . . Does it not seem as if the "many" were all united *in* the "One" in the last resort, and might not this viewpoint be applied to . . . psychic phenomena? [6]

Man is dual, and desirous of being one. He is composed of a fleshly, natural self and a spiritual "supernatural" self. In turn, that latter self contains a changing, individual self pulling against a changeless, universal self. The man inflicted by awareness of his dual personality is one whose whole being encases pursuer and pursued, cause and consequence. Woe to the man whose one self begins to haunt the other. Weal to the author able to make artistic use of the plight of the embattled consciousness that strives to reconcile its selves to itself.

That Henry James made self-hauntedness his artistic weal is easily shown. More significant is the way he continued to use the nomenclature and metaphors long associated with ghostly visitation to convey the psychological truths his generation yearly dragged toward the light. Whether he put the theme to use in his declared tales of supernaturalism, or—having perfected his forms on this lesser ground—put them to work in the treatment of his "big" subjects, James made a reverse transference. He carefully poured newly attained psychological insights into the receptacles of the early romancers, gothicizers, and tellers of fireside tales. Instead of using the fashionable contemporary jargon of the alienists in order to psychologize the tales of the Brothers Grimm, he sought to merge his awareness of psychic aberrations with the inherited language born of literature and legend.[7]

Two Men, Their Own Ghosts: Spencer Brydon

In 1908 James wrote "The Jolly Corner," the last of a series of short tales directly immersed in the supernatural. The story repeats several elements made familiar by James's previous work in the genre: the ghosts whose latent powers to haunt are aroused only by the presence of the living; the haunted house in which the antagonists must meet and make their peace; the "ordinary" setting wherein grows "an 'unnatural' anxiety, a *malaise* so incongruous and discordant, in the given prosaic prosperous conditions, as almost to be compromising." [8] There is also James's usual minute attention to the artistic rendering of his strange materials, as well as a concern for "aboutness" discreetly wrapped in the disguising subtleties of his craft. But something else has entered "The Jolly Corner." Previously the emphasis in James's supernatural tales had been on the man haunted, whether by externally visible ghosts or by invisible apparitions of self. Now there is a noticeable rise of interest in the man who not only finds himself haunted, but haunting others as well.

The dramatic notion of the pursued turned into pursuer made James's own dream about the Galerie d'Apollon both the "most appalling" and yet the "most admirable" of his life. Like that meticulously recalled nightmare, set down at the same time he was at work on "The Jolly Corner" and its literary companion-piece, *The Sense of Past*, the fictional accounts are "about" an "act indeed of life-saving energy, as well as unutterable fear." Galerie dream, "The Jolly Corner," and *The Sense of the Past*, all three, involve the fact

that the "central figure," the subject of the experience, has the terror of a particular ground for feeling and fearing that *he himself is*, or may be, at any moment become, a producer, an object, of this (for you and me) state of panic on the part of others.

James drew a telling conclusion.

It is less gross, much less *banal* and exploded, than the dear old familiar bugaboo; produces, I think, for the reader an almost equal funk—or at any rate an equal suspense and unrest; and carries with it, as I have "fixed" it, a more truly curious and interesting drama—especially a more human one—.[9]

In examining "The Jolly Corner" Leon Edel is perturbed over what he calls James's "curiously inacurate account," which makes it seem as if James "here substitutes the nightmare for the story."[10] Edel overlooks the fact that in Brydon's encounters with the house's *two* apparitions,[11] he does indeed pursue and appall the one "upstairs." More pertinent is Raymond Thorberg's remark that while Brydon is merely curious over approaching what he has *not* been, he is later appalled when he confronts what he *is*.[12] As for *The Sense of the Past*, Ralph Pendrel is able cheerfully to rush back into the past, encountering his ghostly cousins without a qualm; he begins to feel horror and terror only when he sees himself, perceived by others, as the appalling, pursuing ghost. The structural handling in each story of this shift from pleasure to fear is significant, therefore.

According to the criteria set down by Peter Penzoldt, the Galerie dream as it stands in James's memoirs represents a perfect example of the ghostly tale in its simplest, most traditional narrative form.[13] Very short, it contains the briefest of expositions; it is almost all "climax"; there is one ghostly figure, one human mind to comprehend it, one encounter, one ending—and the emotion is mainly that of intoxicating joy over the self's released powers. "The Jolly Corner" as a sophisticated version of the haunter-haunted theme poses a quite different, an almost unique structural problem. Usually, Penzoldt notes, the literary ghost tale works its way through a long and ascending exposition, one which sets up the atmosphere conducive to emotional vulnerability, out of which a strange figure will suddenly emerge. Such a point in the story may be called its "double climax," since the same figure may have materialized several times earlier, but is only now revealed as one of the ghostly kind, or, only now, acts with violence. Forbidden to well-told ghost stories is a structure which presents a long exposition followed by the appearance of one ghost, then another sequence of exposition concluded by the appearance of yet another ghost. James does this forbidden thing in "The Jolly Corner"; he literally gives us a "double climax" by having Brydon lead up to and bring to a close the ghostly encounter "upstairs." Then when Brydon thinks his adventures are over, he, and we, are led downstairs to a sudden and violent encounter with a second presence.

The Sense of the Past, a novel with both the problems and advantages of length, complicates and outrages the conventions of the supernatural narrative, which is traditionally predicated on an emotional effect gained through brevity; it gives us at length Pendrel's encounter in the present with the figure in the portrait, which only then acts to open the way to the novel's main sequence, in which Pendrel, now in the past, moves through a lengthy self-realization of his own status as ghostly figure. The whole focus in the Galerie dream upon the dreamer's "feeling and fearing that *he himself is*, or may be, at any moment become, a producer, as object, of this (for you and me) state of panic on the part of others" becomes, in "The Jolly Corner," part one of Brydon's adventure, and, in *The Sense of the Past*, part two of Pendrel's.

All three—the recorded dream, the story, the novel—start

from the same base: the feeling of the uncanny that comes when one discovers in a previously unrecognized projection the familiar lineaments of one's innermost self; the sense that one is being judged by one's harsher self, even while being granted certain heady powers of release by another, more indulgent self; the sensations of life and death, of terror and horror, which are activated either by the imagining or the experiencing of one's double.[14] The Galerie dream, briefly, and the story and the novel, more fully, reveal by their intricate gradations James's avid interest in the *processes* that the mind imaginatively and experientially goes through when it meets itself and is forced to know itself completely. The characters know *horror*, the paralysis of feeling that halts action, and *terror*, the stimulation of energy. They live through the distinctions between the *dread* that comes just before the ghost is faced and brings hope for the *possibilities* of free choice over how one will act, and the *anguish* that comes at the moment of confrontation and despair over the *necessity* for that choice.[15]

The presences in the house on the jolly corner are asleep and harmless until Brydon comes to arouse them out of his desire for pleasurable dread. He calls them a summation "of all the old baffled forsworn *possibilities*. What he did therefore by this appeal of his hushed presence was to wake them into such measure of ghostly life as they might still enjoy" (my italics).[16] "They were shy," he realizes,

all but unappeasably shy, but they weren't really sinister; at least they weren't as he had hitherto felt them—before they had taken *the Form he so yearned to make them take,* the Form he at moments saw himself in the light of fairly hunting on tiptoe, the points of his evening-shoes. . . . (pp. 740-741; my italics.)

Exchanging the big-game boots, worn during years of aimless self-gratification, for patent evening slippers, Brydon thinks with elation that it is he who is doing the haunting. "People enough,

first and last, had been in terror of apparitions, but who had ever
before so turned the tables and become himself, in the apparitional world, an incalculable terror?" (p. 742). In his rush after
the unseen, only imagined presence fleeing before him through
the blank rooms, he experiences, as never before, the thrill and
flush of real life that comes with feeling one's untapped possibilities a source of mystery and power.

Brydon is proud that his ghostly antagonist is brave enough
to turn to fight. This shows that it (however negated a part of
himself) is "not unworthy of him" (p. 745). He goes to meet it
holding a candle aloft like a sword, but when he comes to the
closed door where waits that self that is what he chose not to be,
the pleasure of dread vanishes. Anguish over the rejected choice
and the present pressure to choose rightly rushes in to take its
place; the immediate effect is horror and its paralysis of action.

> Oh to have this consciousness was to *think*—and to think, Brydon knew,
> as he stood there, was, with the lapsing moments, not to have acted! Not
> to have acted—that was the misery and the pang—was even still not to
> act; was in fact *all* to feel the thing in another, in a new and terrible way.
> (p. 749)

Further emotion comes as part of Brydon's self-realization—
compassion for "the Other." " 'You affect me as by the appeal
positively for pity: you convince me that for reasons rigid and
sublime—what do I know?—we both of us should have suffered' " (p. 750). (If Brydon had earlier permitted "the Other" to
come fully to life, they would have suffered in natural consequence of living; since he never let the other self come to birth,
it can only be seen as a piteous, non-suffering cipher.) Facing for
the first time the result of not being what he might have been,
Brydon declares, " '[M]oved and privileged as, I believe, it has
never been given to man, I retire, I renounce—never, on my
honour, to try again. So rest for ever—and let *me!* ' " (Ibid.). By

taking responsibility for what he is not, Brydon finally suffers, but without crippling remorse. By asking forgiveness of the self he had hitherto denied, he simultaneously increases the pain of his sense of guilt and finds the swiftest way to relieve it. This tale is, indeed, not about a man locked to a sense of what he might have been; it does, however, imply that a man's unused possibilities are forever a part of his imaginative life.

First, Brydon had felt a renewed sense of life through the pursuit of "the Other." Secondly, he experienced suffering of guilt through compassion and the overcoming of guilt by forgiveness. The third step comes when Brydon faces the apparition who is not "Other" but is his actual self. The process of coming to self-knowledge, initially begun in terror and dread, comes to its first climax upstairs before the closed door of what he is *not*. The process culminates significantly in the entry hall, at the second moment of climax, when he experiences horror and anguish over what he *is*. These several stages are necessary ones, however they break the back of the traditional narrative structure. Brydon must experience what he is, as well as imagine what he is not. He must examine pride of possible self and revulsion of actual self before his total self can be known, and once known, accepted.

James used the term "the Others" in two ways in his fiction: to signify the visiting presences of the dead, and to express whatever is not contained completely within a particular man's being. Both the imagined creature of the closed upstairs room and the one encountered in the entrance hall may be viewed merely as haunting presences in the first sense. However, these apparitions paired together also make up the totality of Brydon's true subconscious self and thus are not "Other" at all. To be freed completely into his conscious life, Brydon must finally "die" to both those selves, must force them to cease being "the Others" in the second sense. Before testing the outcome of Brydon's night in the jolly corner (where, after the manner of Thoreau, he runs life into that corner and faces its truth), it will be profitable to survey how Ralph Pendrel endures his series of ordeals.

Two Men, Their Own Ghosts: Ralph Pendrel

Uneven in quality, unfinished in performance, *The Sense of the Past* is still invaluable as evidence for the way James worked over several important matters. The detailed scenario James dictated for this novel ought to be placed beside his notebooks, his prefaces, and his essay "The Art of Fiction" for the view inward it gives upon his practical theories of art. It ought not to be treated merely as one of those unfortunate creations of an author's years of decline that well-wishing friends hasten out of sight. This truncated, often recalcitrant novel has a right to be studied for what it is: James's attempt (made with the flagging energies of an aging man, but energies nonetheless) to make manageable the complexities of time and consciousness, to draw out new literary definitions for realism from events that go far beyond normal standards of reality, and to incise in strong detail how men may menace themselves—the last of which will be discussed here. Through his portrayal of Ralph Pendrel (whether realized actually or only sketched out in its potentials), James presses home a startling extension of the notion that the living may menace the dead and become a ghost to ghosts; he pointed toward one of the most distinctively "modern" literary themes: that of the man so cut off from himself, from society, from time, and from empirical reality, that he comes to question the reality of his own existence.

James seized upon the terrors and pleasures of the double consciousness as profoundly new in the way he rendered them fictionally in 1900, although not new as a recognized condition.[17] James frequently specified that Pendrel would have "the extraordinary experience (the experience *within* the experience) of his

being under observation by his alter ego." Pendrel is to do everything "en double" because it is the representation of "the double
consciousness . . . which makes the thrill and the curiosity of the
affair, the consciousness of being the other and yet himself also,
of being himself and yet the other also." [18]

When Pendrel tells the Ambassador that he is not himself but
somebody else, his sympathetic listener asks whether he is sure
he knows which of his selves is which. Pendrel is sure. He has
studied his own "case" with the avidity amateur psychologists
usually bring to bear.

> "I didn't say, kindly understand, that we have *merged* personalities, but
> that we have definitely exchanged them—which is a different matter.
> Our duality is so far from diminished that it's only the greater—but our
> formulation, each to the other, of the so marked difference in our inter-
> est. The man [Pendrel of 1910] ridden by his curiosity about the Past,
> *can't*, you'll grasp, be one and the same with the man [Pendrel of 1820]
> ridden by his curiosity about the Future." [19]

Ralph Pendrel is familiar as the Man of Imagination whose
strong psychic sensitivity leaves him especially vulnerable to
psychological disturbances, yet one who feels compelled to pursue his other self along the corridors of consciousness in order
to *enact* that experience and to *be* that self.

Until he was thirty Ralph Pendrel had remained quietly
within the "small circle" of his consciousness, further limited by
the fact of being an American.[20] He fruitlessly loves Aurora
Coyne, who has been left immensely rich and free by a stream
of family deaths, herself a golden dawn of coins. The day comes
in their static relations when she is shocked by the news that
Pendrel can now go to England to learn how to live. Aurora has
always said she could never love "the 'mere' person, the mere
leader, of the intellectual life, the mere liver in a cultivated corner" (p. 351). It is "men of action" she admires, men "who've
been through something" (p. 11). Now she fears to have Pendrel

go forth to meet experience in the only way he knows, by going abroad, where there is a past in which to immerse himself.

The would-be lovers are at an impasse until Pendrel decides he must exert "the kind of personal force, of action on her nerves and her senses, that might win from her a second surrender" before she will consent to take him as her second husband (p. 8). He sets out, hoping to gather in new riches of imaginative material for his consciousness to feed upon, even if his mode of action is all in terms of moving backward in time and of dealing with the dead.

Once transported quite literally into the past, Pendrel will come to the point where "his dawning anguish glimmers and glimmers" because he is a truly divided man. Remaining a personage of 1910 even while immersed in 1820, he will discover he feels less a part of existence rather than doubly so,

it being so one thing to "live in the Past" *with* the whole spirit, the whole candour of confidence and confidence of candour, that he would then have naturally had—and a totally different thing to find himself living in it without those helps to possibility, those determinations of relation, those preponderant right instincts and, say, saving divinations. (p. 301) [21]

Such dangers appear to Pendrel only after he makes the movement backward and becomes a ghost of the Future surrounded by ghosts of the Past. Before his excursion this man, who has hitherto only "been," excitedly feels himself "on the eve of a great adventure." [22] Yet he has promised Aurora to return, " 'because I shall want to' " (p. 31). Whether a man's will is sufficient to pull him back from among ghosts and to release him from his own ghostliness proves the vital question.

Pendrel's wandering through the empty house in London fills him with a sense of the silent secrets of the place. They have been given him "as in a locked brass-bound box the key of which he

was to find" (p. 45). Marvelous secrets, but not disclosed without
risk.

> He encountered however on this ground of a possible menace to his
> peace a reassurance that sprang, and with all eagerness, from the very
> nature of his mind. He lived, so far as a wit sharpened by friction with
> the real permitted him, in his imagination; but if life was for this faculty
> a chain of open doors through which endless connections danced there
> was yet no knowledge in the world on which one should wish a door
> closed. (p. 46)

Alone one night in the shadowed house, Pendrel senses that
something remarkable is about to happen. He asks himself "if he
were prepared, if he should 'elect' to be . . ." (p. 83). He does so
elect, and by choosing to be *is* worthy. "He had had his idea of
testing the house, and lo it was the house that by the turn of the
tables had tested him. He had at all events grasped his candle as
if it had been sword or cross, and his attitude may pass for us
as sufficiently his answer or his vow" (p. 84).

Pendrel moves closer to the desired confrontation, and closer
to a right evaluation of the tepidness of his previous mode of
existence. "[W]hat was of course now most present to him was
that he had hitherto grasped of life a sadly insignificant shred.
There were at least as many more things in it for one's philosophy than poor Hamlet himself was to have found in heaven and
earth" (p. 90)—things discovered by both men by means of visiting ghosts.

Pendrel is excited by what he learns. Soon afterward he tells
the Ambassador, " 'I'm so far from intending or wishing to com-
mit suicide that I'm proposing to push my affair all the way it
will go, or in other words to live with an intensity unprece-
dented' " (p. 109).

In this excitement of the strange, Pendrel finds "an inordinate
charm. But if it might be a charm, for the time, as much as one
would, just so it might become later on, and was probably sure

to, a terror . . ." (p. 90). A charm and a terror, but not at first. Upon taking up his role of ghost in 1820 he experiences joy. At last he is really alive, "excited and amused and exhilarated" by the special psychical powers granted him; he is delighted by "the freedom with which he lives and enjoys and sees and knows" what the mere ghosts of the past cannot possibly know (p. 301). But soon the *malaise* toward which James had been heading his plot begins to gather. It comes from that sense of "the gruesome" *"pushed to the full and right expression of its grotesqueness,"* which in turn comes from "the fact of the consciousness of [terror] as given, not *received,* on the part of the central, sentient, person of the story." [23]

James takes care to describe Pendrel's 1820 cousins, Mrs. Midmore and her son Perry, as apparitions (pp. 144, 149). When, unaware of their own nature, ghosts are faced by a much odder kind of ghost, they feel a horror that they transmit to the one who causes it. One of the characters comments, " 'Isn't the impression strange in proportion as it's contrary to nature, and isn't it by the same token agitating or upsetting or appalling, for any relation with such a matter, in proportion as it's strange?' " (p. 102). Strange Pendrel certainly is to the Midmores; appalling he becomes.[24]

James insists upon the fear felt over the hero's presence that leads to Pendrel's fear of himself. "What appealed to me as of an intensely effective note of the supernatural and sinister kind was this secret within his breast . . . of his abnormal nature and of the effect on others that a dim, vague, attached and yet rather dreadful and distressful sense of it produces on *them.*" [25]

The slow growth on the part of the others of their fear of Ralph, even in the midst of their making much of him, as abnormal, as uncanny, as not *like* those they know of their own kind etc., etc.; and his fear just *of* theirs, with his double consciousness, alas, his being *almost* as right as possible for the "period," and yet so intimately and secretly wrong; with his desire to mitigate so far as he can the malaise that he feels himself, do what he will, more and more produce. (p. 295)

Though Pendrel assures the Midmores that he has no "gift of second sight," it is clairvoyancy that first drops a mist of fear between them. All he need do is "to *do* the thing" and it will "'come' right" for him (p. 122). Think of a miniature in his pocket and it appears. Think of the absent Nan Midmore miles away in the act of breaking a precious vase and he sees nearly all the scene. Think of the letters Molly Midmore tells him she wrote, and he promptly envisions her misspellings of "friteful" and "goast" (pp. 188, 189). What begins as a lovely parlor-game of consciousness—"the divinatory gift that so unfailingly flared up in him under stress"—ends by inciting fear (p. 224).

The malaise is further heightened by the accelerating sense of knowing that another knows one knows; it is "an extraordinary communion" that grows out of "the strange long look, the questioning fear" (p. 259). This is communication without comprehension, one that brings unrest, not peace. Suddenly Pendrel sees the Midmores,

during a series of moments, well-nigh as an artful, a wonderful trio, some mechanic but consummate imitation of ancient life, staring through the vast plate of a museum. It was for all the world as if his own interpretation grew, under this breath of crisis, exactly by the lapse of theirs, lasting long enough to suggest that his very care for them had somehow annihilated them, or had at least converted them to the *necessarily* void and soundless state. (p. 213)

Because they think him so "other" and cannot understand what he is, they think him mad. Their Medusa-fear chills them into stone. When Pendrel sees the dehumanizing effect he has upon them, he becomes even more dismayed at the force for paralysis he represents.

James planned to tap home "the silver nail" that makes Pendrel realize he faces the "danger of passing for a madman, or some unspeakable kind of supernatural traitor, to others; and if he accepts the situation, that is, accepts the terror of his consciousness, he becomes the same sort of thing to himself." [26]

. . . the very beauty of the subject is in the fact of his at the same time watching himself, watching his success, criticising his failure, being both the other man and not the other man, being just sufficiently the other, his prior, his own, self, not to be able to help living in that a bit too. Isn't it a part of what I call the beauty that this concomitant, this watchful and critical, living his "own" self inevitably grows and grows from a certain moment on?—and isn't it for instance quite magnificent that one sees this growth of it as inevitably promoted more and more by his sense of what I have noted as the malaise on the part of the others? (pp. 300–301)

It is at this juncture that James's scenario declares that Pendrel becomes wild to leave the past and return to his single self in the present. He becomes desperate with the fear that

he is going to be *left*, handed over to the condition of where and what above all *when* he is; never saved, never rescued, never restored again, by the termination of his adventure and his experience, to his native temporal conditions, which he yearns for with an unutterable yearning. (p. 327)

He feels "so 'cut off,' so now conclusively and hopelessly cut off, from the life, from the whole magnificent world from which he is truant"—that world of "all the wonders and splendours that he is straining back to, and of which he now sees only the ripeness, richness, attraction and civilisation, the virtual perfection without a flaw . . ." (pp. 336, 337–338). (Pendrel has no notion of what the next four years will bring to 1910.) After all, "[his] whole preconception has been that it [his trip into the past] would, that it should, be an excursion and nothing more," from which he could easily extricate himself—an "adventure" that would certainly not lead to such dislocation of consciousness. (p. 367)[27]

How is Pendrel to be rescued from the terrors of his doubleness? How can he be returned to "single blessedness" in the grace and beauty of his own era? If and when he returns, will he be capable of living in the present; for what good would it be if his physical self were plunged back into the present while his consciousness lingered in the past?

One force that helps ready Pendrel for his return is the force within his own consciousness that acts naturally to heal its own wounds and regain its saving balance.

> Don't I see his divination of *that* [the. effect his Past-self has on the Midmores] so affect and act upon him that little by little he begins to live more, to live most, and most uneasily, in what I refer to as his own, his prior self, and less, uneasily less, in his borrowed, his adventurous, that of his tremendous speculation, so to speak—. . . . (p. 301)

However, it takes more than the will of a haunted man to save himself from himself. It is the love of good women which finally does the deed. In James's version, which tentatively accepts the truth of this age-old literary mode of salvation, it is a "psychical" rescue that Aurora Coyne and Nan Midmore perform for Ralph Pendrel. It is the same answer that gives over the "third" climax of "The Jolly Corner" to Alice Staverton. It is in this light that the endings of these two works must be judged. Each proves the strengths inherent in James's attitudes toward the outcome of the ordeal of the haunted haunters; each betrays the weaknesses of these attitudes.[28]

The Flight from Peace

There is yet another "climax" in store for Spencer Brydon before his story's ending. At the moment of encountering his true self, the mutilated figure in the entry hall, Brydon is paralyzed by horror and anguish. He experiences what the elder Henry James would have called the Vastation that redeems, the sweep of self-revulsion that drives Brydon into the relief of unconsciousness. Then he awakens, as if from death, his head cradled protectively in Alice Staverton's lap. Her love had given her the power of psychic sight, and she has watched him exorcise the two presences during the night's sequence of climaxes. Brydon's ordeal over, she welcomes him back into consciousness with the prophetic words, " 'Now I have you.' "

In *The Sense of the Past* Nan Midmore also has the power to end Pendrel's horror and eject him from the past by the force of her psychic sympathy. James intended, as well, for Aurora Coyne, waiting impatiently back in the present, to take her part. Aurora is to rescue Pendrel "on this side of time," just as "the liberation, for rescue of the other side of time" was Nan's. James recorded how the unfinished novel was meant to end.

I want his restoration and recovery to take place actually and literally through [Aurora] having got into such a "psychic" state, passed through such a psychic evolution, over there, that she takes action at last, takes the very action that she sort of defied Ralph to make her take. . . . (p. 351)

Before he left her in New York, Pendrel called Aurora one of *"the* women" who could be counted on to help him if his adventure proved too much for him. She had replied, " '[If] I *am* moved —moved from within and by something now incalculable—you may count on me' " (p. 36). As he drew to the end of his scenario, James's excitement mounted over the way Aurora would be so "moved." It was his "conceit" that Aurora,

left to the aftersense of what has passed between them, gradually feels her "state of mind," state of feeling, state of fancy, say, state of nerves in fine, grow and grow (in a sort of way that is corresponding all the while to the stages of [Pendrel's] experience . . .). (p. 352)

There is strength in this conception that defines the conclusions of both *The Sense of the Past* and "The Jolly Corner" in terms of an evolving consciousness. Pendrel and Brydon must undergo the legendary ordeals that test their valor, sustained in their nights of fear by the love of women who participate in the only way they can—within their hearts and minds. Together, through a doubling of psychic powers, the men win and the women gain their prize.

The weaknesses involved in this new psychological retelling of knightly quest tales (and of moral Darwinism) are only inferred, not seen, but they cannot be ignored. These weaknesses arise out of what, it is implied, will characterize the lives of Spencer Brydon and Ralph Pendrel after the last sentences of their stories have come to a full stop. (Judgment of such matters is made more difficult by *The Sense of the Past* since we have to deal with James's intentions, not with an achieved ending.)

Up to the very end, these two stories rest on the strength of the desire for intensity of life. Both heroes are avid for life while they are pursued and pursuer. It is only at the conclusion, with their victories won, that a suspicious stagnation sets in. Brydon comes back from unconsciousness to find himself cradled by Alice in a *Pietà* position; the passion is over, even if a kind of resurrection has taken place. Pendrel will find himself welcomed back by Aurora with her promise of a lifetime of marriage. There is nothing wrong as such with "happy endings" that push the man into the lady's arms, but one comes away with the unsettling feeling that the men's brave and, for us, interesting struggles against the apparitions of the self have come *only* to this. There is no assurance whatever that the energies and powers that marked their nights of encounter will ever be sustained by Brydon or Pendrel. They will have memories, of course, of their heightened moments of consciousness, and they will possess the present fact of Alice and Aurora with their everlasting psychic powers, but the sense conveyed of the future is sterile when compared with the intense sense of the past and participation in the present they have enjoyed.

In "The Jolly Corner" and *The Sense of the Past*, the heroes are immediately protected from death because they are loved and were sustained by love through their crises of consciousness, but the stories in which they appear are somehow lost—lost in the same way Brydon and Pendrel may be yet lost because the great time of testing and victory is over and will never return. (Consider, too, the endings of *A Farewell to Arms* and *Sons and Lovers*. The heroes walk away from the dead women with whom passionate contention has brought them both joy and pain; they walk into a future flavored by self-pity, morbidity, and sterility, however "saved" they are by their authors' refusal to hand them a happy ending.)

The weakness detected in these two James stories of the supernatural is also present in "Sir Edmund Orme" (with its toss-away reminder that the love of Charlotte Marden and the narrator ends rapidly in death) and in "The Altar of the Dead" when George Stransom finds life through love of the dead at the near moment of his own death. In "The Turn of the Screw" and "The Beast in the Jungle" James escapes such a falling off from once-heightened consciousness. These are stories that refuse to rest in an eternal aftermath of death or static acceptance of what the self has achieved. The future of private hells implied for the governess and John Marcher is the salvation of these stories as fiction. Their sense of the past, of the dead, and of their own self-haunt-edness continues now, and forever, in the intensity of the present.

These comments may indicate an important generalization about James's fiction. As long as it works tensely with coming-to-awareness, with the frictions between past and present, and with the intensities of consciousness, its chances for success as art are great; it is able to roll up the special attributes of the tale of self-haunting and go far beyond it. Once that crucially contested awareness is attained, however—once a captured past is pressed forward into the serene future, and once tranquillities of mind are gained—the special value of James's fiction tends to fall away. His is an art that cannot stand peace. It thrives upon the life of consciousness driven in constant pursuit of the self through the even-duplicating mirrors of the Galerie d'Apollon—"a dream-adventure founded in the deepest, quickest, clearest act of cognition and comparison, act indeed of life-saving energy, as well as in unutterable fear. . . ." [29]

CHAPTER VII

The Heroine as "Sensitive"

The Ladies of E.S.P.

Every era has its heroines whose selection reveals what it values most in women. That generation intrigued by occult matters during the last decades of the nineteenth century raised a long list of female "sensitives" to the rank of real, if sometimes questionable, renown. Beginning with the Fox sisters and Mrs. Hayden, women mediums and telepathists flourished. Among them were Mrs. Leonard, Mrs. Cooper, and Mrs. Palladino (the "Mrs." often assumed with somewhat the same desire for professional respectability found in brothel madams). Far and away the most discussed was the "mental" medium, Mrs. Leonora Piper of Boston. (She was not a "physical" medium like, say, the notorious Eusapia Palladino.) Mrs. Piper's special psychic powers especially fascinated William James.[1] It was, in fact, his cautious attendance at one of her séances in 1884 that first started James upon his sub-career as psychic researcher.[2] As her mentor—almost, one might say, her entrepreneur—James studied her messages for fifteen years in the hope that her abilities as telepathist and clairvoyant might reveal important information concerning spirit survival and the nature of consciousness and ego.

William James was particularly interested in those qualities of consciousness that might either lay a woman low with nervous disturbances or raise her to the heights of near omniscience. After one of his sister's recurrent mental upsets, he wrote Alice James in 1891 to explain that "in these neurotic cases . . . some infernality in the body *prevents* really existing parts of the mind from coming to their effective rights at all, suppresses them, and blots them out from participation in this world's experiences, although they are *there* all the time." [3] Early and late in his long association with her, Mrs. Piper's mind seemed to James remarkably able to exercise its full potentialities, but *how* he could not make out. After she told him many things of a personal nature, relating certain events within his home, he reported, "Insignificant as these things sound when read, the accumulation of a large number of them has an irresistible effect. . . ." He ended, "This is all that I can tell you of Mrs. Piper. I wish it were more 'Scientific'. " [4] Twenty-three years after first making her acquaintance he concluded, "Mrs. Piper has supernormal knowledge in her trances; but whether it comes from 'tapping the minds' of living persons, or from some common cosmic reservoir of memories, or from surviving 'spirits' of the departed, is a question impossible for *me* to answer just now to my own satisfaction." He added, "the electric current called *belief* has not yet closed in my mind." [5]

In an article of 1897, "What Psychical Research Has Accomplished," William James made distinctions relevant to his brother's fiction when he drew the line between the two basic types of mind involved in psychical research. There are the "feminine-mystical" mind and its antagonist, the "scientific-academic" or masculine-critical mind. [6] The "feminine-mystical" mind has powers of institution of the kind Henri Bergson upheld against those who associated intuition "with the preternatural and the arcane, with fortune-tellers and seers." [7] William James also maintained that the feminine-mystical mind is best able to grasp the real facts. (Mrs. Piper vindicated at last!)

When once they [facts] are indisputably ascertained and admitted, the academic and critical minds are by far the best fitted ones to interpret and discuss them—for surely to pass from mystical to scientific speculations is like passing from lunacy to sanity; but on the other hand if there is anything which human history demonstrates, it is the extreme slowness with which the ordinary academic and critical mind acknowledges facts to exist which present themselves as wild facts.

To William James "there [was] no doubt" that the feminine-mystical mind goes "with a gift for meeting with certain kinds of phenomenal experience." He concluded, "In psychology, physiology, and medicine, wherever a debate between the mystics and the scientifics has been once for all decided, it is the mystics who have usually proved to be right about the *facts*, while the scientifics had the better of it in respect to the theories." [8]

What was necessary to William James in his endeavors—the constant testing of the "masculine" intellect by the "feminine" psyche—also proved artistically right for the fiction of his brother that plays off "natural," workaday perceptions against "supernatural" awareness. In either instance—William's science or Henry's art—the last word was generally had by the feminine-mystical consciousness with its ability to go beyond the limitations of visible evidence.

In the world of James's fiction, who has more femininity of psyche than the women characters? No one, except perhaps Henry James himself,[9] who possessed both the "feminine-mystical" mind that intuits and the masculine-critical mind that interprets.

One day in 1895 Henry James made a lengthy entry in his notebooks; it concerned the fictional possibilities of a story about a brother and sister who "see with the same sensibilities and the same imagination, vibrate with the same nerves, suffer with the same suffering: have, in a word, exactly, identically the same

experience of life. Two lives, two beings, and *one* experience. . . ." [10] James turned over the thought that there might
then be "the incident of their dying together as the only thing
they *can* do that does not a little fall short of absolutely ideally
perfect agreement." Theirs was to be "a kind of resigned, inevitable, disenchanted double suicide. It is a reflection, a reduplication
of melancholy, of irony."

The more James thought about it the more the intensity of this
ingrown relationship mounted. When the brother suffers

the sister understands, perceives, shares, with every pulse of her being.
He has to tell her nothing—she *knows*; it's identity of sensation, of
vibration. It's for *her*, the Pain of Sympathy: *that* would be the subject,
the formula.

For James his fiction would increasingly follow out the implications of "sympathy"—that sharing of pain that need never be
voiced aloud in order to be released.

"Sympathy" as a belief in a physical-psychical system of communication between the living had long been part of nineteenth-
century Romanticism.[11] Important passages in *Jane Eyre, The Scar-
let Letter,* and Browning's *Men and Women,* as well as the
contemporary *The Return of the Native,* show how the notion of
occult rapport of minds had been used for artistic purposes by
James's time. James liked to work within existing literary traditions, while expanding possibilities only hinted at by earlier writers or while discovering in them entirely new imaginative
strengths. In the artistic rendering of psychic communication
James tried to avoid certain weaknesses he noted in previous
attempts.[12] He also emerged with a novel variation on the time-
hallowed theme. James's special twist was his observation that
even if men achieve a certain degree of sympathetic knowledge,
they may never hope to reach the peak of psychic reciprocity
possible to a woman.[13]

The constant reader of James sometimes has the uneasy feeling that there would be no need for dialogue if the novels and stories were populated solely by women—they who "subtly intercommunicate." The author would then merely note the responses received by the antennae of his women's vibrating consciousnesses. But since the Jamesian world is filled with clods of men as well as refinements of women, the latter have as their duty to explain "all" to the men. Wives in James's novels have an especially tedious time of it, spelling out to their dullard husbands what they know about what other women know; as with Mrs. Assingham to the Colonel about Maggie Verver; or Mrs. Brook to Edward Brookenham about Nana: " 'Without a syllable said to her she's yet aware in every fibre of her little being of what has taken place.' " [14]

James's *ficelles* lead an even more arduous life. Though Maria Gostrey disclaims to Strether the possession of "the prophetic vision," she was "at this instant the nearest approach he had ever met to the priestess of the oracle. The light was in her eyes." When Maria tells him Chad Newsome is not free, "The air of it held him. 'Then you've all the while known—?' " he asks. " 'I've known nothing but what I've seen; and I wonder,' she declared with some impatience, 'that you didn't see as much. It was enough to do with him there—.' " [15] All a proper Jamesian female need do is *be*. Through her occult vision—formed by intuition rather than reason—she is able to say, "And there we are!" baffling her poor male confidant, who has only the haziest notion where he, or anyone, is.

Intuitive intelligence and the sympathy of suffering gained through the experience of shared life are the minimum requirements for the development of these special powers, which are, of course, human and natural in the fullest secular sense.

James states with authorial concern that Olive Chancellor in *The Bostonians* puts him "under the necessity of imparting much occult information" about her. [16] He feels himself under obligation to show how Olive confronts her guests "with her spectral

face"; how "forebodings were a peculiarity of her organisation";
how she has conveyed to her, "by the voices of the air," the nature
of Verena's Harvard admirer; how she had "a sort of mystical
foreboding" about Basil Ransom's future psychic interference
with her will. In *The Portrait of a Lady* even the relatively stupid
Countess Gemini can recognize what lies in Osmond's past
"without a word said" because her mind is not impeded by the
innocence that negates the fineness of Isabel Archer's intelligence.[17] Even the narrator of *The Sacred Fount* admits that he is
a mere child in swaddling clothes when it comes to the "vision"
women have of others: the vision that consists of "The instinct
of sympathy, pity—the response to fellowship in misery; the
sight of another fate as strange, as monstrous as her own."[18]

The best of Jamesian men may possess some or all of these
eminently humanistic qualities that endow them in turn with
special psychic powers, but never to the degree of James's
women, even the worst of them.[19] This is especially true when
they are women in love.

Intelligence, experience, sympathy, and love combined grant
a woman extraordinary powers. Bluntly put, James believed that
women love better than men. Whether this is so because they are
psychically sensitive to others' consciousness, or whether they
are sensitive because they love, falls under the classic chicken-egg
quandary. It is perhaps sufficient to note these points. The
regularity with which James made use of the notion of feminine
intuitiveness in matters of love, and the way in which James's
belief that women in love are aware of a great deal more than
they have been told, changed in fictional function. What began
for James as a conventional metaphor or surface observation
became a central motif and structuring strategy during the years
after 1880. This was the time when the movement of his plots
came to depend increasingly upon the divulgence of concealed
information by psychically sensitive women able to see and thus
to know and to reveal all. The following brief review marks the

advances Henry James made once the material of psychic concerns became a usable part of his fiction.

In James's first big novel, *Roderick Hudson* of 1876, Rowland Mallet is shown to be nearly as responsive as the women "sensitives" into whose company he is thrown because he, too, loves. He "knew that his companion [Mary Garland] knew, by that infallible sixth sense of a woman who loves, how the beautiful strange girl [Christina Light] she had seen for the first time at Saint Peter's (since when she had asked no question about her) had possibly the power to do her a definite wrong." [20] The relatively dull-witted and unimaginative Charlotte Wentworth of *The Europeans* of 1878 sees why her fiancé, the minister Mr. Brand, wants to perform the marriage ceremony for her sister, for whom he had recently had an infatuation. "Her imagination . . . was not so rapid as her sister's, but now it had taken several little jumps" [21] —because now she loves. In these two early novels the motif is inserted at appropriate points, but it is trite enough; it has no real link with the occult either in the literal sense of that term or in its literary uses.

What James might make of feminine sensitivity is somewhat more apparent in his 1880 novel *Confidence*. The heroine Angela Vivian tells the hero she knew all along the degrading game he and his friend were playing with her. " 'How can a woman help knowing such a thing? She guesses it—she discovers it by instinct—. . . .' " Later, having revealed she "knows all" about yet another veiled matter of love, Angela asserts wearily, " 'Men are so stupid; it's only women that have real discernment.' " [22] It would be the purpose of *Confidence* to use that psychically gained information for its plot movement, even if James failed to fulfill its literary expression.

In an 1883 discussion of Trollope's novels James commented, "Women are delicate and patient observers; they hold their noses close, as it were, to the texture of life. They feel and perceive the

real with a kind of personal tact. . . ." [23] In "The Art of Fiction"
of 1884 he noted that a woman novelist had inspired his admonitions to cultivate the "power to guess the unseen from the seen,
to trace the implications of things. . . ." [24] James's own ideas on
the matter solidified by the 1890's once he learned how to use
feminine powers directly in his fiction.

Julia Dallow of *The Tragic Muse* of 1890 explains why she had
suddenly burst in upon her fiancé's studio to find things as she
had suspected: not up to snuff. " 'I knew it—I knew everything;
that's why I came,' " she declares, and Nick Dormer can only
reply, " 'It was a sort of second-sight—what they call a brain-
wave.' " Soon after in the same novel, Peter Sherringham decides
of Biddy Dormer (who loves him) that she "participated by imagination, by divination, by a clever girl's secret tremulous instincts. . . . He had impressions, possibly gross and unjust, in
regard to the way women move constantly together amid such
considerations and subtly intercommunicate. . . ." [25] In *The Other
House* of 1896 Rose Armiger "knows" what it is Julia Bream
wants her husband Tony (whom Rose loves) to promise before
she dies. When Tony asks Rose how she knew that Julia would
ask him not to remarry as long as their child was alive, she
answers, " 'I haven't needed to be a monster of cunning to
guess!' " [26] It is simply that her love enables her to know, just as
it is her love that turns her into a monster of cunning to hold
the man she loves in her thrall, even to the point of doing murder
to manage it. Fleda Vetch, the lover of *The Spoils of Poynton* of
1896, "almost demonically both sees and feels, while the others
but feel without seeing." [27] Then there is little Maisie Farange,
who is made the heroine of the 1897 novel devoted to what she
"knew" and how she knew it. Maisie knows "for all the world
as if through a small demonic foresight" because she loves—Sir
Claude, Mrs. Wix, the Captain, her mother, and her father. "Maisie knew what 'amour' meant too," but more particularly love
in its sympathetic forms, because even in embryo her feminine-

mystical sensitivity has been led along the far road of consciousness and awareness.[28]

The interest roused by a resumé such as that just given is
probably mild and its value certainly nil if it remains nothing
more than a chronological itemization entitled "References to
Metaphors of Female 'Occultism' in the Novels of Henry James."
Consider, however, the integral part this particular kind of extra-
sensory knowledge plays in the novels written after 1880. In
Confidence and *The Other House* the women's ability to know
beyond the realm of the usual is what conditions the ways in
which the plots are made to turn. In *The Tragic Muse* Julia and
Biddy's "knowledge" is important to the working out of their
relationships to the men they love, as is Fleda's in *The Spoils of
Poynton*. But in *What Maisie Knew* this motif *is* the novel, what it is
about and how all involved are affected. The basic fact that Maisie
loves as she does leads her out of innocence into the first stages
of adult awareness and beyond those adults who do not know
rightly how to love; it shapes her life and tests the flawed loves
of those who circle her with their lesser, loveless knowledge.

The role taken by Nan Midmore in *The Sense of the Past* is
hugely instructive; through his notes for the ghost-novel published posthumously in its unfinished form in 1917 we see James
on the verge of making feminine psychic "sympathy" act as the
turning point of his hero's adventures. Nan Midmore has just
been introduced when the novel's manuscript breaks off, But
James's scenario gives his intentions concerning the girl who was
his "nearest approach . . . in the whole thing to a Heroine" (p.
293).[29] James excitedly prepared plans for the big scene (never
written) in which Pendrel's ghostly character would be affirmed
and his plight and Nan's saving love would be dramatized almost
solely by means of psychic communication. To James "the question is really had out between them without either of them so
speaking, and only by his looking her very hard in the eye, and
her so looking at him, and his keeping it up on this and her

keeping it up on that" (p. 321). Pendrel will learn that Nan "*knows*—and I think he doesn't even quite understand why or how she knows . . ." (p. 324). She has her knowledge "all absolutely through" Pendrel's mind, telepathically transmitted to hers when he "breaks down under the beautiful pity of her divination, the wonder of her so feeling for him that she virtually knows, or knows enough . . ." (p. 326).

James is clear that Nan's "sympathy"—expressed totally in terms of the psychic—proves to be Pendrel's salvation. Knowing and loving, Nan is ready to sacrifice herself for his sake. "The 'sacrifice,' the indispensable, unspeakable sacrifice, on the girl's part," James declared, "is involved in her relation to Ralph *as she now knows him,* and the quintessential 'drama' of it, so to speak, is by the same token involved in *his knowing her* as she knows him, and as, above all, she is known *by* him" (p. 348).

The intricate development of the "plot" (the immolating action that saves the beloved's harassed consciousness from pitching over into the darkness of madness) was to be wordlessly enacted as if a pantomime, with only glances and looks and that "something else" now called *psi.* James's notation also stresses his desire to avoid making specific statements about his lovers' feelings during their important scenes together. He pressed himself "harder and more intelligently" (p. 326) to solve his compositional problems without resorting to dread specificity.

Thematically, James wished to present a remarkable instance of silent sympathy; stylistically, he wished to achieve something uncommon in the way of communication between the written page and its readers. He envisioned the crest of the novel as that at which Nan's unspoken love and Pendrel's unspoken terror— the love assuaging the terror—set up a psychic flow of the kind William James *felt* (even if he could never factually know) was Mrs. Piper's special genius; of the kind Henry James *knew* (because he felt it) was the special genius of his own breed of fictional heroine.

Part Three

LITERARY EXTENSIONS

CHAPTER VIII

The Tale-Teller's Strategies

Conundrums

In 1903 William Dean Howells fashioned an imaginary conversation with a lady reader of the fiction of Henry James. When the lady petulantly asks why it need be so difficult to make out what James is saying, Howells patiently tries to wheedle her into a more generous understanding of James's method.

"[W]hat was I saying just now but that life itself is a series of conundrums, to which the answers are lost in the past, or are to be supplied us, after a long and purifying discipline of guessing, in the future? I do not admit your position, but if I did, still I should read the author who keeps you guessing, with a pleasure, an edification, in the suggestive, the instructive way he has of asking his conundrums beyond that I take in any of the authors who do not tax my curiosity, who shove their answers at me before I have had a chance to try whether I cannot guess them."

Howells's persuasiveness takes a new turn as he moves to flatter the recalcitrant reader.

"It is my high opinion of you that you precisely do like to keep puzzling his things out; that you are pleased with the sort of personal appeal made to you by the difficulties you pretend to resent, and that you enjoy the just sense of superiority which your continual or final divinations give you. Mr. James is one of these authors who pay the finest tribute an author can pay the intelligence of his reader by trusting it, fully and frankly. There you are; and if you are not puzzling out these recondite conundrums which you complain of, what better things, in the perusal of the whole range of contemporary fiction, could you be doing?" [1]

There are many things one can be doing other than reading the fiction of Henry James. Madness looms at the thought of having *only* that to do. What if one were—like Tony Last of *A Handful of Dust* doomed to a lifetime of Dickens—condemned to years in the jungle reading and re-reading *The Golden Bowl?* But there *is* something hugely there when a story-teller possesses an eye for the great extension and tutors himself to use it well.

As James came to annex several worlds to the consciousness— the worlds of immediate social being and of ghostly encounters in the past and present—he also pressed forward certain experiments in narrative strategy for their encompassment. Questions of time projection, of silent communication between the psychically sensitive, of taking in the "more" that life's "destructive element" was rapidly exposing to view—all became immediate questions for both his "daytime" novels and his "nightside" romances.

This is not to say that James's interest in the supernatural *per se* led to the brilliant discoveries in technique for which he is noted; they would doubtless have come about in his writing if he had never turned his hand to a single tale of the ghostly. At no time is this book attempting to transfer artistic cart and horse by making undue claims for the importance of James's interest, real as it was, in the supernatural as a force for his fiction. However, certain lines of discovery worked out in his occult tales run alongside his presentation of consciousness at its most "realistic." A look at three of James's novels and one of his novellas may demonstrate how readily he moved between fictional worlds, once he learned how much he could bring to his major efforts from his *amusettes.*

The Portrait of a Lady

At the opening of *The Portrait of a Lady* (1876) Isabel Archer is dangerously innocent. By the end she has not only suffered (most people accomplish that) and has known in what ways she has suffered (many achieve that minor bit of knowledge), but she has learned why she has suffered and what it means (a rare lesson granted to the fortunate few). The sign that reveals to her what has happened is one that James unobstrusively but carefully sets up as a kind of testing metaphor. At first she is unable to see the ghost of Gardencourt, although naively eager to. After her ordeal the ghost appears to her unbidden, but now understood. By means of brief but telling references to the ghost of Gardencourt, that strong sense of Before and After is achieved that the novel of maturation craves.

Isabel Archer comes from America to England prepared to face the thrilling dangers that await inexperienced young girls. She knows they are true because she has read about them. She is approaching that "strange unseen place on the other side—a place which became to the child's imagination, according to its different moods, a region of delight or of terror" that she had read about in the dark, sealed up house in Albany, New York.[2] Now at Gardencourt, Isabel demands of Ralph Touchett that he bring on visible frights for her appraisal.

"Please tell me—isn't there a ghost?" she went on.
   "A ghost?"
   "A castle-spectre, a thing that appears. We call them ghosts in America."
   "So do we here, when we see them."
   "You do see them then. You ought to, in this romantic old house."
   "It's not a romantic old house," said Ralph. "You'll be disappointed if you count on that. It's a dismally prosaic one; there's no romance here but what you may have brought with you." (III, 62)

When Isabel stubbornly continues to insist that Ralph trot out the ghost for her surveillance,

Ralph shook his head sadly. "I might show it to you, but you'd never see it. The privilege isn't given to every one; it's not enviable. It has never been seen by a young, happy, innocent person like you. You must have suffered first, have suffered greatly, have gained some miserable knowledge. In that way your eyes are opened to it. I saw it long ago," said Ralph.
"I told you just now I'm very fond of knowledge," Isabel answered.
"Yes, of happy knowledge—of pleasant knowledge. But you haven't suffered, and you're not made to suffer. I hope you'll never see the ghost!" (III, 64)

Although she fears to suffer, as she admits to Ralph, Isabel is unafraid of ghosts since she does not yet know the connection between the feeling they elicit and the phenomena they represent.[3] She came to Europe "to be as happy as possible" (III, 65). The question remains open in her mind (although not in Ralph's) whether she can have both the sought-after ghost—that is, knowledge—and happiness.

According to Henry James, Sr., experience is a prerequisite for gaining knowledge. To possess knowledge means one has learned the difference between good and evil; to learn the difference between good and evil demands that one has suffered the experience of each.[4] Henry James accepted the general drift of his father's notation by the manner in which he located Isabel's vulnerability. Her desire for the knowledge of experience is a questionable endeavor as long as she resists the suffering that seems to be the source for that knowledge. " 'No, I don't wish to touch the cup of experience,' " she tells Ralph. " 'It's a poisoned drink! I only want to see for myself.' " Ralph replies, " 'You want to see, but not to feel' " (III, 213). Ghosts, metaphoric or not, must be felt, be experienced, not merely seen and a person must suffer before being able even to encounter one. How then is Isabel to gain the privileged pain of facing the ghost of Garden-court? Only by living through the rest of the novel, living into the experience whose meaning Ralph Touchett understands from the first—both because he has already seen the ghost and because he is, in a sense, a good ghost himself—perhaps the very ghost Isabel has such avidity to see.[5]

Isabel Archer goes forth into the world, meets and marries a man who is in many ways dead, and disappears into the haunted mansion of his mind. Isabel, who thinks her fortune came from one dead man and is actually beholden for her wealth to his dying son, has been continually surrounded by emblems of death that mock her protestations that it is life she wants. Death had excited the young Isabel. It was, she believed, one of those vibrant experiences she had been looking for. Indeed, the "subtle consequences" of Mr. Touchett's death begin a series of meetings that alter her life. Immediately after, Madame Merle returns to console the new widow. A woman for whom it is "likely" her own husband should have died, Madame Merle herself is not alive in the correct sense; she admits she is a ghost of the pre-Revolutionary past. Through her machinations Gilbert Osmond enters the scene, his advent dated "some six months after old Mr. Touchett's death." Osmond's decadence and sterility are symbolically implied in the Capitoline Gallery chapter when Isabel dismisses Warburton (the vanquished Dying Gladiator, "the lion of the collection") and chooses, as it were, what she then thinks "the best"—the Antinous. Osmond's sister, the Countess Gemini, also surrounds Isabel with the aura of death. Her husband is dead, and all three of her children. She was "often extremely bored—bored, in her own phrase, to extinction." The Osmond marriage residence, the Palazzo Roccanera, is a symbol of long centuries of death as well. But it is Osmond who is most truly dead in spirit. He seems to kill all he touches by the fact that he has already buried one wife and that Isabel's child by him dies soon after its birth. But he does far worse in slaying Isabel's living ideas as a sacrifice for his pride. In his youth he had actively pursued sensual pleasure, but even that life-by-lust has dropped away. Now his only gratifications are his sterile contemplation of inanimate art objects, his incestuous regard for his own superiority, and his vampiristic efforts to take all he can from rapidly depleting sources. The only force that can stand him off in the contest over Isabel's consciousness is that of the "good ghost," Ralph Touchett.

Word arrives that Ralph is, at last, ready to end his long dying. During the trip back to England Isabel has "moments indeed in her journey from Rome which were almost as good as being dead"; she feels very much like an Etruscan figure sitting in its ashes in a jar (IV, 391). She leaves the death-in-life of the Palazzo Roccanera, travels as if dead, and passes through London, the dusky city of death (IV, 393), in order to reach the dying man at green and hushed Gardencourt, which is filled with the perfect stillness that presaged Ralph's father's death and now heralds his own (III, 294; IV, 403).

One of the great ironies Isabel has to face is this: Ralph, whom others with pity or contempt have considered as much as dead for years, is the only truly living spirit she has ever known. The money and the freedom of action he gave her she could—and did—misuse. His greatest gift was the he "made her feel the good of the world; he made her feel what might have been." Through feeling, he tried to show her that consciousness can be a weapon for joy, not a blasphemy of life. In this way Ralph, the good ghost, counters Osmond's gift of feeling defined only as horror; he counters Osmond's blighted view of consciousness as totally concerned with suffering and despair. Isabel's new awareness of Ralph's fine consciousness will outlast everything, even if it cannot solve the pain Osmond has brought her or alter her loneliness.

As Ralph lies with "his large unwinking eyes open into her own" (IV, 412), he has one final gift. His is the fixed stare of ghosts that forces the living to look into the most obscure corners of their consciousnesses so they may be able to free themselves from the burden of their own deadening egos. His stare brings Isabel "the knowledge that they were looking at the truth together" (IV, 414).

Only now is Isabel able to see Gardencourt's ghost. When it comes, it is Ralph bringing her his final farewell.[6]

He had told her, the first evening she ever spent at Gardencourt, that if she should live to suffer enough she might some day see the ghost with which the old house was duly provided. She apparently had fulfilled the necessary condition; for the next morning, in the cold, faint dawn, she knew that a spirit was standing by her bed. . . . [At] the time the darkness began vaguely to grow grey she started up from her pillow as abruptly as if she had received a summons. It seemed to her for an instant that he was standing there—a vague, hovering figure in the vagueness of the room. She stared a moment; she saw his white face—his kind eyes; then she saw there was nothing. She was not afraid; she was only sure. (IV, 418)

Isabel goes to Ralph's room, finds him dead as announced by the veridical hallucination, and recognizes the "strange resemblance to the face of his father, which, six years before, she had seen lying on the same pillow" (IV, 419). At that time she had mistakenly believed the father's death had brought her into money, marriage, and misery; he was the one she naively charged with being "the beneficent author of infinite woe!" (IV, 193). The son's death brings her a double legacy, however: the knowledge that the ills she has suffered arise from her own character since evil comes from the land of the living and not from another world over which men have no responsibility; the knowledge that consciousness as vaguely felt suffering can only be countered by consciousness as the saving strength of self-awareness and a commitment to joy.

Isabel Archer is made ready to see Gardencourt's ghost by means of events, characters, and settings drawn from James's (and Isabel's) own taste for reading in the gothic novel. Mrs. Ann Radcliffe would have been quietly pleased with the components of *The Portrait of a Lady*. Surely they would have been familiar to her. Isabel Archer as heroine: a lovely orphaned girl set down in the midst of intrigue and deceit with only her innocence to shield her from hidden evils, that same innocence making her all the more vulnerable to those evils; a reflective girl eager to meet life and yet fearful of overt expressions of its passions; a well-bred girl of unassailable self-esteem who glories in her own rectitude and imagined ability to win out over all; a naif who dotes on mystery and carefully leased-in thrills. Osmond and Madame Merle: the charming gentleman-villain and his accomplished accomplice in wickedness who eventually destroy one another. Lord Warburton: the noble nobleman who seeks the heroine's hand but is spurned. Ralph Touchett: white-faced consumptive who loves in silence and in vain. Henrietta Stackpole and Mr. Bantling: humorous companions whose coarsened, though sympathetic, comments make the delicate sensibility of the heroine seem all the more fine-grained. Pansy Osmond: secondary victim, seemingly all innocence and little will. Gardencourt: English manor house haunted by a family ghost that appears to the heroine only after her soul has been prepared sufficiently by suffering. Europe as general setting: redolent of centuries of civilized cruelty. Palazzo Crescenti in Florence and Osmond's villa: imaged as prisons from whence it might not be easy to escape. Palazzo Roccanera: ominous Italian palace steeped in violence and filled with layers of darkness that flood the innocents' minds with fear.[7] There is even a Roman Catholic convent whose exterior of gracious smiles and sanctity hides the threats of involuntary imprisonment traditional to the essential Protestantism of the gothic genre.

A common motto of many gothic novels is "Had I but known!" Certainly sufficient hints (recognizable to close readers of gothic fiction) concerning the true natures of Osmond and Isabel's dear friend Madame Merle are given, but not until Isabel—like Emily in *The Mysteries of Udolpho*, whisked away by Montoni from gay Venice to the gloom of his secluded palace—is taken from sun-lit Florence and set down in endungeoned Rome does she begin to notice the tell-tale aura of death and decay. With his gothic characters, his symbols, and his setting of potential terror well in hand, James was ready to elaborate the drama of the menaced consciousness.

Isabel Archer admits she does not at all know Gilbert Osmond when she marries him and that she has hesitated to know him too well for fear he might prove to be other than his Christian name implies, the nebulous "bright wish" on whose validity she has risked everything. Even before her marriage the "sublime principle" of her imagination "somehow broke down" and now "hung back" from the "last vague space it couldn't cross—a dusky, uncertain tract which looked ambiguous and even slightly treacherous, like a moorland seen in the winter twilight. But she was to cross it yet" (IV, 21–22).

Isabel crosses the dark and bloody ground of Osmond's consciousness the night after she comes upon Madame Merle and Osmond arranged in positions of such familiarity that she receives the impression that they are together "with the freedom of old friends who sometimes exchange ideas without uttering them" (IV, 165). They are, in fact, in psychic communication of a kind that Isabel's own psychic perceptions cannot immediately grasp. She does grasp it in part as she sits in long meditation through the dark night of her soul, during the actual night when the "ugly possibilities," the "labyrinth" of events roil the surface of her consciousness (IV, 188). Isabel is poised in what F. W. H. Myers later named "the Centre of Consciousness"—that "point from which [the percipient] seems to himself to be surveying some phantasmal scene." [8] She comes to experience, as James's sister Alice did, "the immense extension that is added to life when you are not just immersed in it but also intellectually

detached, when you are aware not only of the immediate moment, but also of your awareness of that awareness. . . ." [9]

Suddenly Isabel finds that "her soul was haunted with terrors
which crowded to the foreground of thought as quickly as a place
was made for them"; she realizes Osmond's "faculty for making
everything wither that he touched . . ." (IV, 188). She tells herself that it was "as if he had had the evil eye," as if he—Borgia-
like—tried to poison her whole being, "as if Osmond deliberately, almost malignantly, had put the lights out one by one" (IV,
188, 190). It is Osmond's *mind* that now seems to her a far more
ominous place than the Palazzo Roccanera. She discovers "she
had lived *in* it almost" (IV, 194); that since "she had followed him
further and he had led her into the mansion of his own habita-
tion, then, *then* she had seen where she really was" (IV, 196). It
is with "incredulous terror" that "she had taken the measure of
her dwelling" (ibid.).[10]

Once she knows where she is (inside Osmond's palazzo and his
mind), she can tell what he is. He has not changed from what
he was; she simply now sees him all. In the very act of describing
his dungeonlike house as if it were a man's mind and his mind
as if it were a gothic house of horror and then, in turn, imagining
that mind as if it were also the menacing presence that haunts
the actual Palazzo, Isabel comes to know Osmond.

Between those four walls she had lived ever since; they were to surround
her for the rest of her life. It was the house of darkness, the house of
dumbness, the house of suffocation. Osmond's beautiful mind gave it
neither light nor air; Osmond's beautiful mind indeed seemed to peep
down from a small high window and mock at her. (Ibid.)

When Isabel sees the "rigid system" by which he wishes her
spirit to live, when she feels it "close about her, draped though
it was in pictured tapestries, that sense of darkness and suffocation of which I have spoken took possession of her; she seemed
shut up with an odour of mould and decay" (IV, 199). She has

been led downward into the dungeon, "into realms of restriction and depression where the sound of other lives, easier and freer, was heard as from above . . ." (IV, 189). Stripped of her innocence, her freedom of spirit denied her, her world-view blighted, Isabel now recognizes that life with Osmond's mind in Osmond's house was "a horrible life" (IV, 202).

Among the distinctions Isabel makes during that night of confrontation with the mental malaise that rises up around and within her is who is haunting whom. "These shadows were not an emanation from her own mind," she decides. "They were a part, they were a kind of creation and consequence, of her husband's very presence" (IV, 190). James is careful, however, to make the point that ultimately Isabel is most afraid of herself. To be afraid of Osmond, she realizes, would merely be her wifely duty. The most insidious thing he has done is to reveal her to herself at her worst, as Ralph Touchett, dying, will reveal her to herself at her best. Through the experiencing of intense suffering she moves toward a self-knowledge that places her in an even darker, lower place than the rooms where Osmond's consciousness resides. Previously, she had known brief moments of fear of herself (III, 156, 157; IV, 18), but only now does she realize fully that if it is a gothic horror to dwell in an actual house of clammy stone and dark passageways, and if it is a worse horror to find oneself locked within the frightening chambers of the blighted mind of one with the power to hold one in thrall, the worst horror is to discover the dungeon of dread that is one's own consciousness.

The novel closes with Isabel having left Osmond's mind on a brief return to Gardencourt and its consciousness represented by the good ghost of Ralph Touchett. That reunion with the finer spirit ended, she has a terrifying sense of being pulled down within the iron consciousness of Casper Goodwood. She extracts herself only with effort, and then moves back toward Osmond's house. In the chambers of whose consciousness she will live from now on is the question that remains unanswered at the novel's end. She has, at least, been shown the way out into life by Ralph's consciousness, even if he had to die for her to experience it fully.

The Bostonians

In 1883 James informed his notebook of his intention "to write a very *American* tale, a tale very characteristic of our social conditions. . . ." [11] Three years later *The Bostonians* was published. Among other things the novel is an exposé—as Howells's novel of 1880, *The Undiscovered Country*, had been one—of the cheap practices of mesmerists and "inspiration" speakers and of the impossible dreams of the more addled believers in the perfectibility of man. It works alongside Francis Parkman's caustic remark about the vulgarity of the new sects based on "spirit rapping" and the new cult of chivalry in the form of " 'woman's rights,' Heaven deliver us." [12] *The Bostonians* is also a very amusing book, its humor based upon urbane manipulation of words and situations that twitch the coverings from incongruities and ironies kept hidden until that moment. By the time James finishes his satiric survey not much grace is left the senior Tarrants and their beguiled followers. Indeed, *The Bostonians* is pointed to by critics as a novel that successfully pulls away the wool thrown over all too many romanticists' eyes.

Specifically singled out for the satirist's belittling treatment are Dr. and Mrs. Selah Tarrant, who participate in "weird meetings" likened to a rendezvous of "witches and wizards, mediums and spirit-rappers, and roaring radicals." [13] When Olive Chancellor takes the hero Basil Ransom to such a motley gathering, Ransom encounters Tarrant, a mesmeric healer who effects "miraculous cures." It was said of Tarrant's healing power that " 'it was all done with the hands—what wasn't done with the tongue!' " (p. 44). To Ransom, sceptic and Southerner, Tarrant —with his "eloquence of the hand"—is "the detested carpetbagger," "false, cunning, vulgar, ignoble; the cheapest kind of human product" (pp. 74, 56).

While Ransom rages James calmly exploits the excellent comic potentialities in Tarrant's tawdry practices. It is when James develops his reductive description of Mrs. Tarrant that the aversion he felt for such cultism is revealed. Mrs. Tarrant was born of solid New England abolitionist stock with an honorable tradition of socially conscious, militantly moral fervor. The lady's moral sense has, unfortunately, dissolved through association with her husband. She knew Selah Tarrant was "very magnetic." It was this magnetism with its unspecified sexual connotations that "held her to him," but she "hated her husband for having magnetised her so that she consented to certain things, and even did them, the thought of which to-day would suddenly make her face burn . . ." (p. 73). Yet she also admired the impudence of this psychic-seducer. This was the worst part of the whole bad business. The "new religion" had led to her moral decay, and she liked it. There could be

no doubt that this poor lady had grown dreadfully limp. She had blinked and compromised and shuffled; she asked herself whether, after all, it was any more than natural that she should have wanted to help her husband, in those exciting days of his mediumship, when the table, sometimes, wouldn't rise from the ground, the sofa wouldn't float through the air, and the soft hand of a lost loved one was not so alert as it might have been to visit the circle. Mrs. Tarrant's hand was soft enough for the most supernatural effect, and she consoled her conscience on such occasions by reflecting that she ministered to a belief in immortality. . . . (Ibid.)

If literary realism defines itself in part by its portrayal of women like Mrs. Tarrant with their baseless pretensions of special powers, if it stresses its handling of ordinary people caught up by ordinary events in an ordinary world, what is the artist to do with those who are somehow "other"? If one of the persistent attributes of art is the way it insists upon dealing with what is "other" than is expected, how can the man more interested in life-as-art-as-truth than in life-as-truth avoid seeking out means to project "thatness" in the midst of a welter of "thisness"?

The Bostonians was written at the time when James had yet to recognize what manner of realist he was to become. The novel abounds with scruffy types, déclassé in their professional mountebankery, and yet "ordinary" with a vengeance for all that. Mr. and Mrs. Selah Tarrant, Mrs. Farrinder, Matthias Pardon, and the rest of their ilk are "little people" in the tradition fast becoming sanctioned by Howellsian "delight" in the "foolish and insipid face" of such specimens of "Real life." R. W. B. Lewis notes that the world of *The Bostonians* is "from the point of view of the literary artist, unavailable to either allegory or legend, and fit primarily for satire and realism." [14] But the Tarrants have a daughter, Verena—the girl for whom the novel was originally to have been named. She is a different creature altogether from her parents. At least James wished to place her apart from the surrounding mediocrity by granting her an aura of something other than the commonplace.

Whatever James's original intention may have been before he changed the novel's title from *Verena* to that of the more inclusive group appellation, *The Bostonians,* Verena scants the fictional figure she ought to be. She is pretty, she is sweet, she is rather vapid and rather a bore. She causes astonishment and ardor in others, but can hardly be said to *be* astonishing or passionate. Because unsuccessfully executed as a character, she remains but one of the great blob of Bostonians who give the novel its special quality of grey wash over drypoint. But Henry James unquestionably tried to do something special with Verena and for the novel as a whole. He tried to make it exude the scent of that differentness he was in the process of discovering as his unique fictional method, even if it would mean redefining the terms of reality he wrote by.

Looks, gestures, and a social role that is "other" can be superimposed upon a fictional character without achieving the final coup of an inner essence that is "other" as well. Verena Tarrant is given the vivid red hair and flawless white skin that make her vibrate in a crowd. She is handed a sweetness of disposition and passivity of mind that make her more susceptible than most to the victimizing tactics of her admirers. As a famed "inspirational speaker" she is put through the paces of commercial success. Had James contented himself with stopping at this point he would have merely had a flamboyant "public personality" with innocuous mind who acts as an obvious counter to the private person of Olive Chancellor. James went much further, however short his depiction came of complete artistic realization. Deeply imbedded in this satiric exposé, which turns its comic malice upon the suspect representatives of Modern Spiritualism, and in marked contrast to the novel's overt realism, James places a fairy-tale about a beautiful young girl. Portrayed as such a rare being she might be called superhuman, Verena Tarrant stands as a tentative new version of that legendary creature who, from century to century, is set down in the midst of mortals to bewilder and to bless.

Morally tarnished and humanly frail as the Tarrants are, their daughter seems endowed by some kind of occult gift. Even Doctor Prance is not quite certain what it is. "Perhaps she could die and come to life again," she quips (p. 44). Perhaps, Miss Birdseye muses, the fact that Verena's mother had hidden a runaway slave in her home for thirty days had "thrown a kind of rainbow over her cradle, and wouldn't she naturally have some gift?" (p. 32). Verena is careful to say that this strange force is not her own doing. Her father is just as zealous to make this clear. "It was some power outside—it seemed to flow through her . . ." (p. 55). It was a voice from the dead "that spoke from her lips" (pp. 55–56).

"With her bright, vulgar clothes, her salient appearance, she might have been a rope-dancer or a fortune teller . . ." (p. 79), but beneath this theatrical calculation Verena has "a strange spontaneity in her manner, and an air of artless enthusiasm, of personal purity" (p. 52). Even more unusual, although "she had grown up among people who took for granted all sorts of queer laxities, she had kept the consummate innocence of the American girl . . ." (p. 121). Amazingly, "Verena was perfectly uncontaminated, and she would never be touched by evil" (p. 84). She had had to do the housework at home, a lowering act if ever there was one in the Jamesian view. Yet such chores "had left no trace upon her person or her mind; everything fresh and fair renewed itself in her with extraordinary facility, everything ugly and tiresome evaporated as soon as it touched her . . ." (p. 173).

As she looks from Verena to the parents and back again, Olive Chancellor cannot get over

the wonder of such people being Verena's progenitors at all. She had explained it, as we explain all exceptional things, by making the part, as the French say, of the miraculous. She had come to consider the girl as a wonder of wonders, to hold that no human origin, however congruous it might superficially appear, would sufficiently account for her; that her springing up between Selah and his wife was an exquisite whim of the creative force; and that in such a case a few shades more or less of the inexplicable didn't matter . . . . Verena, for Olive, was the very type and mode of the "gifted being"; her qualities had not been bought and paid for; they were like some brilliant birthday-present, left at the door by an unknown messenger, to be delightful for ever as an inexhaustible legacy, and amusing for ever from the obscurity of its source. (pp. 114-115)

Even in a world entrenched in the secular and the natural, "There were people like that, fresh from the hand of Omnipotence," Olive mused (p. 115). Most amazing of all was that "Everything she turned to or took up became an illustration of the facility, the 'giftedness,' which Olive, who had so little of it, never ceased to wonder at and prize. Nothing frightened her; she always smiled at it, she could do anything she tried" (p. 176).

When William James wrote to give his opinion of *The Bostonians*, he commented to Henry, "Really the *datum* seems to me to belong rather to the region of fancy, but the treatment to that of the most elaborate realism." [15] Henry had found it necessary to step forward from the novel to confront his readers with the moan that it gave him only "despair" to try to describe Verena's specialness "with the air of reality" (p. 380). It was this very specialness that placed Verena in such an odd personal relationship with Olive. In turn, this fervid relationship made theirs "a tale very characteristic of our social conditions," made it a realistic novel in the sense accepted by Howells and recognized by William James.

Confronted by a psychological attraction as "real" as was the Boston scene, James found the nomenclature of the supernatural the answer to an agnostic's prayer. Terms used by empirical realists were inadequate to reveal that other, inner reality of accute psychic sensitivity. Conceived as a kind of being that even the most sceptical of ages has to accommodate, Verena is placed against the backdrop of fraudulent supernaturalism in order to portray a genuine manifestation of that mysterious power that topples natural laws and grants rarity of form. How he failed with Verena's projected transcendence gives the mark of his success with Milly Theale sixteen years later.

By the time *The Wings of the Dove* appeared in 1902 it was increasingly difficult to distinguish in James's fiction between *datum* and treatment, between fancy and realism—especially as it concerns man's consciousness, to James the most fantastic, yet the most real quality, of man's being.

The Wings of the Dove

To Susan Stringham "an education in the occult—she could scarce say what to call it—had begun for her the day she left New York with Mildred." [16] Susan never forgot "her own first sight of the striking apparition, then unheralded and unexplained . . ." (XIX, 105). To Susan "the charm of the creature was positively in the creature's greatness" (XIX, 112). Wide-eyed Susan is easily impressed by the wonder she observes, thus her responses might be discredited. More importantly, James was also impressed by the thought of what Milly Theale would become and, in so being, could do for the strength of his novel.

With a fatally diseased heroine on his hands, James had to counter the sentimentality or disgust that greets a pasty-faced orphan, susceptible to Victorian vapors, feebly succumbing to disappointment in love. James could escape the treacle by using metaphors that insist upon the presence of powers that come from the fact of Milly having lived and resisted superbly as a human being. She had to be seen in the process of becoming someone special, potentially larger than life while still living, and more than dead once she has died. That James did not fully succeed in his attempt marks whatever weakness the novel contains; that he succeeded as well as he did reveals not only his desired good but the methods by which he so nearly approaches success.

To back Susan Stringham's intuitive awareness of what Milly is, James added the weight of his own authorial concerns. "When Milly smiled it was a public event—and when she didn't it was a chapter of history" (XIX, 118). Milly was "a princess" whose splendor was "a perfectly definite doom for the wearer"—the kind of doom "with its involved loveliness and other mysteries" (XIX, 120). In James's words Milly's is the knack of knowing "the unspoken." Hers the ability to see "round several corners." Hers the "obviously weird charm," the "alertness of vision," the sensibility that is "almost too sharp." Hers the "high, dim, charming oddity," the "daily grace," that art "of being almost tragically impatient and yet making it as light as air; of being inexplicably sad and yet making it as soft as dusk." Hers the "immense range" of the girl whose priceless lace hangs "down to her feet like the stole of a priestess." Hers the great " 'paying' powers" and the deftness to be "the great and only princess" because "at her court" life "does pay."

James's stress upon the elevation of Milly's character—his treatment of her as if she were a sacred vessel of spirit to be lifted up by her priest at the altar of his art—is just so that we may respond even more positively to her decision to "come down." Milly chooses not to stay on the Alpine heights, merely looking out over the kingdoms of the earth; she elects to come down to the life of battle in London where she can be hurt in her mortality. Milly chooses not to stay above in the Venetian palace, but descends the staircase into the midst of the ambush that awaits her below. If James does all he can to make her seem a transcending princess, he does this to mark the passage her wings cover as they carry her, through her choice, back to where she is vulnerable to betrayal—and able to live out the terms of her love. Like Prospero, she must freely break the wand of her special power that would keep her apart from human existence. Having seen where she could have rested—out of harm's way, out of life—we can assess the power of her choice to forgo the sanctuary of transcendence.

Milly Theale realizes she is "so 'other,' so taken up with the unspoken. . . ." Whether at the National Gallery or on the balcony of her hotel, Milly quickly knows without a spoken phrase that Kate Croy and Merton Densher are in some kind of strong relation (XIX, 298, 257, 272). But Milly's particular American brand of psychic perspicuity lacks the strengthening effect of experience; because of this it fails to make her aware of everything, especially what Kate plans for her. Kate's richly intuitive womanliness, in combination with her will-strong, life-proud intelligence and hard-won experience, initially makes her more than a match for anyone else, even if ultimately she falls short of the moral magnitude of Milly's consciousness. Through his enhancement of the "occult" characterization of Kate Croy and Merton Densher—built up by means of motifs of E.S.P. and gothic self-haunting, James gives Milly Theale adversaries whose tonalities do not clash against her own special qualities. He had made Verena Tarrant stand too far out from her novel; she hardly seems of it. Milly, Kate, and Densher are a well-matched set of consciousnesses placed within a novel unafraid to risk strangeness.

To the wondering Densher Kate is "a whole library of the unknown, the uncut" (XX, 62). But she knows him very well, even from their first meeting on the dark London Underground Railway when "her consciousness had gone to him as straight as if they had come together in some bright stretch of a desert" (XIX, 54). At this point Kate is on the verge of love. Soon after, completely committed to that love and thus in the full flush of her psychic powers, she is asked puzzledly by Densher how she knows what she does about him. She replies with another question, " 'What do you expect one *not* to understand when one cares for you?' " (XIX, 87). When Densher tells her he must go off to America for a time, they have a mild tiff about the sending of letters. With exasperation Kate says,

"Men are too stupid—even you. You didn't understand just now why, if I post my letters myself, it won't be for anything so vulgar as to hide them."

"Oh, you named it—for the pleasure."

"Yes; but you didn't, you don't, understand what the pleasure may be. There are refinements—!" she more patiently dropped, "I mean of consciousness, of sensation, of appreciation," she went on. "No," she sadly insisted—"men *don't* know. They know in such matters almost nothing but what women show them." (XIX, 99)

Densher graciously accedes to this. " 'Then that's exactly why we've such an abysmal need of you!' "

Kate continues to be irked over "the amount of light men *did* need!" to understand what women know in a flash (XX, 3). The demand she places upon Densher in reply to his plea that she come to his rooms is that he fully understand what he is to do with Milly. " 'If you decline to understand me I wholly decline to understand you. I'll do nothing,' " she tells him. He asks, " 'And if I do understand?' " She replies, " 'I'll do everything' " (XX, 230–231). Previously he had willed not to understand and had been safe in his lack of knowledge. Once he wills himself to "understand"—once he faces the truth of the way they plan to "use" Milly, a truth Kate has long since had the nerve to confront —guilt lies in this act of will, not in his mere knowing, but in his going forth to know that he knows.

If Kate is life of the world that throbs into willed action, Densher is the still, receptive consciousness, waiting to be acted upon by one kind of life or the other. "He suggested above all, however, that wondrous state of youth in which the elements, the metals more or less precious, are so in fusion and fermenta- tion that the question of the final stamp, the pressure that fixes the value, must wait for comparative coolness" (XIX, 48–49). His character not yet determined, what greater catalyst upon his consciousness than the "handsome creature" that Kate Croy so impressively is?

If Densher as Consciousness needs Kate as Life of the World to complete his being, she needs him just as much.

He represented what her life had never given her and certainly, without some aid as his, never would give her; all the high dim things she lumped together as of the mind. It was on the side of the mind that was rich for her and mysterious and strong; and he had rendered her in especial the sovereign service of making that element real. (XIX, 50–51)

Before knowing Densher's mind Kate had only heard "vague rumors of its existence" (XIX, 51). "The chance had come—it was an extraordinary one—on the day she first met Densher; and it was to the girl's lasting honour that she knew on the spot what she was in the presence of" (ibid.).

Theirs is a reciprocal giving. At the height of the first fine passion they enjoy "a practical *fusion* of consciousness," "the subjective community." [17]

Densher's perception went out to meet the young woman's and quite kept pace with her own recognition. Having so often concluded on the fact of his weakness, as he called it, for life—his strength merely for thought—life, he logically opined, was what he must somehow arrange to annex and possess. This was so much a necessity that thought by itself only went on in the void; it was from the immediate air of life that it must draw its breath. (XIX, 51)

Kate stands for the great worldly life that requires money, but she also needs Densher's mind to make up for the lacks of the great life. However, he intuitively knows he and money will never come together. He possesses as "the innermost fact, so often vivid to him, of his own consciousness—his private inability to believe he should ever be rich" (XIX, 62). Always,

the mark on his forehead stood clear; he saw himself remain without whether he married or not . . . . He was quite aware of how he handled everything; it was another mark on his forehead; the pair of smudges from the thumb of fortune, the brand on the passive fleece, dated from the primal hour and kept each other company. (XIX, 63–64)

Prophetically marked at birth for failure, as fairy-tale heroes are usually marked for success, Densher's consciousness is preordained not to possess the great life that is activated by money. The life he finally gains is of quite another kind, the life of the spirit. Not Kate's kind of life, but Milly Theale's. But first he must gain the sense of guilt that will give him knowledge of that life.

Henry James's father had noted, "Our experience of the spiritual world dates in truth only from our first unaffected shiver at guilt." [18] Merton Densher dates his coming to the truth of the power of Milly Theale's consciousness over his own by the first shivers of guilt he feels; he is forced to face the meaning of that guilt once he admits he alone is haunting himself.

At first, in London, Densher defines menace as an external quality; he images it as the house at Lancaster Gate, whose "heavy horrors"—"operatively, ominously so cruel"—and whose prowling form as "a strange and dreadful monster" cast its appalling shadow across his love for Kate Croy, as well as over the vulnerable Milly. (XIX, 78, 277) A little later, just after arriving in Venice, Densher experiences early twinges of self-doubt when he realizes it was "on the cards for him that he might kill" Milly, and he takes "fear in this thought" which "had come out, with this first intensity, as a terror . . ." (XX, 252). It is in James's rendering of what happens next to Densher—the depiction of his hedging, the protective rationalizations and self-delusions he uses to fend off knowledge of himself as his own haunter—that the novelist shows what he could do with psychological gothicism as an art form.

James's generation had been warned of the dangers that come to the self in the act of observing the non-self. The "I" may become "the last conception that is reached by the conscious subject itself" and the self may be "so absorbed in the object as never to ask itself about itself." [19] Such a situation may be termed the Cuckolded Consciousness: The Last Man to Know Is the Self Most Involved. This definition perfectly fits the terror that begins to rise within Densher from the moment he is turned away from the Palazzo Leporelli with the curt information that Milly is no longer "receiving."

Fully in accord with the tradition of Mrs. Ann Radcliffe's fiction, Densher's emotions rapidly begin to color the scene around him with guilt. "It was a Venice all of evil . . . a Venice of cold lashing rain from a low black sky, of wicked wind raging . . ." (XX, 259). Casting the inward sense of storm and evil outward upon the decaying city, he—like a murderer drawn com-

pulsively back to the scene of his crime—becomes a "haunter"
of the café where he had initially felt the weight of "the catas-
trophe" his duplicity might bring to Milly (XX, 263).

In Saint Mark's Square Densher sees Lord Mark. Immediately
he transfers the blame for the world's ills upon the other man:
"the weather had changed, the rain was ugly, the wind wicked,
the sea impossible, *because* of Lord Mark" (ibid.). Because of him
all seems "sinister," "evil," and "nasty" (XX, 264, 265). Taking
great pains, Densher pretends to himself to judge the situation
critically,

so that if blame were to accrue he shouldn't feel he had dodged it. But
it wasn't he who, that day, had touched [Milly], and if she was upset it
wasn't a bit his act. The ability so to think about it amounted for
Densher during several hours to a kind of exhilaration. The exhilaration
was heightened fairly, besides, by the visible conditions—sharp, striking, ugly to him—of Lord Mark's return. (XX, 264)

Densher names Lord Mark as "brutal," a man who imposed
"stupid shocks" upon Milly that he, Densher, had "so decently
sought to spare her" (XX, 265). Alas, that Lord Mark has not
acted in the "delicate and honourable way" Densher has (ibid.).
When Susan Stringham comes to him, Densher continues to
suppress his growing guilt by a denunciation of Lord Mark as
"the inevitable ass," "a horrid little beast," "a hound," "an idiot
of idiots" who is now "unmasked" for what he is: a man so low
he had the effrontery to suggest that Densher had been up "to
some game," to "some deviltry," to "some duplicity" (XX, 285,
286, 290, 291). In reply to Densher's self-righteous indignation
toward the man whom his accusations have conveniently turned
into a stock gothic menace, Susan replies with quiet irony that
Lord Mark's aspersions upon Densher's motives are "of course"
only "a monstrous supposition" (XX, 291).

Milly dead, Densher's rooms are no longer pleasantly, sensuously haunted—as before—by the hovering sense of Kate's

presence left from the night she came to give herself to him. He finds them haunted by a new ghost. He sees rise before him

a young man far off and in a relation inconceivable, saw him hushed, passive, staying his breath, but half understanding, yet dimly conscious of something immense and holding himself painfully together not to lose it. The young man at these moments so seen was too distant and too strange for the right identity; and yet, outside, afterwards, it was his own face Densher had known. (XX, 342–343)

He has come to realize of whom he is afraid, as he had not at the time of Susan's visit: it is not of Sir Luke Strett, Milly, Susan; not Kate. "He knew soon enough it was of himself he was afraid"—"incontestably afraid" (XX, 282).

Returning to London (at Christmas—that season hallowed by Dickens and other nineteenth-century writers as the time for ghosts to prompt the consciences of the living), Densher is "a man haunted with a memory" (XX, 343). Forced to face the consequences of his now-acknowledged "duplicity," he finds those "consequences"—like his own image—have also assumed haunting forms that loom in the darkness of his room. There his spirit must, at last, deal with them in full self-knowledge. These metaphoric haunters, creatures born of his own acts, came

as close as a pair of monsters of whom he might have felt on either cheek the hot breath and the huge eyes. He saw them at once and but by looking straight before him; he wouldn't for that matter, in his cold apprehension, have turned his head by an inch. (XX, 352)

Not only these self-born monsters roam his rooms; so does the presence of Milly's love—"something sentient and throbbing, something that, for the spiritual ear, might have been audible as a faint far wail" (XX, 396).[20] But if Densher fears the nearness of his own gothic consciousness, he now strives to cherish Milly's presence in the midst of the unearthly stillness as once he had cherished Kate's (XX, 235–237). Milly's love is the conquering ghost, while Kate's guilt-darkened love must be acknowledged as that which agonizingly haunts them both (XX, 401).[21]

Densher is a man afraid: of what he is, of what lies altered past pleasure between himself and Kate, of Milly's psychically-sensed love for him, and of what now ties him to Milly—"*all* the truth" that he now loves her (XX, 403). It is this change of consciousness that Kate characterizes as "wonderful!" The fear Densher feels is wonder-ful and marvel-ous; there is fear in his guilt and fear in his loves, old and new—moral fears represented by psychological-occult metaphors of hauntedness. Densher's fears and attempted evasions of those fears will last him the rest of his life. The neo-gothic novel as developed by James does not end with the once imprisoning dungeon doors swinging open, the night's horrors dispelled by a daytime "natural" explanation, or with the villain slain; not when one's self is the imprisonment, the horror, and the villainy.

The act of reviewing the series of haunting presences encountered by Densher helps us trace the coming to awareness, which is one of the most vital meanings of *The Wings of the Dove*. Densher moves from the prosaic notion that society (symbolized by the Lancaster Gate house) is the source of the evil that steeps the scene with heavy menace, to the knowledge that his rooms were sensuously haunted by Kate's presence. His deluded belief that it is Lord Mark who clouds the world with storm and darkness is torn from him by the appearances of ever new ghostly forms: the man who proves to be his own guilty self and the monsters of the "consequences" that stare with huge eyes out of the dark. Finally, Densher arrives at the farthest point—haunted by the combined presences of the dead Milly, the past love and present guilt that hang over him and Kate, and his own fearful new love for the dead princess.

Through one kind of love Kate knows Densher ("knowledge" both as sexual union and as consciousness) and so is able at first to control him by the overwhelming power of her very real presence. Through another kind of love Densher comes to know Milly by "sympathetic" responsiveness to the intense concern of her spirit ("spirit" both in terms of Milly as disembodied consciousness and as the remembered embodiment of distinct moral qualities), and so is more fully controlled by her *in absentia*.

As partial compensation for the agony of metamorphosis from innocence to awareness he has undergone, Densher is granted some of the powers of women in love; he is, in fact, given possession of a bit of the "feminine-mystical" mind to mingle with his own "scientific-academic" intelligence. (If one does not like what happens to him, it could be said that his new feminine powers are the result of his emasculation by two women.) His power of clairvoyant vision grows most noticeably. When Kate asks how he knows what Sir Luke Strett has done for Milly even though he was never told, he says, " 'I see, I feel' " (XX, 332). The peak of his new prowess comes when he is able to deduce what lies within the unopened letter from the dead Milly. He need not even look at the handwritting on the envelope. " 'But my eyes went straight to it, in an extraordinary way, from the door,' " he tells Kate. " 'I recognised it, knew what it was, without touching it' " (XX, 373).[22] He has by now developed his own ESP about Milly's hovering presence and is both doomed and blessed by it.

The Wings of the Dove falls into that admirable category of the Novel of Moral Maturation. It concerns itself with the journeys of consciousness taken out of innocence into experience by others as well as Densher. (Even Lionel Croy by novel's end peers out of the amoral womb of his lifelong infancy at the approaching experience of death; as a result, he flees to his bed, whimpering, and pulls the covers up over his head as he senses the thing that he is and soon must become—in a kind of travesty of Milly's own deathbed movement toward knowledge.) But Densher's consciousness eventually becomes the main target, replacing the perceptions of Kate and Milly. In the novel's preface James noted that he "had scarce availed [himself] of the privilege of seeing with Densher's eyes." The "point is that I had intelligently marked my possible, my occasional need of it" (XIX, xxi). James used Densher's consciousness once it began to become aware of itself. Milly, who loved and was on her way to awareness, and Kate, who loves and possesses one kind of experience which she is in the process of shedding for yet another kind, press in upon Densher. Under the extraordinary tension of the situation he has been forced to reassess what he considers love to be and from whom he feels it. He changes into what he had never wished to be: a man who must choose.

"The Beast in the Jungle"

John Marcher is a man who chose early in his life to wait for a special fate. The story in which his wish comes true in ways he could hardly have foretold is itself of a special kind; it is neither fully a piece of realistic fiction, nor fully a ghostly tale. To see how it partakes of the occult and of the natural is to measure how far James had brought his experimentations in the art of the inner life by 1903.

In 1901 James confided to his notebook that "The Beast in the Jungle" would prove "a very tiny *fantaisie*." [23] Tiny, but "*about* something" as James felt all good stories must be. About what? He gave few clues. Six years earlier he had asked himself, "What is there in the idea of *Too late*—of some friendship or passion or bond—some affection long desired and waited for, that is found too late?—I mean too late in life altogether." [24] The idea of "too late" and the why of "too late" are overtones in this story, not its controlling themes. The cause and effect of passion deferred too long and love lost are what gives the story its memorable feeling of pathos, not what gives it its overwhelming shock of power.

As usual James played around the edges of the questions raised by his notebook entries. The final answers he left for the readers to detect in the tale itself. True, James was already hinting in 1901 of the woman in the affair who would be Marcher's "2nd consciousness" who "sees." James could mark exactly where the beast would spring for the first time. *"It must come for the READER thus, at this moment"* that a woman's love was "what might have happened, and what *has* happened is that it didn't." [25] But even the preface James later attached to the New York Edition of the story says little more than that it is about "another poor sensitive gentleman" whose career "thus resolves itself into a great negative adventure" and that it is successful "only as its motive may seem to the reader to stand out sharp." [26]

The motive of "The Beast in the Jungle" is indicated by the words in James's notebooks, "With his base safety and shrinkage he never knew," and is proved by the story itself. If this motive comes from James's concern with the necessity of shared experience—that which one must not shrink from out of base safety—the story's success appropriately depends upon the reader's taking up James's challenge to participate in Marcher's anti-experience. If we are worthy of the dare, we gain a "positive adventure" deep inside what we must sense is a new region of consciousness opened to us by a calculated series of master strokes.

James robs his readers of many of the props used to sustain the best of nineteenth-century literature. First he deletes; then he moves toward addition and accumulation.

Few details of setting are given. No specified bric-a-brac of house and landscape are present to particularize Weatherend, May Bartram's parlor, or the suburban cemetery. There is only the general atmosphere, that massive consciousness of place that rushes in to fill the vacuum left by missing chairs and portieres and London villas. When objects do appear—the clock on the mantel and the cold hearth of May's parlor—they are grasped as symbols of lost time and lost passions, not as objects. Conventional details of personal appearance are also absent. Instead of the expected descriptive paragraph granted each new character upon his entrance into the usual Victorian novel, we are given merely the names—John Marcher and May Bartram—and blanks for bodies. Marcher *is* a blank who wears "a mask painted with the social simper" and a "concealing veil" that he dares not lift "from his image" to "people at large." [27] Of course, May is *something* rather than the nothing Marcher seems to represent. Her eyes, if nothing else, embody her somethingness throughout the story, just as the fact of her love is indicated by mention of her silveriness (its offer) and growing fragility (its rejection). Since the story is about non-action, a waiting very still for the beast to approach near where one stands, details that conventionally delineate characters caught up in action are absent; the story becomes wholly a matter of consciousness: Marcher's, May's, and ours.

Much has been taken away that is reassuring, expected, and traditional from "The Beast in the Jungle," but James does not pare, strip, or eliminate details of consciousness. He adds more and more spoor to the "beaten grass" so that *we* can see the beast better, sooner, even while Marcher comes to believe that the jungle has been transformed into a flatlands (p. 710). James invests tremendous energy in accumulating the details that reveal life as consciousness, not as clothes, actions, or social phrases. Pushed on by this accumulation, we see what effects these details of consciousness have upon the characters. For May, who has, out of her love for Marcher, stripped down her days to the bare rudiments of waiting, life is enrichment. For Marcher, who has built up his days to a massive waiting, out of his love for his own specialness, life is loss. [28]

There are many details concerning time as one of the major life-patterns assumed by the consciousness. Time in "The Beast of the Jungle" is not socially or historically defined. Marcher fears "the amusement of a cold world"; he fears being thought an ass, viewed "as the funniest of the funny" (pp. 682–683). He who also believes himself above "the stamp of the common doom" fears he may seem even less than average; he might appear ridiculous (p. 705). To protect himself, he has cut himself off from "human communities" and cultivated "the detachment that reigned beneath" his forms so that he may be "lost in the crowd" (pp. 686, 670). He becomes lost in the sense of not being of it, only *in* it. Existing outside "the real world," both Marcher and May are outside the time that governs it—he because of his fear and contempt for society; she because of her love for him. (Because she loves, May remains actually in time; her body shows the effects of time's passage, while mortal physical decay seems to pass Marcher by.)

Time as consciousness takes its effect in other ways. We know time has passed in the story whenever perceptions are altered and new knowledge has been gained. ("Knowledge" defined not as reasoning, but as those consequences felt within the realm of imagination, and as love.) James's new schema for this story also involves consideration of whether time is to be thought of as fate or as a field for choice.

May believes unquestioningly in time as that period during which an active, self-controlled approach is made toward love. Marcher believes in time as the period spent in passive acceptance of his doom. [29] He drifts, he does not march, except like a squirrel caught on a treadwheel of deterministic time. But if he believes he is an object moved by a fate that cannot be met logically, he also believes he must act in conscience by a logic of right and wrong. Since the payment of conscience-money usually involves behavior in terms of social time, his treatment of May is ironic since it takes her out of that time; doubly so, since in paying her by expending his time on her he actually takes all of her time. May, on the other hand, follows out yet another banking metaphor and so redeems the time where Marcher squanders it. The payment of the money of conscience is replaced in her case by the payment of the money of consciousness.

In writing "The Beast in the Jungle" James had the problem of presenting staggered times of entry into awareness—Marcher's awareness, May's, and the reader's. He also had to see to it that those who enter into knowledge at early points can hold on to the accumulating levels of perception that come later to the more laggard. The story begins at Weatherend, but the fact of the story reaches ten years into the past when Marcher and May first met in Italy. That is where James's own awareness begins: at the very beginning. (This is not a statement absurd in its obviousness. There are works of fiction, great ones, in which we detect the writers only coming to full awareness of their stories' movements and meanings part way through those stories.) "The Beast in the Jungle" proceeds from the point of James's entrance. By the point in the narrative that marks May's birthday she has confirmed herself in the knowledge that she probably suspected soon after the Italian sojourn. As for us as readers, any time after the Weatherend episode we begin to suspect the nature of the beast. Surely we know the truth by the scenes that encircle May's dying; surely we learn before Marcher does, at the very end, in the cemetery.

James had to work with such delayed actions of time, and the various reactions to its bared knowledge, in ways similar to those of the writer of a detective story or of the ghost story. If he had to guard against tipping his hand too soon, he had *fairly* to lay down his clues for even the stupid (Marcher or us) to discover. His clues derive from his techniques: (1) the narrative presented by the authorial voice that both tells us how we are to evaluate Marcher's faulty self-awareness and shows us what the truths are; (2) clues that "appreciations and measurements" give; (3) clues symbolized by the activities of the senses; (4) clues supplied by the story's conversations, whether offered in words or by silences.

The steady narrative voice (which disappears for a time, but always returns) sometimes tells us what we ought to feel about Marcher's fate in a manner quite unlike the way he envisions it. Ironic line-breaks guide us: "This was why he had such good—though possibly such rather colourless—manners; this was why,/ above all,/ he could regard himself,/ in a greedy world,/ as decently—as,/ in fact,/ perhaps even a little sublimely—unselfish" (p. 683). This is immediately followed by, "Our point is accordingly . . ." so that we may know what Henry James thinks about John Marcher's belief in his own decency.

The narrative voice also informs us about what May knows by means of her woman's nerves.

She had no source of knowledge that he hadn't equally—except of course that she might have finer nerves. That was what women had where they were interested; they made out things, where people were concerned, that the people often couldn't have made out for themselves. Their nerves, their sensibility, their imagination, were conductors and revealers, and the beauty of May Bartram was in particular that she had given herself so to his case. (p. 694)

It is Marcher who talks the most, jabbering at times. After many of his incessant deductions, justifications, and phrases of self-applause come the narrator's qualifying tags—"as he might have said" and "as he called it"—which discriminate between Marcher's knowledge and its inadequacies. Discriminations that Marcher cannot make, James makes for him "in fine." "His conviction,/ his apprehension,/ his obsession,/ in short": the implied breaks in such a sentence move to measure the rising force of Marcher's self-deceiving fanaticism (p. 684).

The narrative voice is most content when it pretends to suppress its presence, thus forcing upon each situation its own self-dramatization.

It led briefly, in the course of the October afternoon, to his closer meeting with May Bartram, whose face, a reminder, yet not quite a remembrance, as they sat much separated at a very long table, had begun merely by troubling him rather pleasantly. *It* affected him as the sequel of something of which he had lost the beginning. He knew *it*, and for the time quite welcomed *it*, as a continuation, but didn't know what *it* contained, which was an interest or an amusement the greater as he was also somehow aware—yet without a direct sign from her—that the young woman herself hadn't lost the thread. She hadn't lost *it*, but she wouldn't give *it* back to him, he saw, without some putting forth of his hand for *it* . . . . (pp. 671–672; my italics)

What is the "it" that pulls us through this passage? By the second page of the story we still do not know. We, with Marcher, have yet to learn what May Bartram already intuits about "it."

He had thought of himself so long as abominably alone, and, lo he wasn't alone a bit. He hadn't been, it appeared, for an hour—since those moments on the Sorrento boat. It was *she* who had been, he seemed to see as he looked at her—she who had been made so by the graceless fact of his lapse of fidelity. To tell her what he had told her—what had it been but to ask something of her?/ something that she had given,/ in her charity,/ without his having,/ by a remembrance,/ by a return of the spirit,/ failing another encounter,/ so much as thanked her. (p. 678)

Each flick of a comma, each enforced spacing, moves us on faster even while cautioning us to ponder the quality of what May has given.

. . . and as he waked up to the sense of no longer being young,/ which was exactly the sense of being stale,/ just as that,/ in turn,/ was the sense of being weak,/ he waked up to another matter beside. It all hung together; they were subject,/ he and the great vagueness,/ to an equal and indivisible law. When the possibilities themselves had, accordingly, turned stale,/ when the secret of the gods had grown faint,/ had perhaps even quite evaporated,/ that,/ and that only,/ was failure. It wouldn't have been failure to be bankrupt,/ dishonoured,/ pilloried,/ hanged;/ it was failure not to be anything. (p. 697)

Here Marcher begins to form the shape of the beast. The dramatic drive of the sentences makes it appear, loom, and seem about to spring. But no, Marcher turns aside from the truth that has almost revealed itself. The passage, and his consciousness, pull up short with, "He had but one desire left—that he shouldn't have been sold" (p. 698). When the beast finally does appear to Marcher, years later, the description of its coming becomes the drama of the rising, destructive fever of his final knowledge.

He saw the Jungle of his life and saw the lurking Beast; then, while he looked, perceived it, as by a stir of the air, rise, huge and hideous, for the leap that was to settle him. His eyes darkened/—it was close;/ and,/ instinctively turning,/ in his hallucination,/ to avoid it,/ he flung himself,/ face down,/ on the tomb. (p. 719).

The opening scene at Weatherend is devoted to the "appreciations and measurements" taken by the visiting group that moves into the great house to examine and finger its treasures (p. 671). (Weatherend is rather like the palace of "The Masque of the Red Death" where everyone thinks he is safe from the world outside; everyone there except May Bartram is part of a private world in which he pretends to be alone, while drifting under the spell of "the dream of acquisition"—one which can easily turn into a nightmare of death.) From this point Marcher and May, and we, hang suspended over the void whose depth must be tested by the plummet that James uses as one of the story's constant metaphors. One by one, Marcher's losses are marked and measured: loss of the sense of danger; loss of feeling; loss of the love May offers; loss of his claim to her after her death; loss of the sense of personal value she gave him. We finally mark his gain of suffering, which enables him to measure the life he has had by appreciation of the life he has skirted.

Abysses, plumb-lines, and symbols of "value" measure how much is given and how much is taken away from the relationship held in joint stock by Marcher and by May. Marcher never earns what he has received and so must suffer spiritual bankruptcy. Marcher "knew each of the things of importance he was insidiously kept from doing, but she could add up the amount they made, understand how much, with a lighter weight on his spirit, he might have done, and thereby established how, clever as he was, he fell short" (p. 686).

Only once does Marcher have a premonition that this moral tabulation may go against him. He realizes he cannot remember that he had previously shared his secret with May, and is, therefore, "conscious rather of a loss than of a gain" (p. 676). When he does remember, he is glad, for he "yet could profit perhaps exquisitely by the accident" of having given his secret to her (p. 678). "What he had asked of her had been simply at first not to laugh at him. She had beautifully not done so for ten years, and she was not doing so now. So he had endless gratitude to make up" (ibid.). That he never does make it up, that he is always in the debit column, Marcher finds out "too late." He is afraid "lest he should only give himself away" (p. 677). If he decides that May's knowledge is a "compensation," it is one to him as well, one which "he will profit by . . . to the utmost" (pp. 687, 682).

Self-righteously he takes May to the opera in return for his debts to her "mercy, sympathy, seriousness" (p. 683), but she always repays her debts immediately by asking him to dinner. Both literally and figuratively, she is his "daily bread" (p. 688). She is "unremunerated," with only her amusement to satisfy her (p. 685). When he knows she will die, the thought of her "loss" at not being present when the beast makes its spectacular leap "quickened his generosity" (p. 695). Again and again he preens himself on his ability to guard against egotism. He is oblivious to the fact he has taken over May's life, her time, the "things that might happen to *her*," filling them only with the vacuum of himself (p. 683). Even the "very carpets were worn" down in her parlor by "his fitful walk" and "his nervous moods" (pp. 689, 690).

If Marcher always takes, May gives. Her knowledge is "buried treasure" for which she willingly lets him dig (p. 682). Although he romantically muses that he is the one who makes "sacrifices" to their "real truth," he does not see that the sacrifice of her whole life is real. When he wonders if she feels her curiosity "isn't being particularly repaid," she replies, " 'But too well repaid' "—that is, with her hidden suffering *and* her strong grasp on his consciousness (pp. 688, 689). He asks repeatedly, politely, how he can ever repay her. He never does. The only thing she gains is *him*, which makes her right—" 'humanly, which is what we're speaking of' " (p. 693).

Marcher's desire that he not have been "sold" is matched by his wish to have "something all to [himself]" (p. 679). Then May offers him herself one last time: "she had something more to give him: her wasted face delicately shone with it—it glittered almost as with the white lustre of silver in her expression" (p. 704). Having already taken everything else from her, he refuses her final gift because he is ironically unable to recognize its value.

As they stand in the April evening that separates Marcher from May, the beast springs—unseen by him, all too visible to her. She dies, and he goes away, "spending himself on scenes of romantic interest," only to hurry home "because he had been separated so long from the part of himself that alone he now valued" (pp. 713, 714). That part is her grave, which he possesses by squatter's rights only. Hovering over it, he resembles "a contented landlord reviewing a piece of property" (p. 714). Coming to the cemetery was "a positive resource"; it helped him carry out "his idea of periodical returns" (pp. 714–715). It is while he sits where he does not rightfully belong that he discovers the differences between selfless giving and selfish taking. A grieving man passes, and Marcher enviously asks, "What had the man *had*, to make him by the loss of it so bleed and yet live?" (p. 717). At that moment Marcher comes to the realization what his own "loss" is as the result of his one-sided "taking." Only one thing is now left for him to take: the truth that "the wait was itself his portion" (p. 718). It is typical of Marcher's stupidity that he is, even now, unable to recognize the rich value of that wait.

If value symbols aid in pulling together evidence about Marcher's inadequate "appreciations and measurements," metaphors drawn from the senses also act as agents of discrimination. Like the crowd at Weatherend, Marcher tastes, smells, and digs with his bare hands in his search for the buried treasure of his life (pp. 671, 677, 682). But he fails to use his hands in the most human way for the communion of touch.

Marcher is also afraid to see. James wrote of him in the story's preface. "Like the blinded seeker in the old-fashioned game he 'burns,' on occasion, as with the sense of the hidden things near— only to deviate again however into the chill" (p. x). May is aware of Marcher's inability to see. "He knew how he felt, but, besides knowing that, she knew how he *looked* as well . . ." (p. 686). That is, "looked" not only in the sense of how he appeared to others (deceptive at best), but also how he "saw," which in his case was not at all. " 'You've everything still to see,' " she tells him (p. 691).

Throughout the story James describes the special light that comes from May's eyes. Twice Marcher intercepts its flash, but it leaves him with only the partially understood edge of truth. " 'I'm with you—don't you see?—still' " (p. 702). When she realizes he will remain blind, May closes her eyes. This is the signal for the beast to spring. Marcher does not even see its claws. A ghostly tiger is powerless to hurt one who does not see it, just as May is powerless to save Marcher because he cannot see her. Marcher ignored the force of her "cold sweet eyes;" only "letters of quick flame" from the "smoky torch" of meaning that blazes from the face of the bereaved man at the cemetery can affect him (pp. 703, 717–718). The "final flash of light under which he reads his lifelong riddle and sees his conviction proved" mentioned in the story's preface (p. xi) is the harsh light of the knowledge of the necessity for shared experience. When it comes, as it had to, from "the face of a fellow mortal," Marcher is left "most of all stupefied at the blindness he had cherished" (pp. 716, 718).

"The Beast in the Jungle" is filled with conversations, some propelled by words, others by telling silences. Where May uses words to try to make Marcher see what he must discover for himself, they are often teasing, playful. This is a game she is in, and she will make the most, and best, of it. At that time when she implies that his fate has already come, Marcher says, " 'As if you believed that nothing will now take place.' " She replies, "rather inscrutably, 'You're far from my thought' " (p. 689). Soon after she reaffirms her punning on the fact that nothing has taken place. " 'I've shown you, my dear, nothing' " (p. 701). Dialogue such as the following makes us realize that the woman took what fun she might out of the situation.

> In her own look, however, was doubt. "You see what?"
> "Why, what you mean—what you've always meant."
> She again shook her head. "What I mean isn't what I've always meant. It's different."
> "It's something new?"
> She hung back from it a little. "Something new. It's not what you think. I see what you think." (pp. 702–703)

Statements are made by the one person and repeated by the other. Questions are used to answer questions. The seemingly simple is confused by the complexity of the responses intended to be its affirmation. None of these conversations work in the conventional manner to move Marcher any closer to knowledge. What May and Marcher possess together is the "odd irregular rhythm of their intensities and avoidances" and "the ideas washed away by cool intervals, washed like figures traced in sea-sand" (p. 699). The words and ideas pass; the intensities remain.

In a James story—especially one dealing with a metaphor for hauntedness, clairvoyantly sensed by a psychically acute woman—silences ring more clearly than words. May is introduced at Weatherend in her role as "explainer" of the house's treasures, but it is immediately noted that the sound of her voice and the sense of her silences are more important than her words. What remains unsaid about their past relations in Italy is more important to Marcher and May than the recollections of trivial things. Society demands words which explain what a man's value is and what he does and how he is related to the woman in his life. Marcher and May do not waste words on society, either to describe his unique claim to the beast or his common claim to her presence as man to wife.

Their life of unspoken secrets is spent in watching and waiting in silence. Marcher's secret about his anticipated fate is kept from "the stupid world"; May's secret about her love is kept from him even though "her whole attitude was a virtual statement" (pp. 686, 687). When she periodically breaks the long intervals of silence, her words are controlled, limited, and numbered by her secret's demands. Love needs no words to express itself; no amount of words can reveal love to the unaware. Since May's "intention" is to save Marcher because of her love, and since his "intention" is to save himself, their conversations and silences remain on parallel levels that never merge, even though forever moving in the same direction.

The tale is marked on three major occasions by the possibility that the parallel lines of meaning held separately by Marcher and by May might miraculously meet on the reformed plane of single intention. The first occasion is that birthday after which May senses Marcher has moved into an irrevocable state of ignorance about the nature of the beast. Next comes the April meeting of May and Marcher when they face one another across the cold hearth. She is likened to a sphinx [30] (the silent one who forces response to initiatory riddles) and to a sibyl (the explainer who offers riddles by signs that, however true, are deemed ambiguous by the obtuse recipient). May is also imaged as a lily—"an artificial lily, wonderfully imitated and constantly kept, without dust or stain" (p. 698). Hers is no lily of innocence; it is the Annunciation lily of the Virgin May, whose role is to reveal, by means of revealed love, the laws of the gods that pertain to love. May offers Marcher "the unspoken," that wonder and the strangeness of love that is "soft," "not really dreadful." (This is not the terrible wonder and harsh strangeness of the realization of love forgone that he receives at the end.) May's silent offer "failed to come to him," and Marcher replies, " 'Well, you don't say—' " (p. 704). This is true. She does not say. She can only show, realizing now that neither sounds nor silences are of avail. Their third meeting simply reaffirms that "it" has happened. The beast's spring is given no name, but it now has a date in time. " 'You've *had* it,' " May tells Marcher (p. 707), and he certainly has. Now they can only speak from "the *other* side" of the event (p. 708).

Even in the "horror of waking" from his lifelong dream at the cemetery, when he "hears" the silent message of the grieving man's face, Marcher still depends upon his baser senses (p. 719). He has not been able to weep before. He has been kin to the bewitched, whose inability to cry is evidence of their inhumanity. When tears finally come, it is their taste of life and feel of pain he wants. He still fears sight. As the beast of truth springs, Marcher's eyes "darkened." To protect them from the truth's light, he falls face downward upon the stone bosom of May's tombstone. But that stone has only her two names upon it, which previously he had recognized as "a pair of eyes that didn't know him" (p. 713). If she had been his wife, there would have been three names; that might have been the saving number.

James took great risks in "The Beast in the Jungle." The characterization and the plot structure are dictated by a long waiting for Nothing *to* happen, with yet another delay before awareness comes to Marcher that Nothing *has* happened, therefore he *is* Nothing. The story's reward for its risk of seeming to be about nothing is its final claim to be about a Nothing so shattering it is transformed into something very fine. The story thus escapes one of the dangers that most threatens the literature of consciousness. It resists being unmasked as a trivial waste of time spent inside a narrow mind that proves to be a little nothing. (The older literature of consciousness had social contexts that connected its characters' minds to something outside that gave the stories an air of importance. The characters might be boring, but, oh, what one learned about the coke industry!)

The reward of being Something gives life to "The Beast in the Jungle" as a fictional artifact. The sense of somethingness also extends to the characters within the story.[31] We see that what has happened to May Bartram and Marcher is indeed momentous. That is, we do not have a story that merely dramatizes a life of meaninglessness and spiritual poverty in ways that are meaningful and rich only to its readers. The final revelation the story offers is that the characters have also known the excitement of lives of consciousness lived to a high pitch, however off-key.

The story as a narrative whole, and May and Marcher who act within it, risk being overly pretentious as well as too trivial.[32] If "The Beast in the Jungle" claims to be a story fully realized as art or the depiction of lives extravagantly lived, these claims to value have to be sustained without turning into ludicrous High Seriousness. Central to the problem of pretentiousness the story has to solve in order not to fail is the figure of May Bartram.

"The Jolly Corner" and *The Sense of the Past* (as well as James's "The Altar of the Dead") are ultimately weakened by the nature of the women who stand waiting, watching over the men who have passed through their crises of psychic testing. Theirs is the same weakness that crippled the endings of some of Hawthorne's fiction and much of that of Mark Twain and William Dean

Howells. The American Maiden with her purity and possessiveness is a figure both insipid and frightening, destructive to novels into whose masculine worlds she is suddenly, conventionally intruded. James was very close to the problem of what the genteel lady of American fiction threatened to do to his own writing. He could not accept her wholly, just as he could not find the full answer by using in its unaltered form that other stultifying stereotype, the Continental Mistress. As a "type" May Bartram is far closer in her powers to the lady of cold, clear light than to the lurid flames of the corrupt European adulteress, but the ways in which she is presented reveal her as a creature of passion (passion, characteristically, not defined in terms of the flesh), one of the few realized in American letters before the twentieth century.

May Bartram and John Marcher first meet in the excavations of the treasure tombs of Pompeii. They are reunited at Weatherend, the house of treasures pervaded by "the dream of acquisition." Together they seek a buried life of value outside the barren world of society. May's life contains an everyday "passion" suggested by the fact of her humanly being "his daily bread" and his "communion." But Marcher does not see it; he tries rather to escape being nothing by the artificial passion of living inside the tomb of the imagination of disaster that would single him out as a man of unique fate. He only appreciates and measures the extraordinary; he cannot measure the value of "the stamp of common doom" (p. 705).

For Marcher's sake May sits up throughout her lifetime as at a wake watching for signs of his moral awakening. She hopes against hope that he might yet revive from his *golem* state into true life. He fails her. She dies and, in her death, becomes the only idea that interests him who is both necrophilic and corpselike. Dead as he is, he "haunts" the cemetery where she lies buried in a silent tomb that proves a dull mirror for his ego's reflection. Marcher next tries to find the extraordinary at the tombs of India and Egypt, but soon returns to the London cemetery where he is "everything."

He receives a series of minor revelations that tell him that death and suffering are the ordinary fate which may be all there is to his own fate. He further learns that pain is life. However, we as readers are being urged by James to experience a larger vision than that which comes to Marcher even at the end of the story.[33] What the story tells, but Marcher never quite grasps, is that life is more than pain, that there is more than the imagination of disaster. It reveals that men must be ordinary (that is, to live and love in common, "in fine") so that they may find wonder —all that is strange, overwhelming, natural.

When the harsh torch-flames from the eyes of the mourning man show Marcher that there is a power greater than his ego, he admits his humanness. His awareness ceases here. In despair over the thought of having been nothing because he rejected the woman who made him something, he throws himself in a final, romantic gesture upon the tomb of his meaning. James knows, and we must, that Marcher's denial of the romantic dream of being a hero must be matched by his denial of indulgence in the alternative romantic dream of being a failure. If he could forgo this further stultifying impulse, he might purchase the revealed values of romance with its freedom of wonder and of realism with its responsibilities of human love—even if "too late." He could receive what May knew about the passion that moves beyond tragedy, suffering, and death toward the transcending powers of human love.

To Marcher his life has moved from the insipid belief that he was special to the terrifying awareness that he is unique in his nothingness. He has moved from being a figure in a morality play about conscience to a tragic figure in a heightened state of consciousness.[34] There is a change, therefore, in the readers' own reactions to Marcher: from our conscience to consciousness;

from our enjoyable sense of detached self-righteousness to an enjoyable sense of participation in pity and terror. What Marcher does not recognize, but we must, is that by the telling of the story and the presence of May Bartram, he has lived and is living an extraordinarily intense life. If it has moved him to the tragic realm, it ought to move him still further, into the country of the great extension. He has "had it"—beyond the range of his wildest hopes—but never fully comprehends this.

May Bartram, too, has had everything from the moment she "had" Marcher's secret life of consciousness. She is no angelic woman whose good love has no ambition but to save a man if it could. She is the passionate virgin who completely possessed another's consciousness and thus gave him all the being he has. If Marcher, still limited in his awareness, is overwhelmed at the story's end by the thought of the love he lost, we are overwhelmed by the revelation of May's *total* awareness, love, and consciousness. Hers is the transcending concentration of psyche that supernatural forces have, not that of the angelic, who punish conventionally by conscience. Conscience closes in through wrath and justice; consciousness opens up upon the sinner against love the terrible mercy that comes on the fierce wings of the dove.

What Milly Theale is to Merton Densher, May is to Marcher. Only after the women's deaths do their men come to "see" and thus to suffer and to know, even if they still pull back from knowing all. If neither woman had existed, neither man would have been forced to learn what he is. This is the great irony. An unheroic Baldur, Marcher is slain by the one thing thought harmless—the barbed mistletoe of May's love, thrown by the hand of the blind man—himself. Using Marcher's own metaphor, he was on the "look-around" for a ghostly force he imaged in the form of a beast, but he constantly followed the wrong spoor. Marcher had believed that "a man of feeling didn't cause himself to be accompanied by a lady on a tiger-hunt" (p. 684).

He did not know that this lady's love was the tiger, and that it is always better to take the tiger along when one dives into the jungle, so to have it by one's side. May is the only one who ever loved Marcher; she is the only one able to hurt him after she dies. She is the only one able to make us feel what "The Beast in the Jungle" is most about.

Bibliography

Aldrich, C. Knight, M.D., "Another Twist to *The Turn of the Screw,*" *Modern Fiction Studies*, XIII, 2 (Summer 1967), 167–178.

Allen, Gay Wilson, "William James's Determined Free Will," *Essays on Determinism in American Literature*, ed. Sydney J. Krause (Kent, Ohio, 1964), pp. 67–76.

Andreach, Robert J., "Henry James's *The Sacred Fount:* The Existential Predicament," *Nineteenth-Century Fiction*, XVII, 3 (December 1962), 197–216.

————, "Literary Allusion as a Clue to Meaning: James's 'The Ghostly Rental' and Pascal's *Pensées,*" *Comparative Literature Studies*, IV, 3 (1967), 299–306.

Aswell, E. Duncan, "Reflections of a Governess: Image and Distortion in *The Turn of the Screw,*" *Nineteenth-Century Fiction.* XXIII, i (June 1968), 49–63.

Auden, W. H., *The Collected Poetry of W. H. Auden,* New York, 1945.

Auerbach, Erich, *Mimesis, The Representation of Reality,* tr. Willard R. Trask, Princeton, 1953.

Banta, Martha, "The Quality of Experience in *What Maisie Knew,*" *The New England Quarterly*, XLII, 4 (December 1969), 483–510.

————, "Rebirth or Revenge: the Endings of *Huckleberry Finn* and *The American,*" *Modern Fiction Studies*, XV (no.2, 1969), 191–207.

Barrett, William, and Henry D. Aiken, *Philosophy in the Twentieth Century,* 4 vols., New York, 1964.

Bennett, Sir Ernest, *Apparitions and Haunted Houses, A Survey of Evidence,* London, 1939.

Bergson, Henri, "Presidential Address, Delivered on May 28th, 1913 by Professor Henri Bergson, Authorized Translation by H. Wildon Carr, D. Litt.," *Proceedings of the Society for Psychical Research*, XXVII (1914–1915), 157–175.

Blackall, Jean Frantz, *Jamesian Ambiguity and the Sacred Fount*, Ithaca, N.Y., 1965.

Blackmur, R. P., *Form and Value in Modern Poetry*, Garden City, N.Y., 1957.

Bosanquet, Theodora, *Henry James at Work*, The Hogarth Essays, no date, no city.

Broad, C. D., *The Mind and Its Place in Nature*, London, 1925.

————, *Religion, Philosophy, and Psychical Research*, New York, 1953.

Brooks, Cleanth, *The Well-Wrought Urn, Studies in the Structure of Poetry*, New York, 1947.

Cargill, Oscar, "*The Turn of the Screw* and Alice James," *PMLA*, LXXVIII, 3 (June 1963), 238–249.

Clendenning, John, "Irving and the Gothic Tradition," *Bucknell Review*, XII, ii (May 1964), 90–98.

Costello, Donald P., "The Structure of *The Turn of the Screw*," *Modern Language Notes*, LXXV, 4 (April 1960), 312–321.

Cranfil, Thomas Mabry and Robert Lanier Clark, Jr., *An Anatomy of The Turn of the Screw*, Austin, Texas, 1965.

Crowl, Susan, "Aesthetic Allegory in 'The Turn of the Screw,'" *Novel*, IV, 2 (Winter 1971), 106–122.

Doyle, Sir Arthur Conan, *The History of Spiritualism*, 2 vols., New York, 1926.

Edel, Leon, ed., *The Complete Tales of Henry James*, Vols. I and III, London, 1961 and 1962.

————, ed. *The Ghostly Tales of Henry James*, New Brunswick, 1948.

————, and Gordon N. Ray, eds., *Henry James and H. G. Wells, A Record of their Friendship, their Debate on the Art of Fiction, and their Quarrel*, Urbana, Illinois, 1958.

————, *Henry James, 1870–1881, The Conquest of London*, Philadelphia and New York, 1962.

————, *Henry James, 1882–1895, The Middle Years*, Philadelphia and New York, 1962.

————, *Henry James, 1895–1901, The Treacherous Years*, Philadelphia and New York, 1969.

————, *Henry James, 1843–1870, The Untried Years*, Philadelphia and New York, 1953.

————, *The Psychological Novel, 1900–1950*, New York and Philadelphia, 1955.

————, *The Selected Letters of Henry James*, New York, 1955.

Ellenberger, Henri F., *The Discovery of the Unconscious, the History and Evolution of Dynamic Psychiatry*, New York, 1970.

Ellmann, Richard, and Charles Feidelson, Jr., *The Modern Tradition: Backgrounds of Modern Literature*, New York, 1965.

Emerson, Donald, "Henry James and the Limitations of Realism," *College English*, XXII, 3 (December 1960), 161–166.

Folsom, James K., "Archimago's Well: An Interpretation of *The Sacred Fount,*" *Modern Fiction Studies*, VII, 2 (Summer 1961), 136–144.

Fraser, John, "*The Turn of the Screw* Again," *Midwest Quarterly*, VII, 4 (Summer 1966), 327–336.

Frederick, John T., *The Darkened Sky, Nineteenth-Century American Novelists and Religion*, Notre Dame and London, 1969.

Freud, Sigmund, "Dreams and Telepathy," tr. C. J. M. Hubback, *Collected Papers*, IV, London, 1934.

———, "A Neurosis of Demoniacal Possession in the Seventeenth-Century," tr. Edward Glover, *Collected Papers*, IV, The International Psycho-Analytical Library, no. 10, London, 1934.

———, "The Relation of the Poet to Day-Dreaming," tr. I. F. Grant Duff, *Collected Papers*, Vol. IV, London, 1934.

———, "The 'Uncanny,' " tr. Alix Strachey, *Collected Papers*, IV, London, 1934.

Galton, Francis, *Memories of My Life*, London, 1908.

Gargano, James W., "The Turn of the Screw," *Western Humanities Review*, XV, 2 (Spring 1961), 173–179.

Gauld, Alan, *The Founders of Psychical Research*, New York, 1968.

Geismar, Maxwell, "Henry James: 'The Beast in the Jungle,' " *Nineteenth-Century Fiction*, XVIII, i (June 1963), 35–42.

Girling, H. K., "The Strange Case of Dr. James & Mr. Stevenson," *Wascana Review*, III, i (1968), 63–76.

Gosse, Edmund, *Aspects and Impressions*, London, 1922.

Grattan, C. Hartley, *The Three Jameses, A Family of Minds, Henry James, Sr., William James, Henry James*, London, New York, and Toronto, 1932.

Green, David Bounell, "Witch and Bewitchment in *The Bostonians,*" *Papers on Language & Literature*, III, 3 (Summer 1967), 267–269.

Harlow, Virginia, *Thomas Sergeant Perry: A Biography and Letters to Perry from William, Henry, and Garth Wilkinson James*, Durham, N.C., 1950.

Harris, Wendell V., "English Short Fiction in the Nineteenth Century," *Studies in Short Fiction*, VI, i (Fall 1968), 1–93.

Hastings, James, ed., *Encyclopaedia of Religion and Ethics*, 12 vols., New York and Edinburgh, 1909–1927.

Hawthorne, Nathaniel, *The Blithedale Romance, The Works of Nathaniel Hawthorne*, Vol. I, Boston, 1868.

Hearnshaw, L. S., *A Short History of British Psychology: 1840–1940*, London, 1964.

Heilman, Robert B., "The Lure of the Demonic: James and Dürrenmatt," *Comparative Literature*, XIII, iii (Fall 1961), 346–357.

————, "'The Turn of the Screw' as Poem," *University of Kansas City Review,* XIV, 4 (Summer 1948), 277–289.

Hinchliffe, Arnold P., "Henry James's *The Sacred Fount,*" *Texas Studies in Literature and Language,* II, i (Spring 1960), 88–94.

Hoffman, Frederick J., "William James and the Modern Literary Consciousness," *Criticism,* IV, i (Winter 1962), 1–13.

Howells, William Dean, "Editor's Easy Chair," *Harper's Monthly Magazine,* CVII (June 1903), 146–150.

————, "Mr. Henry James's Later Work," *North American Review,* CLXXVI (January 1903), 125–137.

————, *The Undiscovered Country,* Boston, 1880.

———— and Henry Mills Alden, *Shapes That Haunt the Dusk,* New York and London, 1907.

Humphrey, Robert, *Stream of Consciousness in the Modern Novel,* Berkeley, 1954.

Hyde, H. Montgomery, *Henry James at Home,* London, 1969.

Isle, Walter, "The Romantic and the Real: Henry James's *The Sacred Fount,*" *Rice University Studies,* LI, i (Winter 1965), 29–47.

Ives, C. B., "James's Ghosts in *The Turn of the Screw,*" *Nineteenth-Century Fiction,* XVIII, 2 (September 1963), 183–193.

James, Alice, *The Diary of Alice James,* ed. Leon Edel, New York, 1964.

James, Henry, Sr., *Substance and Shadow,* Boston, 1863.

James, Henry, "The Altar of the Dead, The Beast in the Jungle, The Birthplace, The Private Life, Owen Wingrave, The Friends of the Friends, Sir Edmund Orme, and The Real Right Thing," *Novels and Tales,* Vol. XVII, New York, 1908.

————, *The Ambassadors, Novels and Tales,* Vol. XXII, New York, 1909.

————, *The American, Novels and Tales,* Vol. II, New York, 1907.

————, *The American Scene, Together with Three Essays From "Portraits of Places,"* New York, 1946.

————, *A Small Boy and Others,* New York, 1913.

————, "The Aspern Papers, The Turn of the Screw, The Liar, The Two Faces," *Novels and Tales,* Vol. XII, New York, 1908.

————, *The Awkward Age, Novels and Tales,* Vol. IX, New York, 1908.

————, *The Bostonians,* London and New York, 1886.

————, *Confidence,* New York, 1962.

————, *The Europeans,* Boston, 1879.

————, *French Poets and Novelists,* New York, 1964.

————, *Hawthorne,* Ithaca, N.Y., 1956.

————, *Notes of a Son and Brother,* New York, 1914.

————, *The Other House,* New York, 1896.

————, *Partial Portraits,* London and New York, 1888.

————, *The Portrait of a Lady,* Boston, 1882.

————, *The Portrait of a Lady, Novels and Tales,* Vols. III-IV, New York, 1908.

————, *The Princess Casamassima, Novels and Tales,* Vol. V, New York, 1908.

————, *Roderick Hudson, Novels and Tales,* Vol. I, New York, 1907.

————, "The Reverberator, Madame de Mauves, A Passionate Pilgrim and Other Tales," *Novels and Tales,* Vol. XIII, New York, 1908.

————, *The Sacred Fount,* New York, 1901.

————, *The Sense of the Past,* New York, 1917.

————, "The Spoils of Poynton, A London Life, The Chaperon," *Novels and Tales,* Vol. X, New York, 1908.

————, *The Tragic Muse, Novels and Tales,* Vol. VIII, New York, 1908.

————, "What Maisie Knew, In the Cage, The Pupil," *Novels and Tales,* Vol. XI, New York, 1908.

————, *The Wings of the Dove, Novels and Tales,* Vols. XIX and XX, New York, 1909.

James, William, *The Letters of William James,* ed. son Henry James, 2 vols., Boston, 1920.

————, *The Literary Remains of the late Henry James,* Boston and New York, 1884.

————, *Pragmatism: A New Name for Some Old Ways of Thinking,* New York, 1907.

————, *The Varieties of Religious Experience, A Study in Human Nature,* New York, 1902.

————, *The Will to Believe and Other Essays in Popular Philosophy,* New York, London, and Bombay, 1897.

Jacobs, Robert D., *Poe, Journalist & Critic,* Baton Rouge, 1969.

Jean-Aubry, George, ed., *Joseph Conrad, Life and Letters,* 2 vols., Garden City, New York, 1927.

Johnson, Courtney, "John Marcher and the Paradox of The 'Unfortunate' Fall," *Studies in Short Fiction,* VI, 2 (Winter 1969), 121–135.

Johnson, Raynor C., *The Imprisoned Splendour: An approach to Reality, based upon the significance of data drawn from the fields of Natural Science, Psychical Research and Mystical Experience,* London, 1953.

Jones, Alexander E., "Point of View in *The Turn of the Screw,*" *PMLA,* LXXIV, i (March 1959), 112–122.

Kelley, Cornelia P., *The Early Development of Henry James,* University of Illinois Studies in Language and Literature, Vol. XV (1930), nos. 1–2, ed. William A. Oldfather et al.

Kerr, Howard, *Mediums, and Spirit-Rappers, and Roaring Radicals: Spiritualism in American Literature, 1850–1900,* Champaign-Urbana, Ill., 1972.

Kierkegaard, Soren, *The Living Thoughts of Kierkegaard, Presented by W. H. Auden,* New York, 1952.

Knox, George, "Incubi and Succubi in *The Turn of the Screw*," *Western Folklore*, XXII, 2 (April 1963), 122–123.

Koyré, Alexandre, *From the Closed World to the Infinite Universe*, Baltimore, 1957.

Kraft, James, *The Early Tales of Henry James*, Carbondale and Edwardsville, Ill., 1969.

Krook, Dorothea, *The Ordeal of Consciousness in Henry James*, Cambridge, at the University Press, 1962.

Labrie, Ross, "Henry James's Idea of Consciousness," *American Literature*, XXXIX, 4 (January 1968), 517–529.

Lang, Andrew, "Psychical Research," *Encyclopaedia Britannica*, New York, 1911.

Lang, Hans-Joachim, "The Turns in *The Turn of the Screw*," *Jahrbuch Für Amerikastudien*, IX (1964), 110–128.

Lebowitz, Naomi, " 'The Sacred Fount' : An Author in Search of His Characters," *Criticism*, IV, 2 (Spring 1962), 148–159.

Le Clair, Robert C., *The Letters of William James and Théodore Flournoy*, Madison, Milwaukee, and London, 1966.

Lewis, R. W. B., "The Tactics of Sanctity: Hawthorne and James," *Hawthorne Centenary Essays*, ed. Roy Harvey Pearce, Columbus, Ohio, 1964.

Lind, Sidney, ed., "James's 'The Private Life' and Browning," *American Literature*, XXIII, 3 (November 1951), 315–322.

Lubbock, Percy, *The Letters of Henry James*, 2 vols., New York, 1920.

Lydenburg, "The Governess Turns the Screws," *Nineteenth-Century Fiction*, XII, i (June, 1957), 37–58.

Mackenzie, Manfred, "*The Turn of the Screw:* Jamesian Gothic," *Essays in Criticism*, XII (January 1962), 34–38.

McCarthy, Harold T., *Henry James, The Creative Process*, New York, 1958.

McMaster, Juliet, " 'The Full Image of a Repetition' in *The Turn of the Screw*," *Studies in Short Fiction*, VI, 4 (Summer 1969), 377–382.

Male, Roy R., Jr., "Hawthorne and the Concept of Sympathy," *PMLA*, LXVIII, i (March 1953), 138–149.

———, "*Sympathy*—A Key Word in American Romanticism," *The Emerson Society Quarterly*, No. 35 (II Quarter, 1964), 19–23.

Matthiessen, F. O., *Henry James: The Major Phase*, London, New York, and Toronto, 1944.

———, *The James Family, Including Selections from the Writings of Henry James, Senior, William, Henry, & Alice James*, New York, 1947.

——— and Kenneth B. Murdock, *The Notebooks of Henry James*, New York, 1947.

Mays, Milton A., "Henry James, or, The Beast in the Palace of Art," *American Literature*, XXXIX, 4 (January 1968), 467–487.

Miyoshi, Masao, *The Divided Self, A Perspective on The Literature of the Victorians*, New York and London, 1969.

Monteiro, George, "Hawthorne, James, and the Destructive Self," *Texas Studies in Literature and Language*, IV, i (Spring 1962), 58–71.

Murchison, Carl, *The Case For and Against Psychical Research*, Worcester, Mass., 1927.

Murphy, Gardner, and Robert O. Ballou, ed., *William James on Psychical Research*, New York, 1960.

Myers, F. W. H., *Human Personality and Its Survival of Bodily Death*, 2 vols., New York, London and Bombay, 1904.

Ozick, Cynthia, "The Jamesian Parable: *The Sacred Fount*," *Bucknell Review*, XI, iii (May 1963), 55–70.

Parish, Edmund, *Hallucinations and Illusions*, London, 1897.

Pater, Walter, *Appreciations With an Essay on Style*, London and New York, 1889.

Penzoldt, Peter, *The Supernatural in Fiction*, London, 1952.

Perry, Ralph Barton, *The Thought and Character of William James, as revealed in unpublished correspondence and notes, together with his published writings*, 2 vols., Boston, 1935.

Phillips, Norma, "*The Sacred Fount:* The Narrator and the Vampires," *PMLA*, LXXVI, no. 4 (September 1961), 407–412.

Platzner, Robert L. and Robert D. Hume, " 'Gothic Versus Romantic': A Rejoinder," *PMLA*, LXXXVI, 2 (March 1971), 266–274.

Poirier, Richard, *The Comic Sense of Henry James, A Study of the Early Novels*, New York, 1967.

Rahv, Philip, "The Cult of Experience in American Writing," *Partisan Review*, VII (November-December, 1940), 412–424.

Raleigh, John Henry, "Henry James: The Poetics of Empiricism," *PMLA*, LXVI (March 1951), 107–123.

Reaney, James, "The Condition of Light: Henry James's *The Sacred Fount*," *University of Toronto Quarterly*, XXXI (January 1962), 136–151.

Reilly, Robert J., "Henry James and the Morality of Fiction," *American Literature*, XXXIX, i (March 1967), 1–30.

Remley, David A., "William James: The Meaning and Function of Art," *Midcontinent American Studies*, IV, 2 (Fall 1963), 39–48.

Roberts, James D., *Faith and Reason, A Comparative Study of Pascal, Bergson and James*, Boston, 1962.

Roberts, James L., "An Approach to Evil in Henry James," *Arizona Quarterly*, XVII, i (Spring 1961), 5–16.

Roberts, R. Ellis, "Great James," *The Bookman* (London), LIII (December 1917), 107–108.

————, "The Other Side of the Moon, Introduction to the Mysterious in Literature," *The Bookman* (London), LXXVII (December 1929), Special Supplement, 157–160.

Roellinger, Francis X., Jr., "Psychical Research and 'The Turn of the Screw,' " *American Literature*, XX (January 1949), 401–412.

Rogers, Robert, "The Beast in Henry James," *The American Imago*, XIII, 4 (Winter 1956), 427–454.

———, *A Psychoanalytic Study of the Double in Literature*, Cleveland, Ohio, 1971.

Rosenzweig, Saul, "The Ghost of Henry James," *Partisan Review*, XI, 4 (Fall 1944), 436–455.

Samuel, Irene, "Henry James on Imagination and the Will to Power," *Bulletin of the New York Public Library*, LXIX, 2 (February 1965), 117–130.

Samuels, Charles T., "At the Bottom of the *Fount,* "*Novel*, II, i (Fall 1968), 46–54.

Scarborough, Dorothy, *The Supernatural in Modern English Fiction*, New York and London, 1917.

Schneider, Herbert, *A History of American Philosophy*, New York, 1946.

Schroeder, John W., "The Mothers of Henry James," *American Literature*, XXII, 4 (January 1951), 425–431.

Search, Pamela, ed., *The Supernatural in the English Short Story*, London, 1959.

Sears, Sallie, *The Negative Imagination, Form and Perspective in the Novels of Henry James*, Ithaca, N. Y., 1968.

Solomon, Eric, "The Return of the Screw," *University Review*, XXX (Spring 1964), 205–211.

Sontag, Susan, "Piety without Content," *Against Interpretation, and Other Essays*, New York, 1966.

Spacks, Patricia Myer, *The Insistence of Horror, Aspects of the Supernatural in Eighteenth-Century Poetry*, Cambridge, Mass., 1962.

Spence, Lewis, ed., *An Encyclopaedia of Occultism*, London, 1920.

Spilka, Mark, "Turning the Freudian Screw: How Not to Do It," *Literature and Psychology*, XIII, 4 (Fall 1963), 105–111.

Spiller, Robert E., Willard Thorp, Thomas H. Johnson, and Henry Seidel Canby, *Literary History of the United States*, New York, 1960.

Stafford, William T., "William James as Critic of His Brother James," *The Personalist*, XL, 4 (Autumn, October 1959), 341—353.

Steiner, George, *The Death of Tragedy*, New York, 1961.

Stovall, Floyd, "Henry James's 'The Jolly Corner,' "*Nineteenth-Century Fiction*, XII (June 1957), 72–84.

Tanner, Tony, "Henry James's Subjective Adventurer: 'The Sacred Fount,' " *Essays and Studies*, n.s., XVI (1963), 37–55.

Taylor, Gordon O., *The Passages of Thought, Psychological Representation in the American Novel, 1870–1900*, New York, 1969.

Thomas, Augustus, *The Witching Hour*, New York and London, 1908.

Thorberg, Raymond, "Terror Made Relevant: James's Ghost Stories," *The Dalhousie Review*, XLVII, 2 (Summer 1967), 185–191.

Tompkins, J. M. S., *The Popular Novel in England, 1770–1880*, Lincoln, Neb., 1961.

Tuveson, Ernest Lee, *The Imagination as a Means of Grace, Locke and the Aesthetics of Romanticism*, Berkeley and Los Angeles, 1960.

Twain, Mark, "Mental Telegraphy, A Manuscript With A History," *Harper's New Monthly Magazine*, LXXXIV (December 1891), 95–104.

Tyler, Parker, *"The Sacred Fount:* 'The Actuality Pretentious and Vain' vs. 'The Case Rich and Edifying,' " *Modern Fiction Studies*, IX, 2 (Summer 1963), 127–138.

Ward, J. A., "James's Idea of Structure," *PMLA*, LXXX (September 1965), 419–426.

Wells, H. G., *The Country of the Blind*, London, 1911.

Whitehead, Alfred North, *Science and the Modern World, Lowell Lectures, 1925*, New York, 1962.

Willen, Gerald, ed., *A Casebook on Henry James's "The Turn of the Screw,"* New York, 1960.

Wilshire, Bruce, *William James and Phenomenology: a Study of "The Principles of Psychology,"* Bloomington, Ind., 1968.

Wilson, Edmund, "The Ambiguity of Henry James," *Hound and Horn*, VII (April–June, 1934), 385–406.

Young, Frederic H., *The Philosophy of Henry James, Sr.*, New York, 1951.

Notes

I. Strange Bedfellows

1. Background information for Modern Spiritualism and psychical research is drawn mainly from the following sources: the entries under "Spiritualism" in James Hastings' *Encyclopaedia of Religion and Ethics* (New York and Edinburgh, 1909–1927, 12 vols. and Index), and in *An Encyclopaedia of Occultism,* ed. Lewis Spence (London, 1920); Henri F. Ellenberger, *The Discovery of the Unconscious, The History and Evolution of Dynamic Psychiatry* (New York, 1970); Alan Gauld, *The Founders of Psychical Research* (New York, 1968); *The Letters of William James and Théodore Flournoy,* ed. Robert C. Le Clair (Madison, Milwaukee, and London, 1966); Sir Arthur Conan Doyle, *The History of Spiritualism* (New York, 1926), in two volumes; C. D. Broad, *Religion, Philosophy, and Psychical Research* (New York, 1953); Raynor C. Johnson, *The Imprisoned Splendour: An approach to Reality, based upon the significance of data drawn from the fields of Natural Science, Psychical Research and Mystical Experience* (London, 1953); *William James on Psychical Research,* ed. Gardner Murphy and Robert O. Ballou (New York, 1960); *The Case For and Against Psychical Belief,* ed. Carl Murchison (Worcester, Mass., 1927); the entry under "Psychical Research" in Hastings' *Encyclopaedia,* and Andrew Lang's comments in the Eleventh Edition of *Encyclopaedia Britannica* (New York, 1911), under the same topic; L. S. Hearnshaw, *A Short History of British Psychology: 1840–1940* (London, 1964). A book just published, which I read in manuscript form, also covers this period ably: Howard H. Kerr's *Mediums, and Spirit-Rappers, and Roaring Radicals: Spiritualism in American Literature, 1850–1900* (Champaign-Urbana, Illinois, 1972).

2. W. D. Howell's novel of 1880, *The Undiscovered Country,* deals in part with the contemporary confusion over whether spiritualism had killed

off scientific materialism or was itself a grosser form of the empirical. W. B. Carpenter (who influenced William James's later study of the abnormal) led a new school of physiological psychology in the 1850's. An editorial in *The Nation*, I, 10 (September 7, 1865), 295–296, entitled "Judge Edmonds on 'Spiritualism,' " launched an attack against the "Paleyan materialism" evident even in the Spiritualist movement. The Metaphysical Society founded in 1869 included such natural antagonists as Tennyson, Cardinal Manning, Martineau, Gladstone, T. H. Huxley, Tyndall, Ruskin, Bagehot, Froude, Leslie Stephen, Sully, and Henry Sidgwick. Huxley's pronouncements in 1874 and the founding, in 1882, of the S.P.R., headed by Sidgwick, heightened the conflict between science and religion over whether the "celestial is but a rigid prolongation of the natural and terrestrial" (as phrased in *The Nation* article cited above).

3. Gauld (pp. 66–70, 77) reviews the reasons (entrenched orthodoxy and hostility of the press) that slowed acceptance in Britain until the 1860's.

4. See Herbert W. Schneider, *A History of American Philosophy* (New York, 1946), pp. 321–380, for his discussion of the "psychic" turn taken by evolutionists and speculative biologists. Also note that the years of Modern Spiritualism's greatest growth coincided with the proliferation in America of millennial cults and weird social schemes—many originating in the same upper New York State area from whence the Fox sisters came.

5. Sir Arthur Conan Doyle, "The Psychic Question As I See It," *The Case For and Against Psychical Belief*, p. 15. Subsequent references to this anthology will be made to *Case For and Against*.

6. Frederick Bligh Bond, "The Pragmatist in Psychic Research," *Case For and Against*, p. 30.

7. See Gauld for Myers' letters to J. A. Symonds in 1883 and to Sir Oliver Lodge in 1896 (pp. 142, 311).

8. Myers' obituary for Henry Sidgwick, *Proceedings of the Society for Psychical Research*, XV (1900), 459–460 (hereafter cited as *PSPR*).

9. Doyle, *History*, II, 248.

10. The original group contained both Spiritualists such as Stainton Moses and the unconvinced; by 1886–1887 many of the Spiritualists had split away, and the group around Sidgwick was in full control.

11. Gauld, p. 140.

12. Broad, pp. 95–96.

13. Hearnshaw, p. 160. Gauld gives a detailed discussion (pp. 278–299)

of Myers' theories of the subliminal and contrasts them with various theories of the unconscious.

14. Doyle, *History*, II, 64.

15. F. C. S. Schiller, "Some Logical Aspects of Psychical Research," *Case For And Against*, pp. 215–216.

16. Comment by C. D. Broad, p. 109; pagination for subsequent quotations will be given within parentheses. Gauld also gives ample material on Sidgwick, pp. 47–57.

17. See Gauld's remarks (p. 64) on the contrast between the Cambridge men who left the University in the 1840's and the 1870's. Also see Henry James's letter written in 1863 to T. S. Perry, which refers to a visit to a Presbyterian service conducted by a stalwart old Calvinist: "The brimstone fizzles up in the pulpit but fades away into mush and cologne-water in the pews." Virginia Harlow, *Thomas Sergeant Perry: A Biography and Letters to Perry from William, Henry, and Garth Wilkinson James* (Durham, N.C., 1950), p. 269.

18. Gauld dates the coming together of "the Sidwick Group" as 1873.

19. As a student at the Harvard Medical School in 1869, the first possibility seemed the right one when he wrote a review article in attack against Epes Sargent's book, *Planchette: the Despair of Science*.

20. Bruce Wilshire points out that James's aim in *Principles of Psychology* was to divorce psychology from metaphysics, yet that in the 1892 abridgment James confessed that his natural science was one into which "the waters of metaphysical criticism leak at every joint." Wilshire distinguishes James's "metaphysical" quality of "*description* of the phenomenal facts*" from his rejection of "transphenomenal *explanation* of these phenomenal facts." *William James and Phenomenology: A Study of "The Principles of Psychology,"* Bloomington, Ind., 1968, pp. 10–57. This leakage of a "spiritual something" into James's world made it, in turn, one which (in Ralph Barton Perry's words) "slipped through every ideal container and resisted the impression of every logical mould"—so "unfenced, uncultivated, untidy, and unpredictable" was it. *The Thought and Character of William James, as revealed in unpublished correspondence and notes, together with his published writings* (Boston, 1935), III, 585.

21. See James's provocative argument pro and con "romantic" and "scientific" modes of thought in *PSPR*, XII (1896), 8–9, with its final rejection of the scientific mode that will dismiss out of hand a "personal and romantic view" which is "fed by *facts of experience.*"

22. From "The Confidences of a 'Psychical Researcher,' " *William James on Psychical Research*, p. 322; hereafter referred to as *WJ on PR*.

James's "mixture of exasperation and nostalgia" over being moved away from science and "toward a transcendent affirmation" is noted by Frederick J. Hoffman in "William James and the Modern Literary Consciousness," *Criticism*, IV, i (Winter, 1962), 6.

23. *The Letters of William James*, ed. by his son Henry James (Boston, 1920), I, 310; letter of July 6, 1891. Hereafter this two-volume work will be refereed to as *WJ Letters*.

24. In Robert D. Jacobs' study of Edgar Allan Poe, he likens Poe's "excursions into conflicting epistemologies" to William James's "radical empiricalism"—that is, to James's ability "to concede the possibility of pragmatic truth to any aspect of experience, the most visionary or the most mundane." *Poe, Journalist & Critic* (Baton Rouge, 1969), p. 27. In *Principles of Psychology*, II, 639, James wrote, "There are ideal and inward relations amongst the objects of our thought which can in no intelligible sense whatever be interpreted as reproductions of the order of outer experience."

25. *WJ on PR*, pp. 12–13; subsequent pagination will be given within parentheses.

26. See *WJ on PR*, p. 313, in which James candidly admits having once "cheated shamelessly" on an experiment performed before an audience in order to act "for the *larger* truth."

27. James wrote he wished to "re-instate" the "vague to its proper place in our mental life." He knew that "namelessness" is a common part of our experience and yet that, because we lack a vocabulary to describe subjective facts, we tend to overlook them and all that lies "just around the corner." What really counts—is meaning to us—is aptly imaged as "fringe," "halo," "horizon." Wilshire, pp. 78, 87, 89, 99, 103, 200.

28. See James D. Roberts, *Faith and Reason, A Comparative Study of Pascal, Bergson and James* (Boston, 1962), pp. 30–31, concerning James's "anti-intellectualism" against men, whether Rationalists or Empiricists, who forbade faith in experience. James's stress on possibility, chance (tychism), risk is well annotated in Roberts and in "William James's Determined Free Will," by Gay Wilson Allen, from *Essays on Determinism in American Literature*, ed. Sydney J. Krause (Kent, Ohio, 1964), pp. 67–76.

29. *Pragmatism: A New Name for Some Old Ways of Thinking* (New York, 1907), p. 51. Wilshire contrasts James with the behaviorist B. F. Skinner, in whose world "wonder" is gone (p. 222).

30. Introduction to *The Literary Remains of the late Henry James* (Boston and New York, 1884), pp. 10–11.

31. *WJ Letters,* I, 237.

32. Ibid., I, 250. See Wilshire's concluding remarks (pp. 222–225), in which he attacks Behaviorism (which he opposes to the insights gained by James's psychology) as the unwitting champion of "a new spiritualism" that sets itself "on the trail of occult powers and 'controls' "; the result is "the materialist's bastard spiritualism. . . ."

33. "Report on Mrs. Piper's Hodgson-Control," *WJ on PR,* p. 209. Also see *WJ and TF Letters,* p. 48; letter of September 4, 1895.

34. "What Psychical Research Has Accomplished," *The Will to Believe and Other Essays in Popular Philosophy* (New York, London, Bombay, 1897), pp. 303–304.

35. "The Confidences of a 'Psychical Researcher,' " *WJ on PR,* p. 325. Flournoy wrote James in 1907, concerning their mutual appreciation of Henri Bergson's *L'Evolution Créatrice,* of the interest one has in what a philosopher "has *aimed* at and tried to do—not what he has *proved,* but what he *believes.*" *WJ and TF Letters,* p. 190. This well describes Bergson, Flournoy, and James's contributions. Wilshire also remarks that James raised problems and made mistakes that led later thinkers to important discoveries (p. 217).

36. "Address by the President," *WJ on PR,* p. 62. See Flournoy's letter to James of March 15, 1910, in which he expresses the pity felt at the sight of a fervent believer in Spiritualism who beseeched the spirits at a séance to grant him "one small convincing phenomenon; but nothing happened. . . ." To James, as to Flournoy, it must have been "tragically and comically moving" to witness such unanswered pleas. *WJ and TF Letters,* pp. 228–229.

37. See William Barrett and Henry D. Aiken, *Philosophy in the Twentieth Century* (New York, 1964), Vol. I, 67.

38. See Gauld (p. 32) concerning the implications he draws from data taken for the only religious census Britain had, on March 30, 1851.

39. Wilshire brings the battle up to date: "Materialists and spiritualists, helpless in their mutual dependency, have been like blind combatants hacking away at one another on an empty field. The prize lies in a different arena governed by wholly different rules. [William] James helps to free us because he prompts us to see that an adequate materalism is at the same time an adequate philosophy of the spirit, and conversely" (p. 225).

40. "Psychic Research has about as much to do with religion as golf," wrote the doctor-husband of one of the most popular mediums of the 1920's. "Nevertheless, it is going to be one of the most important factors in changing not religions but religious concepts and beliefs." L. R. G. Crandon, *Case For and Against*, p. 105. Myers wrote Lodge (January 26, 1896) that he had "defined the orthodox scientific religion as neo-Phallicism;—should like to explain this to you:—it is not meant to be insulting! but if you don't know what a phallus is, don't ask!" (Gauld, p. 142 n.)

41. "Mental Telegraphy, A Manuscript With A History," *Harper's New Monthly Magazine*, LXXXIV (December, 1891), 95; the next quotation is from the same source. See Sigmund Freud, "Dreams and Telepathy" of 1922, trans. C. J. M. Hubback, *Collected Papers*, IV (The International Psycho-Analytical Library, no. 10, London, 1934), 410–435, for his disavowal of any observed connection between dream-experiences and telepathic communications and for his indifference to telepathy viewed in its "occult sense."

42. "Presidential Address, Delivered on May 28th, 1913 by Professor Henri Bergson, Authorized Translation by H. Wildon Carr, D. Litt.," *PSPR*, XXVII (1914–1915), 159. The original address printed in French appeared in vol. XXVI (1913), 462–479.

43. Broad, p. 103.

44. *WJ and TF Letters*, pp. 103–104.

45. Doyle, *History*, II, 69.

46. Sir Oliver Lodge, "The University Aspect of Psychical Research," *Case For and Against*, p. 8.

47. Whitehead, *Science and the Modern World, Lowell Lectures*, 1925 (New York, 1962), p. 260.

48. After the turn of the century Hans Driesch, Professor of Philosophy at Leipzig and one-time president of the S.P.R., stated, "We are in the Galvani period: facts without explanation. We want to enter the Faraday period: laws established by experiment." Cited by Crandon, *Case For and Against*, pp. 108–109. In 1947 the F. W. H. Myers Memorial Lecturer stated, "Psychical Research today resembles a number of heaps of material stacked in a builder's yard. Many of the materials are there, but no edifice has as yet arisen." Cited by Hearnshaw, *History of British Psychology*, p. 244. In an address given on February 25, 1965 at the University of California at Santa Barbara, the psychologist Sidney Cohen commented that psychical researchers have accumulated masses of data on E.S.P. but have no theories to explain them. "Facts" cannot displace an old hypothesis; only a new hypothesis can, and this is precisely what

is lacking. Much of what science knows about ordinary sense perception tends to concur with what research into E.S.P. uncovers, but there are no valid methods for the transference of knowns about the ordinary to the uses of extraordinary phenomena, or vice versa.

49. In America, Cooper, Bryant, and Whittier had gathered around the séance table, while in England the list of attentive (if often dubious) authors included Frederick Tennyson, John Ruskin, and the Brownings. "Literary mediums" associated directly with Spiritualism turned out "spirit-written" ouija-board novels. Among the best known were Anita Silvana, Mrs. Elsa Barker, Mrs. Campbell-Praed, Mary L. Lewis, Straford Jolly, Hope Crawford, Robert James Lee, and Caspar Yost. See Dorothy Scarborough, *The Supernatural in Modern English Fiction* (New York and London, 1917), pp. 206–207. See Gauld, p. 18, concerning the general tediousness and stylelessness of the writing, and Ellenberger, pp. 158–170, 282–284, who has much to say concerning the influence of the new "dynamic psychiatry" on continental writers.

50. This seemed to be the breakthrough writers had been searching for since general belief in supernatural manifestations was demeaned by philosophical and scientific scepticism. Patricia Myer Spacks, in *The Insistence of Horror, Aspects of the Supernatural in Eighteenth-Century Poetry* (Cambridge, Mass., 1962), examines the various dilemmas that enlightened century had to contend with before it could produce effective ghostly literature; for if theological positions on the subject were confused, so were the aesthetic. Until the late nineteenth century, writers of the supernatural tale had essentially the same problem: how to let tensions—between intellect, which scoffed at the ghostly, and emotion, which accepted it—generate good fiction, not strangle it. Peter Penzoldt in *The Supernatural in Fiction* (London, 1952), p. 5, also offers a good review of the changes that took place in the minds of public and writers alike before the "modern" tale of the supernatural could mature.

51. Pamela Search, in her introduction to *The Supernatural in the English Short Story* (London, 1959), p. 17, concludes, "Of all these modern types of supernatural fiction, the psychological ghost story seems to me the one with the most interesting future. The horror tale is unlikely to survive except as a crime story, and science fiction proper will soon have a hard job to keep ahead of the scientist. But the new scientific type of psychological tale, studies of mental abnormalities and hallucinations based on modern psychiatry, is coming into its own."

52. Scarborough, pp. 4–5; 199; the next two quotations are from pp. 76 and 113.

53. Pamela Search feels that "half the battle [is] won" for the current writer of the psychological ghost story since the public, no longer terrified by ghosts, is apprehensive of "the dread possibilities of mental disease and hallucination." Today the reaction is seldom, "Thank goodness this isn't me," but "Good heavens, this might happen to me" (pp. 17, 20). Penzoldt asserts that what we most often discuss (the possibility of insanity) is what most frightens. (To speak of it does not assuage the fear.) In line with Leon Edel, Penzoldt also states (p. 7) that writers of the supernatural wrote out of their own neuroses in order to exorcise them. (The result is a "healthy-mindedness" that William James might applaud.) Penzoldt further refers (p. 55) to Jung's inability to specify "the borderline between mental disease and the intervention of genuine supernatural powers." He distinguishes between writers like Walter De La Mare, who wrote of normal psychological states, and William Machen, writing of abnormalities; however, Penzoldt—like Pamela Search —links the twentieth-century ghostly tale with insanity, that modern bogey.

54. In a letter of November 23, 1905, Henry James wrote William, "Philosophically, in short, I am 'with' you, almost completely." *The Letters of Henry James,* ed. Percy Lubbock (New York, 1920), II, 43; hereafter referred to as *HJ Letters.*

55. Any educated man living during these decades who did not have some knowledge of current happenings in spiritualism and psychical research would have had to be particularly dull. This Henry James was not. His awareness went beyond the salon-conversation knowledge that enabled him to refer to Gautier's preface to "Les Fleurs du Mal" as containing mention of "what the Spiritualist newspapers would call Baudelaire's 'mentality.'" From the 1876 review for *Nation;* reprinted in his *French Poets and Novelists* (New York, 1964), p. 59. His attitude was usually one of amused scepticism. See Leon Edel's *Henry James, 1870– 1881, The Conquest of London* (Philadelphia and New York, 1962), p. 26, for details of why James turned for entertainment to evenings of spiritualist demonstrations. James personally knew Lang, Sidgwick, Myers, Gurney, and A. C. Benson; he commented that he found Myers "a very pleasant, gushing, aesthetic Briton, but not powerful" and Lang "a very excellent, amiable fellow, of an infantine simplicity. . . ." Harlow, *T. S. Perry,* pp. 303, 306 (letters of September 14, 1879 and February 22, 1880). See *HJ Letters,* I, 210, in which Henry congratulates William on receiving the presidency of the S.P.R. Also read the exchange of letters

of 1890, which tell of Henry's decision to present a paper on the medium Mrs. Piper before the British S.P.R. in William's stead. R. B. Perry, *WJ*, I, 415–417. Significant are the light tone used in recounting this affair and the emphasis on the theatrical opportunities such an appearance afforded both the reader of the piece and its author. Henry James's tone was not so playful, however, in a letter of 1906 written to describe the emotions felt upon receiving news in England from William's wife about a Boston séance; in this instance, his mother, dead for twenty-five years, supposedly conveyed an intimate message to him which "quite astounds as well as deeply touches me." *HJ Letters*, II, 47–48.

56. From *The Country of the Blind* (London, 1911), pp. v–vi.

57. See Wendell V. Harris, "English Short Fiction in the 19th Century," *Studies in Short Fiction*, VII, i (Fall, 1968), 1–93.

58. A similar pattern is evident in the writing careers of W. D. Howells and Mark Twain. This period produced finished work in Howell's case of the type of fantasy and of the supernatural: *The Shadow of a Dream* (1890); significant passages in *The Landlord at Lion's Head* (1897) and *The Son of Royal Langbrith* (1904); two collections of stories, *Questionable Shapes* (1903) and *Between the Dark and the Daylight* (1907); and *The Seen and the Unseen at Stratford-on-Avon, a fantasy* (1914). It produced a mass of unfinished work in Mark Twain's case: "The Great Dark," "The Mysterious Stranger," "My Platonic Sweetheart," scattered starts at other dream reveries, jottings in his notebooks, letters to friends (especially to Howells), and reminiscences caught in his autobiography or in Albert Bigelow Paine's biography; most concerned supernormal phenomena of dreams or psychic communication.

59. See David A. Remley, "William James: The Meaning and Function of Art," *Midcontinent American Studies*, IV, 2 (Fall, 1963), 39–48, for a review of the exactions laid by William upon art's duty to morality and reform which could never be taken literally by Henry. In 1907 William wrote Henry concerning the style of *The American Scene*, comparing it with his own: "Mine being to say a thing in one sentence as straight and explicit as it can be made, and then to drop it forever; yours being to avoid naming it straight, but by dint of breathing and sighing all around it, to arouse in the reader who may have had a similar perception already (Heaven help him if he hasn't!) the illusion of a solid object, made (like the 'ghost' at the Polytechnic) wholly out of impalpable materials, airs, and the prismatic interferences of light, ingeniously focused by mirrors upon empty space." From *The James Family, A Group*

Biography, together with selections from the writings of Henry James, Senior, William, Henry, and Alice James, ed. F. O. Matthiessen (New York, 1947), 341–342.

60. Or to those tales written by H. G. Wells that stressed an anecdotal, free-floating movement into areas of the weird and wondrous where James chose not to venture (and never in ways so structureless and "more or less"). Wells wrote in *The Country of the Blind* (p. iv) that he worked off the basis of asking, "What if—?" Next, "I found that, taking almost anything as a starting-point and letting my thoughts play about it, there would presently come out of the darkness, in a manner quite inexplicable, some absurd or vivid little incident more or less relevant to that initial nucleus. Little men in canoes upon sunlit oceans would come floating out of nothingness, incubating the eggs of prehistoric monsters unaware; violent conflicts would break out amidst the flower-beds of suburban gardens; I would discover I was peering into remote and mysterious worlds ruled by an order logical indeed but other than our common sanity."

II. *Positive Renunciations*

1. "At the Grave of Henry James," *The Collected Poetry of W. H. Auden* (New York, 1945), p. 129.

2. The following books provide an entrance into the tangled beliefs held by the elder James: Frederic H. Young, *The Philosophy of Henry James, Sr.* (New York, 1951); C. Hartley Grattan, *The Three James, A Family of Minds, Henry James, Sr., William James, Henry James* (London, New York and Toronto, 1932); F. O. Matthiessen, *The James Family* (New York, 1947); Henry James, *Notes of a Son and Brother* (New York, 1914), and *A Small Boy and Others* (New York, 1913).

3. *Notes of a Son and Brother,* p. 165; the quotations in the remainder of this paragraph are from pp. 51, 166, and 229.

4. *HJ Letters,* I, 112.

5. *Notes of a Son and Brother,* p. 167.

6. *A Small Boy and Others,* p. 235.

7. To the adult eye "the American Scene" continued to be marked by "bareness," "invisibility," and "vacancy" when it came to the possibilities for a vivid religious sense. *The American Scene, Together with Three Essays from "Portraits of Places"* (New York, 1946), pp. 24, 83, 381–382.

8. *Notes of a Son and Brother,* p. 174.

9. The account of the elder James's experience of Swedenborgian "vastation" is given in *The James Family*, p. 161.

10. *Notes of a Son and Brother*, p. 174; the quotations in the next two paragraphs are from pp. 228–230; 227; 180–181. Consider Poe's quite different handling of Roderick Usher's library. The listing of numerous titles of occult works, among them Swedenborg, gives the reader clues concerning Usher's morbid state. A momentary "effect" is gained, but no continuing "drama" is set up between the volumes and Usher's mind.

11. From Harlow, *T. S. Perry*, pp. 268–271.

12. Preface to "The Aspern Papers; The Turn of the Screw; The Liar; The Two Faces," *Novels and Tales* (New York, 1908), Vol. XII, xv; subsequent pagination will be given within parentheses. For two good examples of the type of "cases" James rejected, see F. W. H. Myers' *Human Personality and Its Survival of Bodily Death* (New York, London and Bombay, 1904), II, 350, and Sir Ernest Bennett's *Apparitions and Haunted Houses, A Survey of Evidence* (London, 1939), p. 26, as well as any *PSPR* of the period.

13. In a review of Gerald Willen's edition of *A Casebook on Henry James's The Turn of the Screw*, C. B. Ives attacks the "irresponsible" distinctions made by James in his preface to "The Turn of the Screw" (attacks, as well, those critics who take the "romantic position" that the ghosts are supernatural manifestations). Ives believes that James's stated liking for active ghosts is contradicted by their passivity in the story. "They were, indeed, the very type of 'recorded and attested "ghosts" ' that the Preface pretends to abjure." (See Ives, "James's Ghosts in *The Turn of the Screw*," *Nineteenth-Century Fiction*, XVIII, 2 [Sept., 1963], 183-193.) In Chapter 5, in which I take on "The Turn of the Screw," I hope to show how the ghosts are "active" in the ways James responsibly meant them to be.

14. In letters to Flournoy of 1903, 1906, and 1908, William James reiterated the continuing boredom mediums caused him. Elsewhere he remarked that "the minute work over insignificant cases and quiddling discussion of 'evidential values' of which the Society's reports are full, seem insufferably tedious. . . . Taken simply by themselves, as separate facts to stare at, they appear so devoid of meaning and sweep that, even were they certainly true, one would be tempted to leave them out of one's universe for being so idiotic. Every other sort of fact has some context and continuity with the rest of nature. These alone are contextless and discontinuous." From "What Psychical Research Has Accomplished," *WJ on PR*, p. 39. Richard Poirier in *The Comic Sense of Henry*

James, A Study of the Early Novels (New York, 1967), pp. 148–149, works between Henry James's dislike of Zola's "air of tension and effort" (in an 1880 review of the French author's use of scientific notation to build up fictional characterization) and William James's distaste for scientific examiners who possess "little of the grand style," since "these new prism, pendulum, and chronograph-philosophers" "mean business, not chivalry" (from the 1890 *Principles of Psychology*). The presence of style and chivalry, as well as continuity and interest, was more important to the Jameses than exact scientific judgments.

15. This quotation and the one following are from James's 1910 essay, "Is There A Life After Death?," *The James Family*, p. 604.

16. "Nothing is more dramatic than a ghost," says one of the characters in the "Dialogue" attached to T. S. Eliot's *The Family Reunion*, yet when Eliot placed the Eumenides on stage he made the error James avoided. In the play devised of James's tale "Owen Wingrave," the theatrical director first planned to have a ghostly figure in white flit across the darkened stage; James immediately objected.

17. Preface to "The Spoils of Poynton, A London Life, The Chaperon," *Novels and Tales* (New York, 1908), Vol. X, viii.

18. Preface to "The Altar of the Dead, The Beast in the Jungle, The Birthplace, The Private Life, Owen Wingrave, The Friends of the Friends, Sir Edmund Orme, and The Real Right Thing," *Novels and Tales* (New York, 1908), Vol. XVII, xvi. Pagination for the next two quotations from the same source will be given within parentheses.

19. James's comment upon Poe's "The Narrative of Arthur Gordon Pym" in Preface to Vol. XVII, xix.

20. Ibid., xix and xx.

21. *Form and Value in Modern Poetry* (Garden City, New York , 1957), pp. 51 and 223.

22. R. Ellis Roberts, "The Other Side of the Moon, Introduction to the Mysterious in Literature," *The Bookman* (London), LXXVII (December, 1929), 160, Special Supplement.

23. Preface to Vol. XVII, xx–xxi.

24. In *The Sense of the Past* (New York, 1917), the Ambassador asks the hero whether the ghost story he has to tell is a good one. " 'For credibility no. But for everything else,' said poor Ralph, 'lovely.' "

25. *The Notebooks of Henry James*, ed. F. O. Matthiessen and Kenneth B. Murdock (New York, 1947), pp. 361, 362.

26. *The Sacred Fount* (New York, 1901), pp. 22–23. The next quotation is a continuation of the same passage. Certain crucial problems concern-

ing the authenticity to be granted this character and the novel as a whole will be discussed in Chapter 4.

27. Gustav Fechner (whose theories of consciousness greatly interested William James) hoped to make formulaic equivalents between sensations (bodily facts) and sensibility (conscious facts), thus transforming psychology into as precise a discipline as mathematics.

28. Entry under "Consciousness," Hastings, *Encyclopaedia*, IV, 51.

29. F. W. H. Myers defined "Centre of Consciousness" as "The place where a percipient imagines himself to be. The point from which he seems to himself to be surveying some phantasmal scene." *Human Personality*, I, xv. Poised at this "Centre," the self of the artist can join with the life being lived by the characters performing before him; the union of the two creates an experience of life where there has previously been a void. David Hume believed that "the mind is a kind of theatre, where several perceptions successively make their appearance; pass, re-pass, glide away, and mingle in an infinite variety of postures and situations." Paraphrase used in Hastings, *Encyclopaedia*, IV, 50. In citing Hume the entry-writer points out that we seem to be confronted by "a unique kind of thing—a thing which seems at the same time to be knower and known, actor and spectator, a show and the spectator for whom the show is." So it was in part for James, who often portrayed in quasi-Yeatsian terms both the dancer and the dance, since he was himself both actor and spectator.

III. *Fairy*, Fantaisic, *or Psychical?*

1. See Masao Miyoshi, *The Divided Self, A Perspective on The Literature of the Victorians* (New York and London, 1969), p. xii.

2. Robert L. Platzner, from " 'Gothic Versus Romantic': A Rejoinder," *PMLA*, LXXXVI, 2 (March 1971), 267.

3. Cited by James Kraft, *The Early Tales of Henry James* (Carbondale and Edwardsville, 1969), p. 42.

4. *The Selected Letters of Henry James*, ed. Leon Edel (New York, 1955), p. 93.

5. Preface to *The American, Novels and Tales* (New York, 1907), Vol. II, x; subsequent pagination will be given within parentheses.

6. Poirier, *Comic Sense*, p. 36.

7. Freud, "The Relation of the Poet to Day-Dreaming," 1908; translated I. F. Grant Duff, *Collected Papers*, Vol. IV (London, 1934), 183.

8. If the romantic enlarges the range of one's life, it almost makes it seem " 'cut off' and shut up to itself;" the vaunted sense of freedom may be false since it is merely the result of the artist working up "a positive illusion of the largest liberty" (ibid., xxii, xxiii). Contradictory perhaps, but necessary for the complexity of definition James gave the word "romantic." Significant, because it demonstrates how he continued to force repeated looks at the whole matter of reality.

9. *HJ Notebooks*, p. 397.

10. Preface to Vol. XXI, ix. James Kraft's comment (*Early Tales*, p. 42) suggests how James could make the artistic experience of Strether's mind—designated by supernatural terms—move toward a universal, an extended vision. "It makes little difference *what* you examine as a writer, but it does matter what your examination *leads* you to. If, for instance, the artistic experience and the supernatural are by nature concerned with the realm of the universal—of truth, of the nonmaterial—then the particulars of art and the supernatural are excellent means to lead to this universal."

11. *Notes of a Son and Brother*, p. 369; subsequent pagination will be placed within parentheses.

12. Preface to "The Reverberator, Madame de Mauves, A Passionate Pilgrim and Other Tales," *Novels and Tales* (New York, 1908), Vol. XIII, xviii, xxi.

13. *HJ Selected Letters*, p. 69; letter of March 30, 1887 to Howells in defense of the unhappy but "realistic" ending of *The American*. The eighteenth century was marked by the rise of the novel of social realism; it was also threaded by the debate over the difference between Fancy and Imagination. Correspondence between Mrs. Elizabeth Carter and Miss Catherine Talbot in the mid-1700's noted that Fancy is associated with the artificial world of the city, the great house and the fashionable life characterized by self-interest and practical reason: this, in contrast to Imagination, more typical of rural free minds that rise above common concerns. This contrast nicely indicates the general difference between the Bellegardes and Christopher Newman before he, briefly, becomes mastered by Fancy and loses his power of Imagination. See my article, "Rebirth or Revenge: The Endings of *Huckleberry Finn* and *The American*," *Modern Fiction Studies*, XV (No. 2, 1969), 191–207. For the material drawn from the correspondence of Mrs. Carter and Miss Talbot, see Ernest Lee Tuveson, *The Imagination as a Means of Grace, Locke and the Aesthetics of Romanticism* (Berkeley and Los Angeles, 1960), p. 162.

14. Preface to Vol. XVII, xvii; subsequent pagination will be given within parentheses.

15. In 1748 David Hume worried over "the strong propensity of mankind to the extraordinary and the marvelous," while T. E. Hulme told the twentieth century that it was inevitable that "wonder must cease to be wonder" once men inoculated themselves against it through familiarity. Hume was afraid that wonder would never be eradicated; Hulme was glad it would be. Their attempts to define reality are therefore different from that of James. His rested on "that blest faculty of wonder" that comes from the "strange passion planted in the heart of man for his benefit, a mysterious provision made for him in the scheme of nature." Preface to Vol. XVII, xvi. In "The Sea and the Mirror," W. H. Auden has Caliban speak out in pure Jamesese to distinguish between the child (one who finds all things full of wonder and thus no one thing miraculous) and the adult (one for whom the spell has been broken but who remembers what it was like). The difference between the child's sense of total possibility and the adult's puzzling mixture of possibility (the actual) and impossible possibility (the wonderful) is implicit in James's portrayal of life.

16. For James, the concerns of literary supernaturalism such as Dryden's "decorum" and Walpole's "probability" (responsibilities of the intellect) were replaced by non-intellectual matters of "the human attestation." See Tuveson, p. 124.

17. John Clendenning writes that "James learned to subjectify all that [Monk] Lewis had to objectify. . . ." From "Irving and the Gothic Tradition," *Bucknell Review*, XII, ii (May 1964), 90.

18. R. Ellis Roberts, "Great James," *The Bookman* (London), LIII (December 1917), 107; the next quotations are from pp. 107–108.

19. "Editor's Easy Chair," *Harper's Monthly Magazine*, CVII (June, 1903), 149. T. S. Eliot and Wright Morris have noted the same tendency toward the "mystic" in James. As Eliot wrote in 1924, "He was possessed by the vision of an ideal society; he *saw* (not fancied) the relations between the members of such a society." (See Dorothea Krook, *The Ordeal of Consciousness in Henry James* [Cambridge, England, 1962], p. 2.)

20. "Human 'knowledge' which comes not from 'mental' activities but from 'spiritual' life is a concern of novelists, if not of psychologists. Knowledge, then, as a category of consciousness must include intuition, vision, and sometimes even the occult, so far as twentieth-century writers are concerned." Humphrey, *Stream of Consciousness in The Modern Novel* (Berkeley, 1954), p. 7.

21. "The Art of Fiction," *The James Family*, p. 360.

22. R. B. Perry, *WJ*, I, 424–425; letter of November 23, 1905.

23. Cited in *The James Family*, p. 504; subsequent quotations in the next two paragraphs are from the same source.

24. Donald Emerson, "Henry James and the Limitations of Realism," *College English*, XXII, 3 (December 1960), 161, cites the frequent references James made from the 1860's on about the need for "a ray of idealism" to light "an age of dingy realism." Richard Poirier notes how elegiac (or to use James's words of 1883, how "cheerfully hopeless" a "protest in the name of the ideal") James's assertions were of the value of an idealism unlikely to be attained in life (pp. 249, 255, *Comic Sense*). Still, they were assertions to be made.

25. Letter of October 1–5, 1887, included in R. B. Perry, *WJ*, I, 399–400. The "Editor's Easy Chair" comment of 1903 shows Howells's recognition of a greater world of experience; also see his later redefinition of the importance of the supernatural in men's lives in his introduction to *Shapes That Haunt the Dusk*, ed. by Howells and Henry Mills Alden (New York and London, 1907), pp. v–vi. Note that James refers to Howells's "standpoint," which gave him "too small a point of view." In the eighteenth century the stress was upon "enlargement" of vision, rather than "elevation" alone. Addison and Dugald Stewart's new aesthetics of the sublime (which included the effects of terror upon the imagination) wished men to push back the walls of the room into which they had been set by Locke's spatial concept of the mind. See Tuveson, *Imagination as Means of Grace*, pp. 105, 184. James's interests were not at one with the eighteenth century, but he had a common feeling for vision that moves horizontally for enlargement's sake.

26. Cited by H. Montgomery Hyde, *Henry James at Home* (London, 1969), p. 209. Poirier has noticed the use by James of imagery of openness pitted against images of enclosure in *The American*, while Susan Crowl sees the same important use of these images in "The Turn of the Screw." Poirier, p. 69; Crowl, "Aesthetic Allegory in 'The Turn of the Screw,' " *Novel*, IV, 2 (Winter 1971), 113.

27. *Literary History of the United States*, ed. Robert E. Spiller, Willard Thorp, Thomas H. Johnson, and Henry Seidel Canby (New York, 1960), p. 1046. *Pace*, Susan Sontag, she who rightly distrusts the loose application of the term "religious": "Piety Without Content," in *Against Interpretation, and Other Essays* (New York, 1966).

28. This overlook is not to be confused with "the 'overbeliefs' that we generally associate with morality" and which Robert J. Reilly insists

are absent from James's fiction. See "Henry James and the Morality of Fiction," *American Literature*, XXXIX, i (March 1967), 25. Also see John T. Frederick's chapter on James in *The Darkened Sky, Nineteenth-Century American Novelists and Religion* (Notre Dame and London, 1969).

29. *Notes of a Son and Brother*, p. 82.

30. "Is There A Life After Death?," *The James Family*, pp. 610–611; the next quotation is from p. 611.

31. See *From the Closed World to the Infinite Universe* by Alexandre Koyré (Baltimore, 1957), pp. 111, 116, 147, 156, 199.

32. See Tuveson, *Imagination as Means of Grace*, especially pp. 105–107, 146–147, 160, 184.

33. Reilly, *American Literature*, XXIX, i (March 1967), 21; the next quotations are from pp. 24, 25.

34. *Ordeal of Consciousness*, p. 17.

35. *French Poets and Novelists*, pp. 276, 81.

36. Sallie Sears is one, in her aptly titled study, *The Negative Imagination, Form and Perspective in the Novels of Henry James* (Ithaca, N.Y.), 1968.

37. *Stream of Consciousness*, p. 2. Also see Gordon O. Taylor, *The Passages of Thought, Psychological Representation in the American Novel, 1870–1900* (New York, 1969), and Ross Labrie, "Henry James's Idea of Consciousness," *American Literature*, XXXIX, 4 (January 1968), 517–529.

38. Richard Ellmann and Charles Feidelson, Jr., *The Modern Tradition: Backgrounds of Modern Literature* (New York, 1965), p. 540.

39. Hastings, *Encyclopaedia*, IV, 54.

40 James's letter to T. S. Perry of November 1863 (Harlow, pp. 269 ff) gives an example of his early awareness of those mental processes that act unperceived by men and result in fixing them in illogical, "squinted at" positions of mere opinion. Stirred up by Perry's questions concerning "prejudice," à la Locke, the twenty-year-old James gives a detailed and intensely serious review of how the mind can arrive at base conclusions unaware of how they came about. Yet James here also fears the results of trying consciously to uproot these unconscious opinions by reason alone. Man would most likely be "crushed under the collapse of his ruined beliefs." If one could believe only what one's reason showed one consciously to be true, "he would end by believing nothing at all." Between scepticism and superstition, the young James could make no ready choice. Later he would reach a third position more tenable for him—the conscious touch upon the spring of intuition.

41. *Notes on Novelists* of 1914; cited by Edel, *Henry James, 1895–1901*,

The Treacherous Years, Vol. IV (Philadelphia and New York, 1969), p. 353, where Edel goes on to compare James's hotel-corridor image with Beerbohm's simplifying cartoon.

42. "Attentive readers of the novels may perhaps find the distinction between these two groups less remarkable than it seemed to their writer. They may even wonder whether the second marriage was not rather a silver wedding, with the old romantic mistress cleverly disguised as a woman of the world." *Henry James at Work* (The Hogarth Essays, n.d., no city), p. 254. Robert Langbaum detects one major genre in modern literature, the Poetry of Experience, that carries on the tradition of nineteenth-century romanticism. Miss Bosanquet used "Experience" superficially to represent literary realism, while indicating its nearness to the romantic. She and Langbaum are observing the same general phenomenon, one which places James within both the Romantic tradition and the common definition accorded to Realism.

43. From James's essay on D'Annunzio: Edel, *HJ, Treacherous Years,* p. 354.

44. Preface to Vol. XVII, xiv, and Preface to Vol. V, xx.

45. J. A. Ward, "James's Idea of Structure," *PMLA,* LXXX (September, 1965), 426. Ward's article is devoted to establishing the vigor with which James's ideas and style moved toward the effect of harmony in the midst of chaos. His conclusion is that "Coherence is not a cancellation of one or more of the heterogeneous elements or a last page revelation that the opposition has been illusory" (ibid.).

46. Once, however, James longed to go as far as Mars in his imagination. A letter of September 23, 1902 to H. G. Wells begs to be allowed to collaborate on just such a work of science fiction. See Edel and Gordon N. Ray, eds., *Henry James and H. G. Wells, A Record of their Friendship, their Debate on the Art of Fiction, and their Quarrel* (Urbana, Ill., 1958), pp. 80–81.

47. "Is There A Life After Death?" *The James Family,* p. 611.

48. What the writer of the biblical story "produced, then, was not primarily oriented toward 'realism' (if he succeeded in being realistic, it was merely a means, not an end); it was oriented toward truth." Erich Auerbach, *Mimesis, The Representation of Reality in Western Literature,* translated Willard R. Trask (Princeton, 1953), p. 14. Subsequent pagination will be given within parentheses.

49. R. B. Perry, *WJ,* I, 270–271; letter of April 13, 1868. In a letter of January 26, 1900, James said that by the act of writing "We open the door to the Devil himself—who is nothing but the sense of beauty, of

mystery, of relations, of appearances, of abysses, of the whole—and of *expression.*" See Edel, *HJ, The Treacherous Years,* p. 355. Indeed, he worshiped Jehovah or the Devil, but not Baal!

IV. *The Vampire Breed*

1. Quoted by Leon Edel in *Henry James, 1843–1870, The Untried Years* (Philadelphia and New York, 1953), p. 164; also see *Notes of a Son and Brother,* pp. 93–94. In 1762 Mrs. Elizabeth Montagu wrote her friend, Mrs. Carter, "I am sure it is a great advantage to a Poet to have the belief and prejudices of the nursery to assist his fictions; they have a sacred horror which is one of the great sources of the sublime. . . . The things we but half believe, and but half understand, are fine ingredients in poetry. . . ." (Letter reproduced by permission of the Huntington Library, San Marino, California, MO, 3084, letter of Mrs. Elizabeth Montagu to Mrs. Carter, dated 1762.) See Tuveson, *Imagination as Means of Grace,* p. 159. James did not respond to eighteenth-century notions of the sublime, but he did to the "sacred horror" left over from the nursery.

2. *A Small Boy and Others,* p. 176.

3. Frederick Bligh Bond, *Case For and Against,* pp. 62–63.

4. Augustus Thomas, *The Witching Hour* (New York and London, 1908), p. 97.

5. See Irene Samuel, "Henry James on Imagination and the Will to Power," *Bulletin of the New York Public Library,* LXIX, 2 (February 1965), 117–130, for her excellent comments on the struggle between those "doomed to success" (the members of Philistia) and those imaginative persons defeated in wordly terms while gaining "the exhilaration of expanding vision." James's prefatory remarks to *The Spoils of Poynton* point to "the awful Mona Brigstock, who is *all* will, without the smallest leak of force into taste or tenderness or vision, into any sense of shades or relations or proportions. She loses no minute in that perception of incongruities in which half Fleda's passion is wasted and misled. . . . Every one, every thing, in the story is accordingly sterile *but* the so thriftily constructed Mona . . ." (Vol. X, xvii). That is, those persons who are constituted solely of will act with fertile economy, while those like Fleda are the sterile ones because they see around too many corners (many of them dark and misleading) and dissipate their powers in refinements of actions and thought. James as a writer abhorred artistic leaks, whatever was uneconomical and sterile. Did not he see that he ought

to be like Mona (concentrated, single-minded will that drives straight to its artistic goal because it keeps its moral blinders on), rather than like Fleda (nuances and delicacies of consciousness, which is vulnerable to ambiguities, "seeing" too much ever to get where it is going)? James would have liked to have both (economy and nuances), and he seems to have realized he could never reconcile these polar impulses.

6. The following is typical of Edel's comments concerning James and his cousin Minny Temple. "If she was the 'heroine of the scene' then he could not be the hero. One or the other had to give way in Henry James' equation. The time was to come when he would equate his improving health with Minny's fading radiance." *HJ, Untried Years,* p. 238. In *Henry James, 1882–1895, The Middle Years* (Philadelphia and New York, 1962), p. 384, Edel sees the same tension developing between James and Constance Fenimore Woolson. Edel's conclusion is that to James "To be led to the marriage bed was to be dead." *HJ, Untried Years,* p. 55. However, Edel also notes of James's story, "Osborne's Revenge," that "a woman who seemed a flirt and a vampire turns out to be noble and virtuous and innocent of all designs attributed to her by the vengeful hero" (ibid., p. 257).

7. Cleanth Brooks, *The Well-Wrought Urn, Studies in the Structure of Poetry* (New York, 1947), p. 87.

8. James took great care not to encroach upon others' privacy (see *HJ and HG Wells,* p. 118 n., and *Henry James At Work,* p. 276), while yet recognizing the artist's need for such curiosity (see Preface to "What Maisie Knew, In the Cage, The Pupil," *Novels and Tales* [New York, 1908], Vol. XI, xx). Arnold P. Hinchliffe, "Henry James's *The Sacred Fount," Texas Studies in Literature and Language,* II, i (Spring 1960), 88, remarks that that novel "contains a conflict between two principles which he himself regarded as sacred: the technical device of the observer and the thematic principle of the sanctity of the individual."

9. *HJ Notebooks,* p. 113; entry of October 23, 1891. James never turned this material into a fictional version. It appears straight in his account of his cousin Henry Wyckoff in *A Small Boy and Others,* pp. 144–153. With his inevitable biographical slant, Edel likes to explain the "usurpation theme" as a working out of the sibling rivalry between Henry and William James; when the first-born is absent the younger will try to take over, but must pay "with his life or with defeat." *HJ, Untried Years,* p. 251.

10. The entry under "Vampire" in Hastings, *Encyclopaedia,* Vol. XII, 589, defines this creature in its traditional form as (1) the spirit of the

dead person, or (2) the corpse that is reanimated either (a) by the spirit of the dead person, or (b) by a demon that returns to sap the life of the living by depriving them of blood or some essential organ in order to increase its own vitality.

11. *The Blithedale Romance, The Works* (Boston, 1868), Vol. I, 231–232; subsequent pagination will be given within parentheses.

12. James disagreed with those involved in the Brook Farm experiment who accused Hawthorne of staying there "as a sort of intellectual vampire, for purely psychological purposes"; thus he makes himself an early critic of the notion that Hawthorne and Coverdale are precisely interchangeable. *Hawthorne* (Ithaca, N.Y., 1956), p. 69. It might be well to keep this separation in mind when considering James and the narrator of *The Sacred Fount.*

13. The ineptitude of the writing seems to have led an important early critic of James astray. "Professor Fargo" is called one of those "odd sticks" that "need not delay us long" as it is "simply one of the 'queer cases' in James's stories which we are to meet now and then and wonder not only why he wrote it, but how he could have done it." Cornelia P. Kelley in *The Early Development of Henry James* (University of Illinois Studies in Language and Literature, Vol. XV [1930], nos. 1–2, ed. William A. Oldfather et al., pp. 168, 169). Miss Kelley also dismisses "The Last of the Valerii" and "The Ghostly Rental" as being "outside the main stream of [James's] development" because freaks in the romance tradition (p. 246 n.). She does not allow for the possibility that they might be minor, but true, items in James's main line of progression.

14. "Professor Fargo," *The Complete Tales of Henry James,* ed. Leon Edel, Vol. III (London, 1962), 260–261; subsequent pagination will be given within parentheses.

15. Red hair as a traditional mark of the devil is attributed to Peter Quint in "The Turn of the Screw." But red hair is also the flaming sign writ large of the special, quasi-supernatural qualities possessed by Verena Tarrant and Milly Theale.

16. *The Undiscovered Country* (Boston, 1880), pp. 53, 179; subsequent pagination will be given within parentheses.

17. *The Bostonians* (London and New York, 1886), p. 80; subsequent pagination will be given within parentheses.

18. Selah Tarrant is especially afraid of Olive's earnestness. "The people he had ever seen who were most in earnest were a committee of gentlemen who had investigated the phenomena of the 'materialisation' of spirits, some ten years before, and had bent the fierce light of

the scientific method upon him" (p. 154). Olive's single-minded "study" of Verena's case could be likened to Mrs. Henry Sidgwick's if that lady had ever become personally engrossed in Mrs. Leonora Piper.

19. See David Bounell Green, "Witch and Bewitchment in *The Bostonians,*" *Papers on Language & Literature*, 3 (Summer 1967), 267–269, and his conclusion: "Nobody would contend that *The Bostonians* is a study of witches and their spells. But this imagery does help set forth one of the principal themes of this book. . . ."

20. In a letter written to J. R. Osgood, James emphasized, "The tale relates the struggle that takes place in the mind of [Verena]." Transcribed in *HJ Notebooks*, p. 47; entry of April 8, 1883.

21. "Mr. Henry James's Later Work," *The North American Review*, CLXXVI (January 1903), p. 135.

22. "Henry James: The Poetics of Empiricism," *PMLA*, LXVI (March 1951), 119.

23. Blackall, *Jamesian Ambiguity and The Sacred Fount* (Ithaca, New York, 1965), p. 21. Mrs. Blackall's book offers a full bibliography for articles written to 1965. I shall mention only those articles that generally seemed helpful and provocative, however at odds with one another. Robert J. Andreach, "Henry James's *The Sacred Fount:* The Existential Predicament," *Nineteenth-Century Fiction*, XVII, 3 (December 1962), 197–216; James K. Folsom, "Archimago's Well: An Interpretation of *The Sacred Fount,*" *Modern Fiction Studies*, VII, 2 (Summer 1961), 136–144; Naomi Lebowitz, " 'The Sacred Fount' : An Author in Search of His Characters," *Criticism*, IV, 2 (Spring 1962), 148–159; Cynthia Ozick, "The Jamesian Parable: *The Sacred Fount,*" *Bucknell Review*, XI, iii (May 1963), 55–70; James Reaney, "The Condition of Light: Henry James's *The Sacred Fount,*" *University of Toronto Quarterly*, XXXI (January 1962), 136–151; Norma Phillips, *"The Sacred Fount:* The Narrator and the Vampires," *PMLA*, LXXVI, 4 (September 1961), 407–412; Tony Tanner, "Henry James's Subjective Adventurer: 'The Sacred Fount,' " *Essays and Studies*, n.s., Vol. 106 (1963), 37–55; Parker Tyler, *"The Sacred Fount:* 'The Actuality Pretentious and Vain' vs. 'The Case Rich and Edifying,' " *Modern Fiction Studies*, IX, 2 (Summer 1963), 127–138. Together with Mrs. Blackall's book, which is certainly the single most important discussion of James's novel, I rank highly Dorothea Krook's comments in *The Ordeal of Consciousness* and Charles T. Samuels's article, "At the Bottom of the *Fount,*" *Novel*, II, i (Fall 1968), 46–54. Both Mrs. Krook and Mr. Samuels stress the dual interpretations necessitated by the novel's meaning. As Samuels puts it (p. 47), "Either it is about morality or it is about thinking.

Unfortunately, it is about both." It is two novels, "a moral allegory of ultimate evil and an epistemological comedy of ultimate imperception" (p. 48). Mrs. Krook (in taking exception to Edel's reading, given in his introduction to the Grove Press edition) insists on the unresolved contrast between "the reality *or* appearance apprehended by the inferential ('phantasmagoric') powers of the artistic imagination and the reality *or* appearance apprehended by sense perception or common sense (the 'evidential')." (*Ordeal*, p. 177.)

24. To several critics the narrator either consciously or unconsciously represents James. Through the ways they choose to look at him, either James's nasty voyeuristic streak is exposed or his highminded martyrdom to the requirements of his art affirmed. There is no clear evidence that this novel is primarily an "artist story," although it offers strong parallels to certain problems any artist faces. It seems reasonable to assume that James was engaged here with the larger problem of how far one ought to allow one's consciousness to range in its desire to know about the not-self. By holding himself aloof from his novel's narrator, James could simultaneously sympathize with the narrator's wish to make significant connections via his psychic sensibility, be amused by the narrator's folly of belief that he could ever deduce a conclusive "larger" law, and ultimately warn against the consequences of an unbridled drive to take possession of others' secrets and selves. We fall into the *Hamlet* dilemma here: how far may a man take himself as self-appointed champion of truth? Of course, we are our brother's keeper, and no man is an island, and so on. Perhaps critical sanity is saved by imposing that norm which denies value to anything taken to excess, and from this conclude that the narrator sins more than he saves. Following the heed of an article by Philip Rahv—"The Cult of Experience in American Writing," *Partisan Review*, VII (November-December, 1940), 412–424, George Monteiro questions the value given the cult of awareness: "Usually accepted as a good in itself, awareness is destructive when the idea of it, becoming essential, is emphasized to excess." "Hawthorne, James, and the Destructive Self," *Texas Studies in Literature and Language*, IV, no. 1 (Spring 1962), 61. Certainly there is much in James that indicates his realization of the precarious tightrope which acute awareness walks between being a "good" and an "evil" will.

25. *The Sacred Fount*, pp. 65–66; subsequent pagination will be given within parentheses.

26. Mrs. Blackall and Samuels take positions opposed to Norma Phillips's concerning the vampire motif. Miss Phillips states (p. 411), "The

vampire theme of fruition and depletion, far from being illusory or superficial, is fundamental to the whole conception of the novel in that it is the very means by which the collapse of the narrator is effected." Samuels believes that James tried to separate the fount theory from sexual matters and so denied it as a metaphor. Once the narrator took the fount literally and decided that May Server was sacrificing her wit and Brissenden his youth, a "fanciful element" was added to a realistic novel and the fount theory "withers into a mere figure of speech." Samuels concludes that by making evil "a literal vampirism James side-steps his dilemma" of identifying the nature of evil in this novel. To use vampirism as a symbol, and a useless one since it refers to an "impossibility," the fact of evil's commonness disappears in "the evanescent mists of fancy" (pp. 49, 53). Mrs. Blackall also sees the vampire motif as a threat to the novel's strength. The narrator, who coddles his belief that vampirism is abroad at Newmarch, is exposed to the perceptive reader as a self-deluded fool. Further, James's original stress on vampirism as the novel's *donnée* in his notebooks dissolves as, during the actual writing of the novel, his attention turned toward other matters (the narrator's reliability, the mad-Wagner-artist, the comic impulse). Just as I agree with the excellent overall conclusions reached by Samuels, I concur with Mrs. Blackall's cogent conclusion that we are meant to see the narrator as a participant who suffers and causes to suffer out of his misconceptions. However, I question Samuels and Mrs. Blackall on one important point. Samuels is convinced that the very use of "literal vampirism" (the belief that one person can drain another's force) is a mistake since it mars a "realistic" novel by the intrusion of the "fanciful." Mrs. Blackall makes the same derogatory evaluation, although in reverse; she sees the novel, "whatever other failings it may have," as "saved from becoming one of the comparatively superficial ghost stories" when James accounted for "his fantastical equations in realistic terms" (p. 157). To Mrs. Blackall James's shift from his original notion of "vampires to the character of the narrator launched him into quite a different story from the simple, anecdotal ghost story that *The Sacred Fount* might have been . . ." (p. 162). I agree that the ambiguities of *The Turn of the Screw* have the same origin as *Fount*, and that they work much better in the former; but I cannot fully see why they are right when used in a "ghost story" but are wrong for the novel that is grounded "much more firmly in the explicable" (p. 174). The success or failure of *The Sacred Fount* (and I feel it is more a failure than otherwise) rests on errors other than James's use of "rank fantasy" in a "realistic" novel. But as long as critics are upset by the very fact of the seeming mix, they will lay the blame for James's artistic failures on this basis, just as they will seek to explain his successes on its absence. The mere presence or absence in James's fiction of such themes as vampirism ought not to sidetrack his readers into evaluations based on the high merits of the realistic as opposed to the shabby demerits of the fantastic.

V. *The Ghostly Encounter*

1. Poe's Dupin knew the superior man in his role as detective must be both mathematician and poet, but James's divinity student believes he need only be the analytic man. Robert J. Andreach's article, "Literary Allusion as a Clue to Meaning: James's 'The Ghostly Rental' and Pascal's *Pensées,*" *Comparative Literature Studies,* IV, 3 (1967), 299–306, is a helpful survey of James's references to and intuitive understanding of the ironic implications involved in the story's narrator as student-manqué of Pascal. Andreach's conclusions (that the student can never reconcile the powers of heart's intuition and head's analysis as Pascal would have him do; that this tale is "an early model for what becomes a typical Jamesian character: the bewildered narrator whose narration is an attempt to understand the past and, ultimately, himself"; and that James also takes on "the introduction to the darker forces in the universe with the consequent loss of naïveté and innocence" and "the criticism of the schizophrenic approach to experience") are coupled with his appreciation of the fact that even in 1876 the young James could "grasp from his reading or the intellectual climate or a conversation the material from which he could create a dramatic tale" and thereby gain "ironic dimension."

2. *The Ghostly Tales of Henry James,* ed. Leon Edel (New Brunswick, N.J., 1948), p. 105; subsequent page references will be given within parentheses.

3. See Henry James's letter of 1883 included in Harlow, *T. S. Perry,* pp. 269, 271.

4. Even as a child James was able to distinguish between the "mere mean blackness" he found in Geneva and the *"rich* blackness" he avidly sought. *Notes of a Son and Brother,* p. 7. Unlike Miss Deborah's empirical observations, James's mode of awareness looked into the spirit of the place. But what he had been able to do privately as a child he was as yet unable to execute artistically in this early story.

5. In his 1879 survey of Hawthorne's generation James paused, hopefully enough, in his assessment of the years ahead to say of "the good American" that he would be "an observer" who "will remember that the ways of the Lord are inscrutable, and eventualities . . . will not find him intellectually unprepared." *Hawthorne*, p. 114.

6. *HJ Ghostly Tales*, p. 145; subsequent pagination will be given within parentheses.

7. This same process is used in *The Portrait of a Lady*; see Chapter 8 of this study.

8. Both Isabel Archer and the governess of Bly will have to reshape previous notions of their conception "of a young lady's universe" under the pressure of the ghosts of Gardencourt and Bly.

9. An entry of January 22, 1879 shows James thinking of a girl who would eventually be Charlotte (*HJ Notebooks*, pp. 9–10). At this point he states she does see the ghost. By 1891 he seems to have had second thoughts about being this specific, and left the matter to the reader to decide. Also note that the inception of the story came soon after the writing of "The Ghostly Rental," but that it was not developed for twelve years.

10. There are ironic dimensions here, surely, in the spring of the hero, and his instinctive act of covering and veiling his beloved to keep her from the very knowledge of terror that James himself does not want her wholly to avoid.

11. Edmund Wilson, "The Ambiguity of Henry James," *Hound and Horn*, VII (April-June, 1934), 385–406; revised for first edition of *The Triple Thinkers* (1938); further revised for the 1948 edition; 1959 postscript added to the article when included in Willen's edition of *A Casebook on Henry James's "The Turn of the Screw."* Robert Heilman, "The Freudian Reading of *The Turn of the Screw*," *MLN*, LXII (November 1947), 433–445, and "*The Turn of the Screw* as Poem," *University of Kansas City Review*, XIV, 4 (Summer 1948), 277–289.

12. Krook, *Ordeal of Consciousness*; Mark Spilka, "Turning the Freudian Screw: How Not to Do It," *Literature and Psychology*, XIII, 4 (Fall 1963), 105–111.

13. The article by C. Knight Aldrich, M.D., "Another Twist to *The Turn of the Screw*," *Modern Fiction Studies*, XIII, 2 (Summer 1967), 167–178, elicited an Editor's Postscript. It noted that whereas Dr. Aldrich "proved" scientifically that Miles and Flora are the uncle's illegitimate children by Mrs. Grose and that the housekeeper calculatedly drives the governess mad out of her own evil jealousy, a previous article (Eric

Solomon, "The Return of the Screw," *University Review*, XXX [Spring 1964], 205–211) had "proved" Mrs. Grose to be both villainess and murderess by means of an extended spoof of current literary critical methods. Less delirious in their interpretations but equally lopsided (because of the extraordinary weight given to biographical data alone) are Oscar Cargill's article, "*The Turn of the Screw* and Alice James," *PMLA*, LXXVIII, 3 (June 1963), 238–249 (which reads the story as a concealed exposé of Alice's nervous condition), and Leon Edel's latest reading in *HJ, Treacherous Years*, pp. 201–214 (which has James writing the story out of his horror and sense of doom over having purchased Lamb House). Both articles, however perceptive in their notations of James's personal life, continue to prove the banality imposed upon any literary work by a single-minded biographical bias. (Such slants are as boring as Dorothea Krook finds Wilson's Freudian reading to be.) For a history of Edel's various interpretations (which, like Wilson's, have undergone a series of shifts), see Alexander E. Jones, "Point of View in *The Turn of the Screw*," *PMLA*, LXXIV, i (March 1959), 112–122; Oscar Cargill, *PMLA* (1963); *An Anatomy of The Turn of the Screw*, ed. Thomas M. Cranfil and Robert L. Clark, Jr., Austin, Texas, 1965.

14. To my mind the best single new piece is "Aesthetic Allegory in 'The Turn of the Screw,'" by Susan Crowl, *Novel*, IV, 2 (Winter 1971), 106–122. Equally helpful in the perspective it places upon the literary traditions (both thematic and structural) out of which this story grows is Hans-Joachim Lang's "The Turns in *The Turn of the Screw*," *Jahrbuch Für Amerikastudien*, IX (1964), 110–128.

15. Harold T. McCarthy, *Henry James, The Creative Process*, New York, 1958, notes that "Screw" "may almost be used as an index of critical techniques and of shifting fashions in evil." Lang (who cites McCarthy's statement) adds (*JFA*, p. 110), "There is a trend in recent criticism towards blurring former sharp distinctions. Critics such as J. J. Firebaugh and John Lydenberg, who cordially hate the governess, no longer blackball the ghosts, and and other critics, who defend her, for example A. E. Jones or Dorothea Krook, more and more admit her imperfections." (Cargill's dual-reading is a peculiar one since he begins by showing the governess as a sick and dangerous woman, but concludes by declaring her a heroine since James had to have her so as she represented for him his sister.) If the pro- and con-ghost factions are learning not to make formulas out of "good governess" plus "ghosts-as-real" or "evil governess" with "ghosts-as-illusions," many also tend to agree with Dorothea Krook's notion that the "real, indisputable co-presence of

elements so grossly incompatible" as real innocence and real corruption is what "accounts for the peculiar mystery and horror of the phenomenon" (*Ordeal,* p. 109), and that "the heart of the tragic predicament" lies in the fact of the governess and the children being possessed by the dual nature of goodness and evil (p. 131). Sallie Sears in *The Negative Imagination* (p. 35) believes that Wilson's oft-repeated question, "Which is the correct interpretation?" is the wrong one; one ought "to take as its *donnée* the fact that the work sustains the double possibility and proceed from there."

16. In his 1909 article, "Final Impressions of a Psychical Researcher," William James wrote, ". . . I confess that at times I have been tempted to believe that the Creator has eternally intended this department of nature [occult phenomena] to remain *baffling,* to prompt our curiosities and hopes and suspicions all in equal measure, so that, although ghosts and clairvoyances, and raps and messages from spirits, are always seeming to exist and can never be fully explained away, they also can never be susceptible of full corroboration" (*WJ on PR,* p. 310). Lang (p. 113) sees a close analogy between the effect the "Screw" has upon its readers and that which occult phenomena had upon William James.

17. Cranfil and Clark's Introduction to *Anatomy of the Screw* and A. E. Jones's *PMLA* article list the major apparitionists and non-apparitionists.

18. Spilka, himself an enlightened Freudian critic, chides those Freudians who impose personal subjective predilections and "confidently assume that James adopts their modern attitudes" (*Literature and Psychology,* XII, 108). However, see Ellenberger, *Discovery of the Unconscious,* p. 295, for evidence that child sexuality was well known in some circles.

19. See Hyde's account (*HJ at Home,* pp. 186 f) of a gala event given by Stephen Crane on December 28, 1899 during which the playlet, "The Ghost," was presented. This piece concerns a giant apparition that appears in 1950 before tourists who have traveled to Brede Place to see the haunter of Crane's house. "The Ghost," in which one of the characters is named Peter Quint Prodmore Moreau (in honor both of "The Turn of the Screw" and *Nigger of the 'Narcissus'*), was dashed off by Crane, who pretended he had nine collaborators involved "with this crime." They included James, Conrad, A. E. W. Mason, H. G. Wells, George Gissing, and Rider Haggard, most of whom attended the performance of this pleasant Christmas-time ghostly tale. The origin of the idea for "Screw" is still unsettled. James said he visited the Archbishop of Canterbury on

January 10, 1895 and picked up the anecdote he used three years later. (See Edel, *HJ, Treacherous Years*, 88–90.). But Cargill (*PMLA*, 239) insists James never heard such a story from the Archbishop.

20. Susan Crowl and Donald Costello side for the ghosts since they believe the story's style insists upon them. Mrs. Krook and Heilman see the ghosts as there for the sake of the children, not the governess; their presences create the excruciating sense of beauty and horror that surrounds what is both innocence and corruption. Spilka believes the ghosts are excellent representations of the biological and social facts of inborn sexuality and its repression. None of these critics makes his choice on grounds as flimsy as Cranfil and Clark (who are against the ghosts since, to them, the governess is more interesting if thought to be mad) or E. E. Stoll (who is for the ghosts simply because tradition makes their presence possible). When I say I believe the story is more interesting with the ghosts, and that tradition was behind James's use of them, I trust I am not resting on an inadequate basis of persuasion.

21. Cranfil and Clark, *Anatomy of the Screw*, pp. 36–37, note that a book by Edmund Parish, *Hallucinations and Illusions*, had been published in London in 1897 just as James began to work on "Screw." There is no proof he read it; but if he did he could very likely have reacted to it negatively in terms of his art.

22. Preface to Vol. XII, xx; subsequent pagination for quotations on the next two pages will be given within parentheses. George Knox in "Incubi and Succubi in *The Turn of the Screw*," *Western Folklore*, XXII, 2 (April 1963), 122–123, points out the analogies between Quint and Miss Jessel and the ancient incubi-succubi tradition. It would be nice to think James knew of this tradition, since he could respond to it more strongly than to S.P.R. ghosts.

23. C. B. Ives criticizes Quint's and Miss Jessel's passivity and silence (*NCF*, XVIII, 186–189). Mrs. Krook (p. 130) remarks, on the other hand, that "they speak never a word, say literally nothing—not even as little as Iago—to 'explain' themselves and their actions; and this is the principal reason for their being apparitional—that is, the kind of apparition or 'demon-spirit' that James speaks of in the Preface." Representative of "the terror of absolute evil," they are made their particular kind "in order that the mystery of evil may retain unimpaired the inexplicable, inexpressible mysteriousness." Freud's 1919 article on "The 'Uncanny'" (*Collected Papers*, IV, 407) refers to "the factors of silence, solitude and darkness" common to fictional apparitions as "elements in the production of that infantile morbid anxiety from which the majority of

human beings have never become quite free." Silence considered alone
as a ghostly attribute, therefore, is characteristic of fictional or laboratory ghosts. The question rests on the quality of the effect of the ghostly
presences: whether they elicit indifference or dramatic response. It is
incorrect to assume, as Ives does, that apparitions that stand around in
silence have no fictional force; all depends on the responses of the living
characters to them. Silent and still of movement, but full of menace and
meaning, Quint and Miss Jessel are ghosts after James's own heart. Peter
Penzoldt (p. 34) describes the shift from the gothic spectre ("usually a
pallid, helpless shade") to the modern ghost (which is "active and generally wreaks its vengeance by the cruellest possible physical means").
James's ghosts are in between: they do not physically touch their victims' bodies (can you easily imagine any Jamesian figure *touching?*), but
they are far from helpless in their menace.

24. Early volumes of *PSPR* contain ten cases of the appearance of
apparitions to children. Francis X. Roellinger, Jr.'s article, "Psychical
Research and 'The Turn of the Screw,' " *American Literature*, XX (January, 1949), 401–412, brings together other instances of current psychical
research that James could well have read and used if so inclined.

25. A delicate technical problem looms here for the writer of ghost
stories. As opposed to the fairy-tale, in which all the characters are
unreal, and no terror is aroused, the modern ghostly tale must mix "real"
characters with apparitions whose intrusive "unreality" is the factor
that makes the story succeed in raising terror. See Raymond Thorberg,
"Terror Made Relevant: James's Ghost Stories," *The Dalhousie Review*,
XLVII, 2 (Summer 1967), 185–191; Pamela Search, *The Supernatural in
the English Short Story;* Freud, "The 'Uncanny' "; and Peter Penzoldt, *The
Supernatural in Fiction.*

26. James here reasserts issues concerning the freedom granted by the
"romantic" raised in his preface to *The American*. James L. Roberts in
"An Approach to Evil in Henry James," *Arizona Quarterly*, XVII, i
(Spring 1961), 6, makes use of James's own balloon metaphor to describe
the way readers ought to approach his tales of evil: "James's world is
indeed a world floating above this earth, and, although anchored to the
earth by a strong chain, it is also a delicate chain which will not allow
the critic to climb from the earth to James's world and back again in
order to make critical comparisons." H. K. Girling's article, "The
Strange Case of Dr. James & Mr. Stevenson," *Wascana Review*, III, i
(1968), 63–76, is instructive, however, in showing how much more "realistic" James was in "Screw" than the "romanticism" he criticized in

R. L. Stevenson's "Dr. Jekyll and Mr. Hyde" of 1886. James stood for fiction that is "true" because it leaves an "impression," is filled with "complexity," and thus can "compete with life."

27. Susan Crowl (*Novel*, IV, 111–112) and Juliet McMaster (in " 'The Full Image of a Repetition' in *The Turn of the Screw*," *Studies in Short Fiction*, VI, 4 [Summer 1969], 377–382) comment on the two audiences built into James's story: the sensation-seeking women who are sent out of the room, and the select audience that remains to hear Douglas read from the manuscript. Surely, James would have liked to deny admittance to readership to those incapable of accepting the story on the particular terms it insists upon.

28. See Lang (p. 118) and Walter Isle, "The Romantic and the Real: Henry James's *The Sacred Fount*," *Rice University Studies*, LI, i (Winter 1965), 32, concerning the uses of first-person narration in order to intensify a sense of looseness, subjectivity, and ambiguity. Also see A. E. Jones (p. 121) and Cranfil and Clark (p. 18) concerning the textual changes James made between 1898 and the New York Edition, which place stress on how the governess *felt*.

29. If James held out against absolutistic conclusions, and thereby created one kind of tension between possibilities in his story, he also liked "extremes" (as Sallie Sears notes in *The Negative Imagination*, p. 16). We are constantly forced both to blur and to render distinct the elements of either-or; we may not rest easily in either clarity or ambiguity.

30. Cargill (*PMLA*, p. 242 n) stresses that any degree of unreliability on the part of the governess makes it impossible for readers to know what is true or false. A. E. Jones (*PMLA*, p. 122) points out the absurdity of such a position; how are we to trust Douglas or James himself if we can credit nothing the governess says; how then to believe a Huck Finn or an Ishmael if we cannot believe her in some part?

31. No critical version of what was seen at Bly could pass an investigating board of the S.P.R. Take the following statements from C. D. Broad's *Religion, Philosophy and Psychical Research*, p. 104. Then run through these testing statements both the conflicting reports given by the story's characters and James's comments made outside the text. This exercise is as stimulating for the literary critic as for the S.P.R. men for whom it was designed. "Now it is known that the main sources of error [in reporting psychical phenomena, or the interpreting of literary texts] are the following: (1) alteration and heightening of a story that passes through a chain of narrators; (2) errors of memory even in first-hand

reports; (3) failure to observe relevant details and tendency to mistake inferences for observations; (4) lastly, if another person beside the witness was present he may have produced an illusion in the witness' mind. Therefore we have to consider (a) any facts about the observer which might tend to make him the victim of an illusion, and (b) any facts about the second person which make it likely that he was able or willing to produce an illusion in the witness."

32. While James Gargano in "The Turn of the Screw," *Western Humanities Review*, XV, 2 (Spring 1961), 173–179, overly exonerates the governess, he is correct in placing her in the long line of Jamesian characters who "launch into passionate pursuit of knowledge inaccessible to obtuse or even ordinarily active minds" (p. 177). Donald Costello in "The Structure of *The Turn of the Screw,*" *Modern Language Notes*, LXXV, 4 (April 1960), 312–321, usefully points out how the story's structure alternates between what is *represented* directly and what is made of the events by means of the governess's *interpretations*. We move both in and out of her experience (of course, allowing for the fictional fact that the representations are part of her experience, though not as subjectively rendered as her subsequent evaluation of the action).

33. See Peter Penzoldt's dismissal of "Screw" as prime ghostly fiction (pp. 219–223). Critics working from outside the supernatural tradition praise or blame James on the basis of whether they think his work psychologically valid; Penzoldt, an insider, who comes upon James as merely one of a long line of practitioners of the ghostly, much prefers the tales of Walter de la Mare. Basic to his objections is his sense (a correct one) that to James "the ghost is the touchstone with which he tests the reactions of his characters." He concludes that James's tales are "far more psychological than they are ghost stories, and thus rather unconvincing as psychical ghost stories" (p. 221). What pleases most Jamesians, therefore, is what displeases a "supernaturalist."

34. *HJ Letters*, I, 297.

35. *Appreciations With an Essay on Style* (London and New York, 1889), p. 247.

36. Critics who stress the undefinable reality of Evil at Bly (such as Robert Heilman in "*The Turn of the Screw* as Poem," and "The Lure of the Demonic: James and Dürrenmatt" [*Comparative Literature*, XIII, iii (Fall 1961), 346–357]) have an able opponent in Mark Spilka. Heilman's contempt is evident for those who reject the notion of an innate world-evil which is "ubiquitous, mysterious, and, though of limited scope, eternal." (*CL*, 346–347.) Spilka rejects just this notion of Original Sin (as

he does any Freudian belief in Original Innocence). He bases his fine reading on a "social-psychological approach" to the problem of evils resulting from Victorian repression of infant sexuality because of adherence to those admirable virtues of "duty, sacrifice and sexless love" (*L. & P,* p. 107). Interestingly, Spilka's view is just as inexorable and fateful as that of Heilman (or of Mrs. Krook). Given Victorian society, and its creations—the governess and the children—the outcome is as inevitably tragic as if ruled by a struggle between God and Satan. Whether we tend to the gothic view of evil (as defined by Robert L. Platzner [*PMLA,* 267]) or a Christian one (as held by Heilman and Mrs. Krook) or Spilka's social-psychological view, the intensity and seriousness of the conflict are unquestioned.

37. Preface to Vol. XII, xvii-xviii, xxii.

38. "The Turn of the Screw: Jamesian Gothic," *Essays in Criticism,* XII (January 1962), 37.

39. Briefly stated, my interpretation of the story's whatness is this: the governess is sensitive, susceptible to the high romantic, and sane— thus responsible for her actions. She believes in her specialness and her right to protect those she loves from harm. Both vampire and saint in part, she meddles, is overly possessive and finely sacrificial. Increasingly, she moves into a world imaged by the fanciful, artificial, and theatrical, in which the children are far more adroit at acting than she. Innocent and morally blind, the governess has too much of the right kind of imagination wrongly used. With the uncle unwilling to aid her and Mrs. Grose unable to, she stands alone to face the ghosts—sadly unprepared for the task.

40. See Bruce Wilshire, pp. 173–175.

41. After reading "Screw," H. G. Wells wrote James, "The story is not wrong—I was." Wells had originally attempted to correct the "impossible" quality of the story, then came "to enlightenment" that nothing about it could be rearranged. *HJ and HG Wells,* p. 58; letter of January 16, 1898.

42. Lang (*JFA,* IX, 122), McMaster (*Studies in Short Fiction,* IV, 379), and E. Duncan Aswell ("Reflections of a Governess: Image and Distortion in *The Turn of the Screw,* " *NCF,* XXIII, i [June 1968], 49–63) have noted that the ghosts are projections of the governess's inner conflicts; her doubling relation with the children has not been examined as I do it here.

43. See Wilshire, p. 117.

44. See Sigmund Freud, "The 'Uncanny,' " *Collected Papers,* IV, 388.

45. *HJ Ghostly Tales*, p. 488; subsequent pagination will be given within parentheses.

46. In "The Turn of the Screw Again," *The Midwest Quarterly*, VII, 4 (Summer 1966), 327–336, John Fraser traces how Miles moves from being seen as a theoretic entity to a person. I agree that by the final scene Miles is no longer an untouchable angel, but is a human boy who can suffer and die.

47. Notice the similarity to the way Jean Martle in James's novel *The Other House* (New York, 1896; p. 13) first envisions Rose Armiger. "At the other end of the place appeared a young woman . . . bent low over a table at which she seemed to have been writing. Her chair was pushed back, her face buried in her extended and supported arms, her whole person relaxed and abandoned." But it is Jean who, surprisingly, seems an "apparition" in Rose's eyes.

48. Susan Crowl (*Novel*, IV, 114) uses the term "chinese boxes" to indicate the doubling quality she generally finds in the story.

49. William James believed that "the thinker is all the things in the world which are judged by him to be his. . . ." (Wilshire's paraphrase, p. 127.) What is a psychological generalization, neutral in its implications, is made baleful by Henry James's stress on the effects of spiritual possessiveness.

50. James's 1868 story "DeGrey: A Romance" indicates the need to stand fast against horrors in league with another. When Margaret Aldis learns the secret of the curse of the DeGreys, she pridefully decides to face it down alone. As a result her fiancé dies in her arms while she goes mad in a melodramatic version of the ending of "Screw." See *The Complete Tales*, I, 425, for the final thoughts of self-denunciation Margaret has in recognition of her vampiristic role.

51. John Lydenberg, "The Governess Turns the Screw," *NCF*, XII, i (June 1957), 57, and Mrs. Krook (p. 125) would agree on the activating powers of the governess's presence. Spilka (p. 107) believes that the conflict between sexuality and saintliness is inevitable since written into the fabric of Victorian society; no particular person arriving at a particular spot is needed to bring it to life.

52. Susan Crowl, p. 117.

53. Preface to Vol. XII, xxi.

54. Comments about James's innovative use of the narrative-frame tradition made by Lang (pp. 117–118) are much more useful than Cargill's (p. 246). The latter's insistence that the governess is proved a heroine by the details of the Prologue forgets that by the time the end

gration in Victorian literature. Robert Rogers offers further suggestions in *A Psychoanalytic Study of the Double in Literature* (Cleveland, Ohio, 1971).

7. In his preface to Vol. XVII (xxiii–xxiv) James remarked of "Sir Edmund Orme" that he wished to gain an effect of "the bright thought of a state of unconscious obsessions or, in romantic parlance, haunted-ness. . . ." Aware of both the "realistic" psychological parlance and the "romantic" phrase that traditionally describes the same state, he chose to dramatize in terms of the latter while exploiting his generation's knowledge of the former.

8. Preface to Vol. XVII, xxiv.

9. *HJ Letters*, I, 356; letter of August 9, 1900 to Howells.

10. *HJ, The Untried Years*, p. 75.

11. Floyd Stovall's article, "Henry James's 'The Jolly Corner,' " *Nineteenth-Century Fiction*, XII (June 1957), 72–84, strikes me as the best over-all interpretation we have in its argument that there are two presences, the self Brydon might have been and the self he is.

12. "Terror Made Relevant," *Dalhousie Review*, XLVII, 188.

13. *Supernatural in Fiction*, pp. 16–19.

14. See Freud's "The 'Uncanny,' " *Collected Papers*, IV. His remarks are useful for an understanding of the way literature can make use of the "uncanny"—that which was once as familiar as ourselves, but, once forgotten, brings fear on its reappearance. He relates Otto Rank's definition of the two stages of the double to his own notions concerning the mind's movement from pleasure to fear, from the sense of life and release to death and chastisement. With Freud and Rank's insights as a suggestive background, not a formula, we can see how James worked out artistically the *stages* of Brydon's and Pendrel's intricate encounters with their several selves.

15. Kierkegaard and Sartre furnish the useful distinctions between dread and anguish. Several definitions are available for horror and terror. Peter Penzoldt, together with Algernon Blackwood and Boris Karloff, sees horror as the stress upon loathsome physical realities, and terror as confrontation with the ghostly. (*Supernatural in Fiction*, p. 9.) "Clean terror" (Karloff's term in his edition of *Tales of Terror*) is considered the superior literary mode. Robert D. Hume associates terror with suspense and horror with shock; he sees the shift from the former to the later in the gothic novels of 1764–1820 period "as probably the most important factor in the evolution of the genre." (From " 'Gothic Versus Romantic': A Rejoinder," *PMLA*, LXXXVI, 268.) To me, James, who chose "clean" over "dirty" physical embellishments, further intensified

his effects in "The Jolly Corner" by showing Brydon moving from horror to terror within a single night's encounter with the ghostly.

16. *HJ Ghostly Tales*, p. 740; subsequent pagination will be given within parentheses.

17. Thoreau, for one, had written he was "sensible of a certain doubleness by which I can stand remote from myself as from another." Dickens, for another, had worked out this sense of doubleness in his last novels.

18. *The Sense of the Past*, p. 342; *HJ Notebooks*, p. 364. Although he commented in *Notebooks* (ibid.) that, as a novel, *Past* "is so different and so much more ample" than the story which followed it, James scrupulously worked out the interlocking analogy between the two fictions, which rest upon the idea that a living man may become a ghost to ghosts. The composition history of both works (extending from 1899 to 1915), together with the commentary James made on his ambitious intentions, helps point up the direction in which he was taking his supernatural fiction at the same time he was tracking deeper into the baffling consciousnesses of his characters in *The Ambassadors*, *The Wings of the Dove*, *The Golden Bowl*, and *The Ivory Tower*. See *Notebooks*, pp. 364, 367–368; *HJ Letters*, I, 354–359; and the scenario included by Lubbock in the 1917 edition of *Past*. Never disenchanted with the idea basic to this novel, James gave no indication that he might be forced—as he earlier warned himself (*HJ Letters*, I, 356)—"to 'chuck' the supernatural and the high fantastic."

19. *The Sense of the Past*, pp. 105–106; subsequent pagination will be given within parentheses.

20. Pendrel tells his 1820 cousins, " 'I'm not a prophet or a soothsayer, and still less a charlatan, and don't pretend to the gift of second sight—I only confess to have cultivated my imagination, as one has to in a country where there is nothing to take that trouble off one's hands' " (p. 251).

21. Two years after *The Sense of the Past* was published, T. S. Eliot's essay "Tradition and the Individual Talent" appeared. In it Eliot wrote that the consciousness of the past by the present includes far more than the past could have had of itself at the moment of its inception. It was Pendrel's discovery of this truth while in a reversed situation that brought him his unsettling sense of doubleness and homelessness; by continuing awareness of the present while one resides in the past, one is led to an expanded and haunting consciousness of time.

22. *HJ Notebooks*, p. 365.

23. Ibid., p. 300.

24. James makes a neat "social" comment when he shows that the cloddish Perry fears the "unknown" quality in Pendrel that calls on his own "quasi-brutish instincts of danger and self-defense" (*Past*, p. 154). What is "unknown" about all men like Pendrel—ever feared by the world's Perrys—is their intelligence and high imagination.

25. *HJ Notebooks*, p. 364.

26. Ibid., p. 368.

27. Ibid., p. 367.

28. My conclusions may be compared with those of Saul Rosenzweig, "The Ghost of Henry James," *Partisan Review*, XI, 4 (Fall 1944), 436-455; John W. Schroeder, "The Mothers of Henry James," *American Literature*, XXII, 4 (January 1951), 425–431; Robert Rogers, "The Beast in Henry James," *The American Imago*, XIII, 4 (Winter 1956), 427–454; Milton A. Mays, "Henry James, or, The Beast in the Palace of Art," *American Literature*, XXXIX, 4 (January 1968), 467–487.

29. *A Small Boy and Others*, p. 348.

VII. *The Heroine as "Sensitive"*

1. And irked him too. William James's correspondence with his fellow S.P.R.-men is interspersed with the sense of redundancy he felt about Mrs. Piper's undramatic, styleless "muchness." See R B. Perry, *WJ*, II, 159, 164-167; letters of 1893, 1895, 1897.

2. Gauld, *Founders of P.R.*, p. 252.

3. *WJ Letters*, I, 310–311.

4. From James's essay "Certain Phenomena of Trance," *PSPR*, VI (1889–1890), 658, 659; *WJ on PR*, p. 110.

5. *WJ Letters*, I, 287; letter of 1907.

6. "What Psychical Research Has Accomplished," *WJ on PR*, p. 27.

7. Barrett, *Philosophy in the Twentieth Century*, III, 139.

8. "What Psychical Research Has Accomplished," *WJ on PR*, pp. 27, 28.

9. An acquaintance of James observed, "He seemed to look at women rather as women looked at them. Women look at women as persons; men look at them as women." Quoted by Edel, *HJ, Conquest of London*, p. 359. Contrast this with Otto Weininger, who, in *Sex and Character* (1903), looked at women not as persons, but as born prostitutes. (See Ellen-

berger, *Discovery of the Unconscious,* p. 293; also p. 294 for his remarks about late nineteenth-century views of the "femme inspiratrice," the "femme fatale," and the "Virgin-Mother.")

10. *HJ Notebooks,* p. 182; the quotations used in the rest of this paragraph and the next are from the same page. James never worked out this story idea, but Thomas Mann later did a version of it in "The Blood of the Walsungs," just as Poe had earlier in "The Fall of the House of Usher."

11. Roy R. Male, Jr. has written two useful studies on the subject: "Hawthorne and the Concept of Sympathy," *PMLA,* LXVIII, i (March 1953), 138–149, and *"Sympathy*—A Key Word in American Romanticism," *The Emerson Society Quarterly,* No. 35 (II Quarter, 1964), 19–23.

12. James considered as real defects Hawthorne's vague references to Priscilla's "Sibylline attributes" and use of unexplained terms like "spheres" and "sympathies." *Hawthorne,* pp. 108, 95.

13. This belief is seemingly affirmed by recent *psi* experiments whose data indicate that the female is more effective as a percipient, while men do better as agents. Johnson, *Imprisoned Splendour,* p. 141.

14. *The Awkward Age, Novels and Tales* (New York, 1908), Vol. IX, 454.

15. *The Ambassadors, Novels and Tales* (New York, 1909), Vol. XXI, 133, 168.

16. *The Bostonians,* p. 10; the next four quotations are from pages 24, 78, 150, and 275.

17. *The Portrait of a Lady, Novels and Tales* (New York, 1908), Vol. IV, 364.

18. *The Sacred Fount,* p. 224.

19. Even the morally shaky Mrs. Brookenham declares, " 'It's by one's sympathies that one suffers.' " *The Awkward Age,* Vol. IX, 463. Even the kind of love Serena Merle feels for Osmond enables her to possess knowledge of "things of which she had no need to be told—things as to which she had a sort of creative intuition." This passage, which does not appear in the drastically rewritten Chapter XXIX of the New York Edition, is from the first edition (Boston, 1882), p. 267.

20. *Roderick Hudson, Novels and Tales* (New York, 1907), Vol. I, 384.

21. *The Europeans* (Boston, 1879), p. 269.

22. *Confidence* (New York: Universal Library, 1962), pp. 154, 196.

23. "Anthony Trollope," *Partial Portraits* (London and New York, 1886), p. 101; first appeared in *Century Magazine,* July 1883.

24. "The Art of Fiction," *The James Family,* p. 360.

25. *The Tragic Muse, Novels and Tales* (New York, 1908), Vol. VIII, 69, 94–95.

26. *The Other House*, p. 41. Rose demonstrates more of her self-vaunted powers when she informs Tony that Mrs. Beever is watching them from across the way. He is astonished she knows this since her back is turned. She replies, " 'It's with my back turned that I see most' " (p. 307).

27. Preface to Vol. X, xv.

28. *What Maisie Knew*, Vol. XI, vii, 285. With a heroine so acutely occult, the author deplores his "rough method"; he must "so despair of courting her noiseless mental footsteps" that he can but "crudely give you my word" for what happens (pp. 280–281). See my article, "The Quality of Experience in *What Maisie Knew,* " *The New England Quarterly*, XLII, no. 4 (December 1969), 483–510.

29. *The Sense of the Past*, p. 299; subsequent pagination will be given within parentheses.

VIII. *The Tale-Teller's Strategies*

1. "Mr. Henry James's Later Work," *North American Review*, pp. 136–137.

2. *The Portrait of a Lady*, III, 30. Subsequent pagination for Vols. III and IV will be given within parentheses.

3. See *The Spoils of Poynton*, Vol. X, 249–250, for the conversation between Fleda Vetch and Mrs. Gereth concerning why there are ghosts at Ricks and none at Poynton, with Fleda seen as authority on the connection between human suffering and the metaphoric sense of ghostly presences.

4. The elder James's comments on this subject are given in his work, *Substance and Shadow* (Boston, 1863).

5. Ralph Touchett tells his father, " 'I can exercise very little influence upon her life' " (III, 260) and cautions himself, "This power he could exert but vaguely" (III, 206), but he notifies Isabel he will devote his life to watching her (III, 211). This is all ghosts can do—watch and warn, while fated to remain unheeded by the living. He senses the evil of Osmond and Madame Merle and is clairvoyantly aware of the life Isabel leads with Osmond (" 'From the voices of the air! Oh, from no one else . . .' " [IV, 305]). Wandering alone through his darkened townhouse surrounded by "a ghostly presence" of past social gatherings and a "hint of the supernatural" (III, 197), Ralph is given many of the tradi-

tional characteristics of the good ghost. He is tender, knowing, ineffectual, "a bright, free, generous spirit" who lives "on air" and is kept on earth only by "the fact that he had not yet seen enough of the person in the world in whom he was most interested . . ." (IV, 60, 75, 146). Until he is satisfied that Isabel might save herself, Ralph will not die in body. He also knows that the sign of her salvation will be to see the ghost of Gardencourt for what it really is: in part himself, in part that knowledge gained by those who have come through suffering to knowledge and the ability to make choices according to that knowledge.

6. This was James's way of describing one kind of psychic phenomenon his brother and the S.P.R. were studying: the "veridical hallucination." The *Oxford English Dictionary* credits F. W. H. Myers as the first to use this term, in the psychological sense, in 1884. *Webster's New International Dictionary*, Second Edition, defines it as "A hallucination corresponding to some real event, as when the apparition of an image of any absent person is coincident with his death." Henry James also made this phenomenon figure prominently in his ghostly tale of 1896, "The Friends of the Friends," but, as usual, he tried to keep free of the deadening taint of the "case study."

7. See the earlier edition of *The Portrait of a Lady* (Boston, 1882), p. 215, for material descriptive of other haunted Italian houses that was deleted from the New York Edition. Also see Vol. IV, 100–101 for Rosier's musings on the subject.

8. *Human Personality*, I, xv. J. M. S. Tompkins, in *The Popular Novel in England, 1770–1800* (Lincoln, Neb., 1961), pp. 258–259, speaks of Mrs. Radcliffe as "the poet of apprehension" whose "heroines are timid but steadfast. They have no enemy within; they are sure that innocence will be divinely shielded, and they never doubt their innocence." From Isabel's position at the "centre of consciousness," such invulnerability is impossible.

9. Matthiessen's comment in *The James Family*, p. 84.

10. Gordon O. Taylor, *The Passages of Thought*, p. 67, remarks that James's stress on the process by which new ideas displace old ones in Isabel's mind offsets "the archaic ring of the omniscient phrase 'her soul was haunted.'" If Taylor sees James as moving away from archaic terminology, Richard Poirier (*Comic Sense*, p. 202) in speaking of Isabel cautions us not to view James as more modern than he was in psychological matters. To Poirier James's concern was over his characters' "emblematic qualities" and their "intense moral consciousness," which

"often has little to do with what we now consider psychological motivation."

11. *HJ Notebooks*, p. 47; entry of April 8, 1883.

12. Cited by Dixon Wecter, *Literary History of the United States*, p. 503. R. W. B. Lewis in "The Tactics of Sanctity: Hawthorne and James," *Hawthorne Centenary Essays*, ed. Roy Harvey Pearce (Columbus, Ohio, 1964), p. 290, observes the shift that took place in America's attitudes; in the years between Hawthorne's *Blithedale Romance* and James's novel, religion became ideology.

13. *The Bostonians*, p. 5; subsequent pagination will be given within parentheses.

14. *Hawthorne Centenary Essays*, p. 295.

15. Cited in *The James Family*, p. 328.

16. Vol. XIX, 104; subsequent pagination will be given within parentheses.

17. Preface to Vol. XIX, xvi, xx.

18. *The James Family*, p. 27.

19. Entry under "Consciousness," Hastings, *Encyclopaedia*, IV, 56, 57.

20. Here we are back for a new look at "The Fall of the House of Usher"—the similar use of the sentient presence, a similar faint far wail expressive of a dead woman's demanding love, and the uneasy thought for some that perhaps Densher will deaden his life by unconscious necrophilia.

21. Dorothea Krook points out that while Kate's psychic powers are strong because of her romantic love for Densher, Kate lacks the understanding that would be hers if, in addition, she loved "spiritually"—as Milly does. Kate, therefore, is "capable both of inferring accurately from the minimal signs she receives what the experience has done to him and of drawing the inescapable conclusions," while yet "totally deficient in moral sensibility in having to the end no knowledge of what Densher's transforming experience might have been. . . ." *Ordeal of Consciousness*, p. 228. Kate understands, however, what it means to their relationship, and is willing to face its effects; this knowledge Densher is, to the end, trying to stave off, since he is still a man afraid of knowledge.

22. In speaking of "The Friends of the Friends," James's ghost story of 1896, Mrs. Krook finds arresting "the connexion of the 'supernatural' part with the denouement of *The Wings of the Dove*." She also cites the importance of James's testing his "too late" theme in "Friends" before developing it in "The Beast in the Jungle," "The Jolly Corner," and *The*

Ambassadors. This habit of trying out an idea in minor pieces was invaluable for its eventual "definitive rendering." *Ordeal of Consciousness*, p. 333. I submit that James continually used his "occult" fiction as dry-runs for his more ambitious "natural" fiction.

23. *HJ Notebooks*, p. 311; entry of August 27. A long entry of 1894 records James's attempts to work out the general theme of death-in-life. Edel wonders if James came across notes written by Constance Fenimore Woolson after her suicide, which also projects the "too late" idea. *HJ, Middle Years*, p. 370. In 1899 James included a fable called "The Golden Dream" in a letter that further searches out its possibilities. *HJ Letters*, I, 329–330. By the 1901 entry his interest had hardly reduced itself to a "tiny" residue; not with *The Ambassadors* as proof to the contrary.

24. *HJ Notebooks*, pp. 182–183; entry of February 5, 1895.

25. Ibid., p. 311. Like "The Jolly Corner," "Beast" has two climaxes: the first comes when, with May, we see what Marcher will never be; the second comes at the end when, with Marcher, we see him seeing what he is.

26. Preface to Vol. XVII, ix and x.

27. *HJ Ghostly Tales*, pp. 686, 685, 711; subsequent pagination will be given within parentheses. Marcher does not realize these are not actually masks and veils. If they were they could be removed from his face, but he has none. Nature abhors a vacuum, but Marcher's head is a void with blank holes for eyes through which May peers as a surrogate self in her concern to help him "pass for a man like another" (p. 693).

28. Mrs. Krook contrasts two principles of "poetic idealisation": Wordsworth's "stripping principle" and James's principles of "addition." *Ordeal of Consciousness*, pp. 19–21. In this story we are made aware of what James has removed before we see what has been added. Thoreau's life-process of "economy" and "extravagance" is practiced by this other Henry quite literally in his style.

29. Marcher finds himself "under the so mixed star of the extreme of apprehension and the extreme of confidence." Preface to Vol. XVII, x.

30. See Courtney Johnson, "John Marcher and the Paradox of the 'Unfortunate' Fall," *Studies in Short Fiction*, IV, 2 (Winter 1969), 121–135. Pico della Mirandola said the sphinx stood for those "divine things" that "should be concealed in riddles and poetical dissimulation."

31. Raymond Thorberg, "Henry James's Ghost Stories," pp. 190–191, points out the paradoxes that the more obsessed Marcher is to lead the rich, full life, the more incapacitated he is to gain it; that through the

achieved agony of guilt he feels at the story's end over not having lived, he gains his strongest sense of a consciousness of life.

32. Typical of Maxwell Geismar's response to the tale is this (to me) unwarranted statement, in which Geismar rightly (I believe) recognizes the presence of a passionate conception of romantic love. "Perhaps James was as falsely romantic in his notion of 'passion' as he was infantile and neurotic in his rejection of it." From "Henry James: 'The Beast in the Jungle,' " *Nineteenth-Century Fiction*, XVIII, i (June 1963), 41.

33. Marcher exemplified the only evil Emerson recognized—that of rejecting Being and becoming Nothing. He stands for what James's cousin Mary Temple disliked when she wrote of that "sickening introspection, analysis of myself and yourself, that exhausting and nauseating subjectivity, with which most of my other friends see fit to deluge me, thereby taking much that is refreshing out of life." *Notes of a Son and Brother*, p. 501. Marcher is also Henry James, Sr.'s definition of the Swedenborgian anti-hero. The elder James's sins of self-consciousness included the greed to take and never to give; to be static, doing neither good nor evil; to attempt to distinguish oneself in the belief one is different from others; to deny reality by assuming the disguises of appearances; to be morally blind to one's own spiritual evils and so to refuse communion with others. However, it is our error if we keep our view of Marcher on the level fixed by these moral pronouncements.

34. Joseph Conrad defined tragedy thus: "What makes mankind tragic is not that they are the victims of nature, it is that they are conscious of it. . . . [As] soon as you know of your slavery, the pain, the anger, the strife—the tragedy begins." *Joseph Conrad, Life and Letters*, ed. George Jean-Aubry (Garden City, N.Y., 1927), Vol. I, 226; letter of January 31, 1898.

Index

M